HOME PLANNERS, INC.

23761 RESEARCH DRIVE, FARMINGTON HILLS, MICHIGAN 48024

1- 800- 848 - 2550

Dear Reader,

Contemporary design "breaks the box" of traditional residential styling with special concessions to modern lifestyle. Often that means more window view and better indoor-outdoor relationships. Often that means more open space and more rooms for our increasingly complex interests today. Of course, that includes more leisure time and enjoyment of backyard living, hobbies, and privacy.

Innovative designers have influenced styling of Contemporary houses today, but coast-to-coast market popularity keeps them in vogue. Our Home Planners designs in this book reflect current market tastes. Our homes have been built in all fifty states and even in foreign countries.

Complete working blueprints with materials lists are available for all these designs at a reasonable price. (See Page 282.) If Contemporary design suits your lifestyle, we are certain that you may find the home of your dreams somewhere in the following pages . . .

Sincerely yours,

Charles W. Talcott

President, Home Planners, Inc.

Publisher's Foreword:

9/87 @ 9.95

134490

Index to Designs

Contents

Edited by Von Br

Published by Home
All designs and illus
rights reserved. Rep
States of America. I

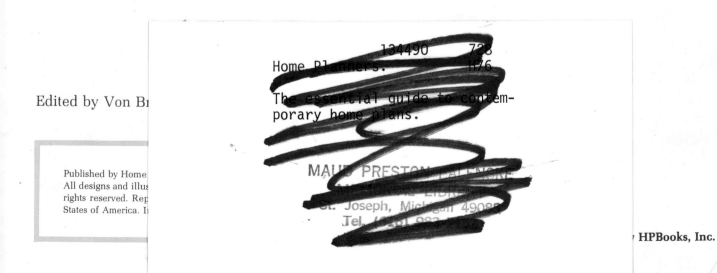

HPBooks, Inc.

Guide to Contemporary Design..

Y ou can tell a lot about people, historians say, by the type of homes they choose for living. Contemporary architecture certainly tells a lot about Americans and their lifestyle.

Modern technology plus availability of new building materials have dictated to architects and designers how buildings look today. Of course, such artistic innovators as Frank Lloyd Wright have set new trends that Contemporary designers today follow.

Market popularity of Contemporary variations has encouraged modern designers to continue these architectural trends. People choose to live in Contemporary homes, because the designs do fit their lifestyle. That includes their love of outdoor space, views, home recreation, multiple leisure interests, privacy, time-saving home maintenance, and a simple yet brash outlook on life in general.

Hence most Contemporary homes feature large vertical windows, open

Design T72791, Pg. 44

GABLED ENDS - Multiple gabled roof lines of English Tudor Styling have been redefined for Contemporary homes. Here a large glass area extends into the gable, set in structural wood. End gables often encase windows for design accent in this manner. Half-timbering is employed. Eaves generally are broadened to create a new sense of shelter.

space, efficient kitchens, roofs easily maintained, many large bathrooms, balconies, patios, multi-purpose rooms, and simple yet bold lines that thrust skyward or trail in woodsy overhangs. The slogan of Contemporary designers became "form follows functions," later revised to read, "form and function are one."

Our Contemporary homes suggest that people today spend much of their time in the back of their homes where terraces, patios, large glass viewing areas, and side balconies offer personal time alone. Fronts of Contemporary homes suggest that people today are more private. That seems especially true in the suburbs and country – Contemporary domains where neighbors see less of each other by design. Indeed, Contemporary frontals today often expose less of the private home to the street with smaller window space. The smaller windows often are used to cast interesting natural lighting effects on the home's inner sanctum.

Earlier Contemporary architecture, still popular in many parts of the country, seemed to offer more large window view in the front of the home. Today with seclusion-minded suburbanites, back-to-nature enthusiasts, and baby-boomers now middle-aged and seeking security in a crowd, we see more backyard living and less openness to the world out front. However, a challenge for Contemporary planning is to provide sound living patterns and good indoor-outdoor relationships with concern for site and solar orientation. While modern families now live much of the time in the rear of their

Design T72244, Pg. 77

GABLE WITH MODERN FLAT ROOF - Here is a design popular in the Pacific Northwest. A steep gabled roof has been combined pleasantly with a modern flat roof. The design likely originated in Pacific Island climates. It has migrated also to the American Southeast climates where light rainfall presents little problem to water buildup.

homes, homes continue to face the south in most urban developments, with rear living areas facing the cold north.

Contemporary homes naturally vary with regions and their many variations in common vernacular. Like a living language of a people, Contemporary architecture is idiomatic and constantly changing almost too rapidly to classify. You can see traces of European, Early American, and Later American period architecture in many Contemporary designs. If you look closely, you'll even see some Cubism, International Styling, and Modernist design. In today's Contemporary marketplace, what works and proves popular continues to sell.

So many Contemporary homes contain nostalgic traces of Tudor styling, Georgian, Salt Boxes, Cape Cod design, or other period architecture. These represent the classics, and people who like classics are willing to accept minor constraints in smaller window size, exacting materials specifications, and other building details to live in their classic.

Contemporary innovators borrowed heavily from the Modernist and International Styling periods that immediately preceeded their new art form. Consequently, large-glass openness, geometrical shapes, and bold, yet elegant lines entered their new creation's equation. Their new mix of styles, however, also reflects America's mixture of people in

Design T72431, Pg. 268

THE A-FRAME - This hardy Northwest innovation has persisted to this day and may be found in many updated applications. Often this involves recreational retreats or cabins, but can include sturdy year-round homes. The design easily weathers heavy snowfall and rain. The downpour just runs off its back. Note the side balcony in the illustration. Original A-frame designs included a side carport.

Design T72256, Pg. 89

GABLED ENTRY - Here the English gabled roof line is employed as a gabled entry. Again, notice the expansive use of vertical glass. Typical of much Contemporary design, lines of this house are horizontal. A deck extends the house with a railed overhang unto a backyard terrace, demonstrating Contemporary integration of indoor-outdoor relationships.

Design T71756, Pg. 106

CALIFORNIA RANCHERO - This early California ranch-style house is Spanish in origin and flavor. Notice the secluded courtyard and covered walkway to the front door. There are wide overhangs, exposed rafter tails, and a spacious sense of openness with this rambling house.

(Cont'd. From Pg. 5)
the new melting pot of cultures. So one sees Americans' favorite aspects of many traditional architectural forms in their redefined boxes. One sees the Tudor roof line shape dramatically maintained and supported by effective glass gable exterior walls. One sees Cubism of an earlier period restated in Contemporary terms as bold geometric shapes. And one certainly sees Classic International Styling with its walls of glass in much Contemporary design.

Contemporary architecture sometimes is called modern architecture. While Contemporary design certainly is modern, it should not be confused with Post-Modern Design, a modernistic architecture that takes a backward glance at charming styles of old in applying a new facelift. Typically, Gothic Victorian style of the mid-19th Century is treated to a neo-Gothic look with vertical lines, steep roofs, and variety of gables reminiscent of the grand houses of yesteryear. The bold new angular shapes and interior, however, are designed for today's housing market and should be included in a discussion of modern design.

Asymmetrical, angular Contemporary architecture "breaks the box" of traditional design, marking Americans' break with their European ancestry. It's no small coincidence that Contemporary architecture blossomed after World War II with a new sense of Americanism. With

Design T71754, Pg. 99

U-SHAPED RANCH HOUSE - This practical ranch design, reminiscent of Northwest Vernacular, employs split shingle roof and efficient zoning of household activities. Notice the private enclosed courtyard, low pitch, and wide overhangs. These are typical features of many Contemporary homes.

world victory and modern technology, Americans took new nationalistic pride in their expansive, bold lifestyle. New Contemporary architecture reflects that change as a truly American art form.

New Americans wanted more than their immigrant parents: more rooms for their increasingly complex interests, more command of spectacular enjoyment, more boldness in personal statements. And so their new Contemporary design homes became their personal statements. Americans had arrived as world leaders, trend setters – no longer simple immitators. Now they would redefine their world and settle into a lifestyle of enjoyment.

While Contemporary homes may be found throughout the United States, modern design is most readily rooted in the Pacific Northwest, Spanish Southwest, and Midwest.

Particularly in the Northwest, climate, materials, designers, builders, and especially consumers showed early preference for Contemporary design. The western frontier, of course, represented a world of wide open spaces, spectacular nature view, raw timber, and new thinking. There pioneers carved themselves a new lifestyle befitting their new world and pioneer thinking.

By contrast, the American Northeast and Southeast generally have retained popular interest in classic Early American architecture with some integration

Design T72557, Pg. 251

ECLECTIC SOUTHWEST CONTEMPORARY - Much Southwest Contemporary design emphasizes outdoor living and employs Spanish styling, often in combination with styles from other cultures. Styles that adapt well to desert climate have been incorporated into much Southwest design.

Design T72595, Pg. 81

WING-SHAPED HOUSE - The roof line and horizontal lines of this house are reminiscent of most ranch-style houses, but the building has been extended in a wing shape. It almost looks like three combined bunk houses back on the ranch. This wing shape allows zoning efficiency of household activities with the spaciousness of open ranch-style living.

(Cont'd. From Pg. 7)

of Contemporary design concepts. This includes incorporatoin of wider windows, modern construction systems, and Contemporary floor plans on Early American homes that may appear classic on the outside but updated on the inside.

The Northwest

The rustic Contemporary architecture of the Northwest reflects its woodsy surroundings in the land of the great outdoors. Consequently, much modern Northwest architecture includes extended wood beams, exposed rafter tails, heavy shake roofs, dark-stained wood exteriors, woodpanel walls, rough-cut siding, wide overhangs, large view windows, and balconies. Indeed, much Northwest architecture resembles the classic "house in the woods" or leisure homes with year-round residents. As with all successful architecture, Northwest modern homes fit their woodsy surroundings and building materials employ readily accessible natural resources.

The Southwest

Homes of the Southwest incorporate Spanish and Indian design in addition to Contemporary styling. The nomadic, eclectic Southwest also has incorporated design features from other places around the world including Egyptian, Mediterranean, English, and French styling.

Masonry walls and concrete block or adobe are employed, often washed with stucco finish to protect the surface. Southwestern Contemporary homes often incorporate roof decks, porches, sheltered "ramada" terraces, shady overhangs, and blank walls that face west away from the burning sun. Desert climate has dictated design, with need for year-round environmental control. Floors often are tile, quarry, or scored concrete to weather the heat. Central patios feature fountains with plants.

The ranch house continues to be popular in the Southwest with modern addition of varied roof lines, new materials, and Pacific styling adopted from Japanese and Hawaiian climes.

Generally, the composit Contemporary homes of the Southwest are simple, open, comfortable, and informal. Modern homes there fit their environment and the people who live there.

The Midwest

In the American Midwest, the western ranch house was introduced after World War II, although changed from original rough-cut timbered look of the west to brick and asphalt and changed from long, low lines to mass of refined detailing and Midwest character.

Much Midwest farm architecture still reflects a sense of mass or self-enclosure with rambling buildings of various roof lines and pitches all leaning toward a central point. The Midwest continues to combine design from both east and west with practical substitution of Midwest materials.

The sophisticated beauty of International Styling's walls of glass and Cubism continue in urban pockets of the Midwest, just as International's post and steal-beam glass houses persist in the Southwest. Many Midwest buildings also reflect the Twenties' European Cubistic concept of man's overcoming nature with Modernistic buildings on platforms above ground.

Modern Midwest architecture, however, is becoming more informal with emphasis on aesthetic values over disciplined art forms in quest of space, freedom, and outdoors. The Midwest compromise has given birth to a new refined, yet informal Contemporary house. Classic architectural forms also are altered to accommodate a more informal and modern Midwest lifestyle. Stately brick, readily available in much of the Midwest, continues its popularity as a building material.

The Northeast

In the Northeast, Early American design often is integrated with modern styling, although adaptations of authentic Early American period architecture continues to show popularity in this region. Many New England homes today are reminiscent of traditional styles on the outside with modern floor plans and wider windows than traditional styles of which they are copies. Other Contemporary lifestyle features have been integrated for modern livability.

Once simple Cape Cod cottages of few rooms and sleeping attic have been modified to larger homes. Often these are sheathed in aluminum or steel, brick, plastic-coated plywood, and chemically treated hardboards on concrete block.

The high-pitched roof continues to be a feature of modern Cape Cod cottage adaptations popular in New England. Northeast climate dictates steep roofs to shed snow and thick walls against cold.

Market popularity of traditional Early American styles continues to reflect the European roots of New Englanders who prefer to preserve their ancestral past.

(Cont'd. Pg. 9)

Design T72747, Pg. 80

EXTENDED RANCH HOUSE - This "rambling ranch" exploits the cluster house concept for add-on buildings for more rooms. Contemporary lifestyle dictates additional rooms for increasingly diverse use of leisure time. Zoning in this extended house also allows isolation of some rooms.

The Southeast

In the South, what's architecturally Contemporary often demonstrates a compromise of traditional styling and modern lines, marking the reverence for traditional preservation of the region. International Styling influences modern design almost as much as Contemporary's use of natural materials and integration of building and environment.

Southern Contemporary homes often employ rough, natural materials and variety of shapes in informal designs. Many modern Southern homes employ stone, stained rough wood and other natural materials for texture.

Pictures Tell the Story

Labels sometimes are confusing in describing any art form as dynamic as lifestyle habitat. Many people use the terms Modern and Contemporary interchangeably, just as people sometimes use terms Southern Colonial and Greek Revival or even Colonial and Early American interchangeably. We try to cut through this confusion in semantics with pictures that tell the story in this book and its companion book, *The Essential Guide to Early American Home Plans.* Architects themselves sometimes disagree on the labels, but examples show the story of how Americans today choose to live and the styles of homes they choose for living. Our illustrations depict the actual designs for homes being built today with blueprints available from the publisher. The exteriors and floor plans featured in this book are examples of the diverse nature of our readers' tastes and preference for Contemporary styling. ∎

Design T72793, Pg. 36

HORIZONTAL LINES - The horizontal lines, typical of much Contemporary design, are illustrated by the house at the right. Notice the alternating use of wood, masonry, and glass for textured look of the exterior. Also note the modern cuts in the roof at right. These are not skylights, but openings to allow light and rain to fall easily on plants in an open area.

Design T72895, Pg. 118

BALCONY EXTENDS HOUSE - Contemporary homes generally are horizontal and sprawling. In the illustration at right, center, a long balcony is used to extend the horizontal lines of a two-story house and also add walk-out to enjoy the outdoors. Notice the skylights cut into the roof, and the effective use of contrasting exterior building materials for texture. Used in good proportion, these varied materials creates·walls with clean lines.

Design T72526, Pg. 134

THE NATURAL LOOK - The livable Contemporary home at the bottom demonstrates use of rugged exposed beams, vertical windows for natural lighting, woodsy overhangs, and alternating use of wood, masonry and glass. This is the natural look. Notice also the effective use of a lower level entry.

Design T72848, Pg. 126

Design T72874, Pg. 298

GEOMETRIC SHAPES - Dramatic shapes of component elements in the house above demonstrate how Contemporary designers continue to "break the box" of symmetrical traditionalism. The shapes often make dramatic statement. Here diagonal and vertical wood siding is employed. Notice the backyard balcony, view windows in rear, and lower level terrace used as a patio.

POST-MODERN DESIGN - New modernistic architecture takes a backward glance at charming styles of old in applying a new facelift (See house at left). Often Gothic Victorian style of the mid-19th Century is treated to a neo-Gothic look with vertical lines, steep roofs, and variety of gables reminiscent of the grand houses of yesterday.

VERTICAL GLASS - The outstanding feature of the practical, little 1½-story house below seems to be the vertical expanse of glass afforded by a small upper floor. The tiny upstairs offers today's family space to grow with extra bedrooms or storage, as their lifestyle and needs change. Essentially this house is designed to function as a one-story home.

Design T72822, Pg. 63

Design T71428

Design T72418, Pg. 265

CIRCULAR GLASS HOUSE - The beam-supported walls of glass in the modern glass house above are reminiscent of the Classic International Styling that has influenced Contemporary design. International Styling was dominant the early half of the century.

WINGED ROOF - The swept wing curve of the modern roof at left illustrates how roof lines today often are used to make statements with geometric shapes in residential architecture. This house looks prepared for flight. Here it's used as a house on the beach, a perfect setting for seagulls, sandpipers, and wing-roofed houses.

WIDE OVERHANGS - The house below illustrates that wide overhanging roofs are popular in much Contemporary design today. Eaves, rear balconies, and the basic roof line all provide overhang. The simple roof line is extended to provide a carport. Notice the natural look of rough lumber mixed with stone.

Design T72546, Pg. 116

Design T72123, Pg. 188

DRAMATIC SIMPLE ROOF - This simple split shingle roof sweeps down in a dramatic statement that is typical of much Contemporary design. Of course, the roof also is economical and easily maintained. Notice the use of large vertical window door cut into the roof line to bisect the shape almost symmetrically.

Design T72135, Pg. 42

CENTRAL MASS - Varying roof lines and components converge to a center point in this rambling house. This is not just an architectural statement. For the residents, the design allows excellent zoning of many rooms. Some areas of the house may be quiet areas. Others may be for various group and personal activities. Notice the courtyard and exposed beams. Here an atrium is located in the center.

Design T72392, Pg. 108

ENCLOSED MASS - Varying roof planes and textured blank wall mass converge. The house at left, top appears private from the front. In the rear, it unfolds with balconies, view windows, and covered patio to provide residents with splendid indoor-outdoor livability. The rough-cut lumber construction and woodsy overhangs give the house a "house in the woods" personality.

LOWER-LEVEL PATIO - Often balconies cover lower level terraces to form covered patios, as illustrated by the house at center. Notice how dramatic roof lines form geometric shapes. Overhangs and rough-cut lumber construction also make a statement. This house celebrates the great outdoors.

THE MODERN GREENHOUSE - Solar-oriented designs for sun rooms or greenhouses have become very popular in Contemporary homes. The illustration below shows how the entire rear of a house has been encased in glass for maximum exposure to glorious sunlight. Special upper clerestory windows trap and circulate heat around the inner shell. The flip-top windows give the design popular name of envelope house.

Design T72511, Pg. 107

Design T72884, Pg. 32

Design T72830, Pg. 22

SOLAR-ORIENTED DESIGN - The passive solar design above combines a solarium with passive solar heating devices and optional active energy collectors. Typically, sun through large windows heats a rock wall. The heated wall, in turn, keeps the rest of the home's walls warm for hours. Skylights in the roof help capture sun. Other more active solar designs use a collector and apparatus for storing and dispersing collected solar energy. Many Con-

temporary homes now employ elements of simple passive solar design.

EARTH SHELTER DESIGN - The roof of the house below is covered by earth and the entire house oriented toward the south for maximum sun in this energy-efficient design. Notice the skylights. The sun's warmth is tapped, and the ground holds the warmth. Also notice the sunken patio or terrace this design affords.

Design T72860, Pg. 54

'Sun passes through large southern windows to heat walls, keeping the home warm inside for hours . . . .'

Design T72384, Pg. 83

MANSARD CONTEMPORARY - This French roof of the house at left is growing increasingly popular in Contemporary design. With western cedar shakes, it's woodsy and easily maintained. Note the various overhangs and sloping roof plane in this L-shaped ranch house.

1½-STORY HIP ROOF - The practical variation of the French Mansard roof (below) allows a small second story for today's smaller family. The cedar shake roof is very woodsy, very western, and very Contemporary.

'The cedar shake roof is very woodsy, very western, and very Contemporary. It's growing increasingly popular . . . .'

Design T72309, Pg. 193

Design T72858, Pg. 29

Design T72893, Pg. 135

COMPOSITE "TREND" HOUSE -
Contemporary designs that incorporate many of the modern lifestyle needs and luxuries often are called Trend Houses (See example above). They represent the new state of the art in pleasing today's home builders. Observe how this house has been designed for a south-facing site. It provides indoor-outdoor livability to the front. Afternoon southern sun is allowed to reach the back yard through the glass.

CLEAN LINES - The elegant Contemporary home at left illustrates the clean walls and clean lines of many Contemporary homes today. Not all modern designs are angular with exposed beams. Excellent proportions of the alternating walls of brick and glass create both clean lines and controlled texture. Note the balcony. This is a home for modern living with plenty of sun, view, and fresh air. Careful planning attention has been given to indoor-outdoor relationships.

Recommended reading:

- *The American House* by Mary Mix Foley, drawings by Madelaine Thatcher (Harper & Row, 1980, paperback) 299 pages with glossary.

- *Home Planners' Guide to Residential Design* by Charles W. Talcott (McGraw-Hill, 1986, paperback) 218 pages with glossary.

- *The Illustrated Guide to the Houses of America* by Richard M. Ballinger and Herman York (Hawthorn Books, Inc., 1971, hardback) 260 pages with glossary.

TREND HOUSES Solar-Oriented Livability

... Increasing building costs, awareness of solar-orientation, and technology are combining to change the way we live. Trend houses are new housing configurations whose floor plans break from convention with modern extras including high ceilings, glass expanses, and great rooms.

Design T72827 1,618 Sq. Ft. - Upper Level
1,458 Sq. Ft. - Lower Level; 41,370 Cu. Ft.

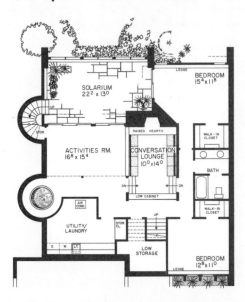

● The two-story solarium with skylights above is the key to energy savings to this bi-level design. Study the efficiency of this floor plan. The conversation lounge on the lower level is a unique focal point.

A Sunspace Spa Highlights this Trend House

● Contemporary in exterior styling, this house is energy oriented. It calls for 2 x 6 exterior wall construction with placement on a north facing lot. Traffic flows through the interior of this plan by way of the foyer. Not only is the foyer useful, but it is dramatic with its sloped ceiling and second floor balcony and skylight above. Excellent living areas are throughout. A spacious, sunken living room is to the left of the foyer. It shares a thru-fireplace, faced with fieldstone, with the study. Sloped ceilings are in both of these rooms. Informal activities can take place in the family room. It, too, has a fireplace and is adjacent to the work center. Two of the bedrooms are on the second floor with a lounge overlooking the gathering room below. The master bedroom is on the first floor. A generous amount of closet space with mirrored doors will enhance its appearance. Study the spacious master bath with all of its many features. Its direct access to the sunspace spa. will be appreciated.

Design T72900 *2,332 Sq. Ft. - First Floor; 953 Sq. Ft. - Second Floor; 46,677 Cu. Ft.*

Passive solar benefits will be acquired from the spa. It transmits light and heat to the other parts of the house. Heat stored during the day, by the stone floor, will be circulated at night by mechanical means. Shades may be used to control the amount of heat gain. This spa provides a large area where various activities can be done at the same time. Note the bar, whirlpool and exercise area. It will be a cheerful and spacious family recreation area. There are 551 square feet and 9,200 cubic feet in the sunspace spa which are not included in the above totals.

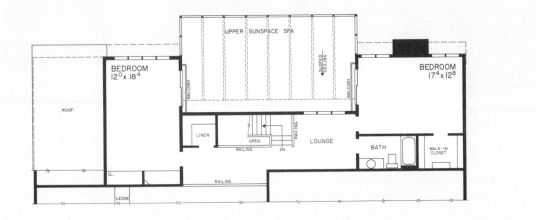

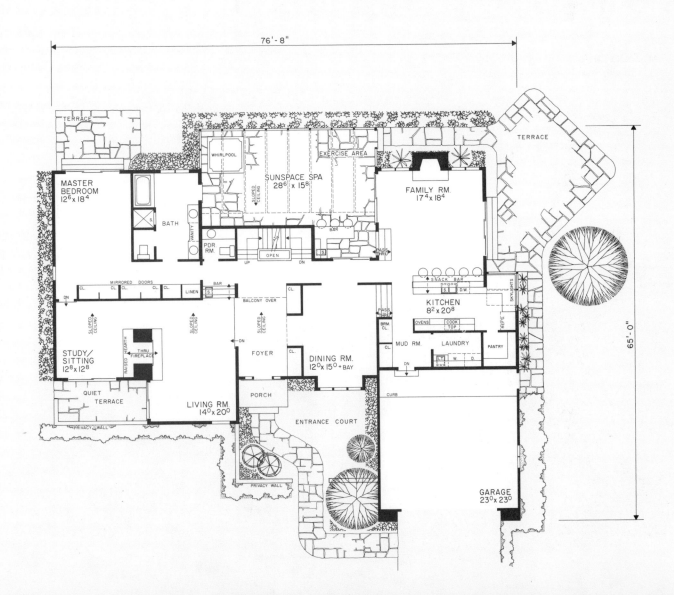

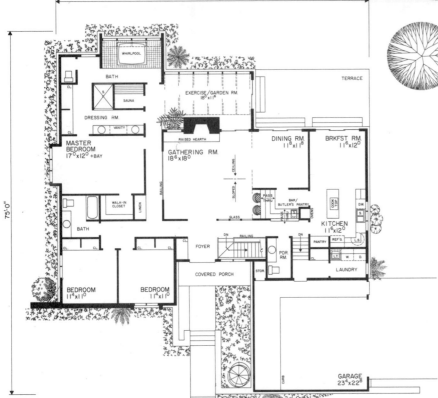

Design T72873
2,838 Sq. Ft.; 58,960 Cu. Ft.

● This modern three-bedroom home incorporates many of the Contemporary features so popular today. A large gathering room with cozy raised-hearth fireplace and sloped ceiling is central focus and centrally located. Adjacent to the gathering room is a dining room that adjoins a bar or butler's pantry. This handy service area also has pass-thru entry to the central gathering room. Just off the pantry is a large modern kitchen with central cook-top island and adjoining breakfast room. The master bedroom suite is especially luxurious with its own sauna, whirlpool, dressing room, bay window, and adjoining exercise room. This adjacent exercise room could double as a lovely garden room. It's located just off the back terrace. There's even a powder room for guests in front, and a covered porch to keep visitors dry. A laundry is conveniently located off the spacious two-car garage. Note the large view glass off the rear exercise/garden room. This is a comfortable and modern home, indeed.

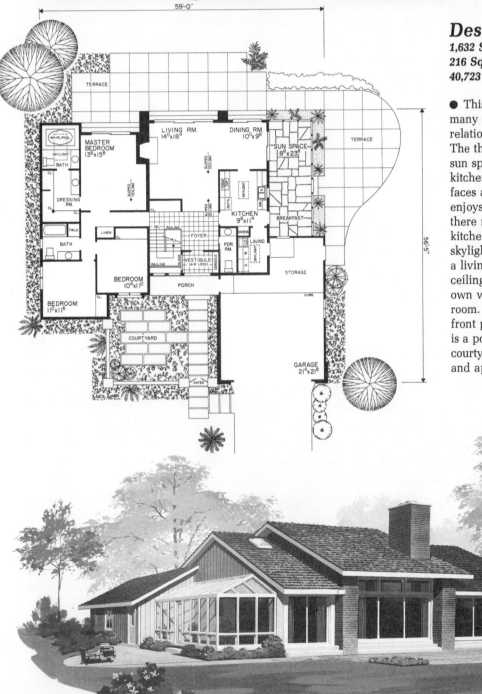

Design T72902
1,632 Sq. Ft. - Living Area
216 Sq. Ft. - Sun Space
40,723 Cu. Ft.

● This modern trend home captures many of the comforts and indoor-outdoor relationships sought by families today. The three-bedroom home incorporates a sun space just off the breakfast room, kitchen, and dining room. The sun space faces a side terrace. The modern kitchen enjoys its own skylight to make work there more cheerful. Adjacent to the kitchen is a handy laundry with its own skylight. The formal dining room opens to a living room with fireplace and sloped ceiling. A master bedroom suite enjoys its own whirlpool, skylight, and dressing room. An air-locked vestibule buffers the front porch from foyer. Just off the foyer is a powder room for guests. A front courtyard further enhances the comfort and appearance of this sunlit, cozy home.

Design T72830   1,795 Sq. Ft. - Main Level; 1,546 Sq. Ft. - Lower Level; 49,900 Cu. Ft.

● Outstanding contemporary design! This home has been created with the advantages of passive solar heating in mind. For optimum energy savings, this delightful design combines passive solar devices, the solarium, with optional active collectors. Included with the purchase of this design are four plot plans to assure that the solar collectors will face the south. The garage in each plan acts as a buffer against cold northern winds. Schematic details for solar application also are included. Along with being energy-efficient, this design has excellent living patterns. Three bedrooms, the master bedroom on the main level and two others on the lower level at each side of the solarium. The living area of the main level will be able to enjoy the delightful view of the solarium and sunken garden.

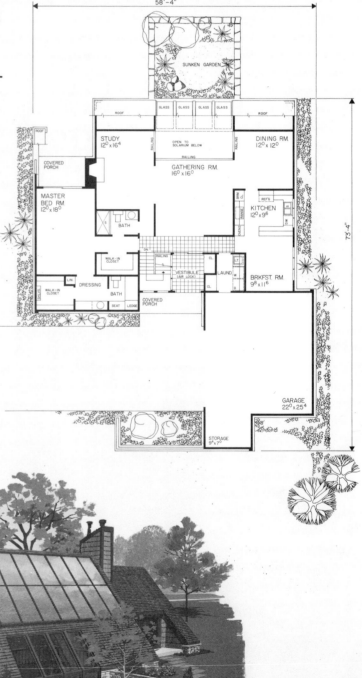

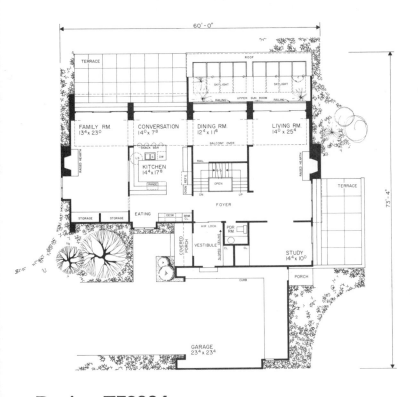

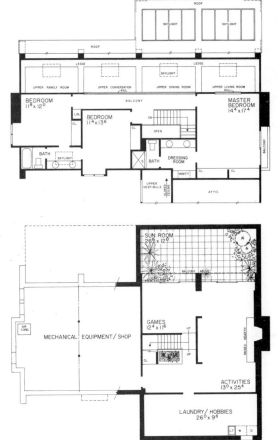

Design T72834
1,775 Sq. Ft. - First Floor; 1,041 Sq. Ft. - Second Floor
1,128 Sq. Ft. - Lower Level; 55,690 Cu. Ft.

● This passive solar design offers 4,200 square feet of livability situated on three levels. The primary passive element will be the lower level sun room which admits sunlight for direct-gain heating. The solar warmth collected in the sun room will radiate into the rest of the house after it passes the sliding glass doors. During the warm summer months, shades are put over the skylight to protect it from direct sunlight. This design has the option of incorporating active solar heating panels to the roof. The collectors would be installed on the south-facing portion of the roof. They would absorb the sun's warmth for both domestic water and supplementary space heating. An attic fan exhausts any hot air out of the house in the summer and circulates air in the winter. With or without the active solar panels, this is a marvelous two-story contemporary.

23

Clutter Room, Media Room To The Fore

● Something new? Something new, indeed!! Here is the introduction of two rooms which will make a wonderful contribution to family living. The clutter room is strategically placed between the kitchen and garage. It is the nerve center of the work area. It houses the laundry, provides space for sewing, has a large sorting table, and even plenty of space for the family's tool bench. A handy potting area is next to the laundry tray. Adjacent to

the clutter room, and a significant part of the planning of this whole zone, are the pantry and freezer with their nearby counter space. These facilities surely will expedite the unloading of groceries from the car and their convenient storing. Wardrobe and broom closets, plus washroom complete the outstanding utility of this area. The location of the clutter room with all its fine cabinet and counter space means that the often numerous family projects

can be on-going. This room is ideally isolated from the family's daily living patterns. The media room may be thought of as the family's entertainment center. While this is the room for the large or small TV, the home movies, the stereo and VCR equipment, it will serve as the library or study. It would be ideal as the family's home office with its computer equipment. Your family will decide just how it will utilize this outstanding area.

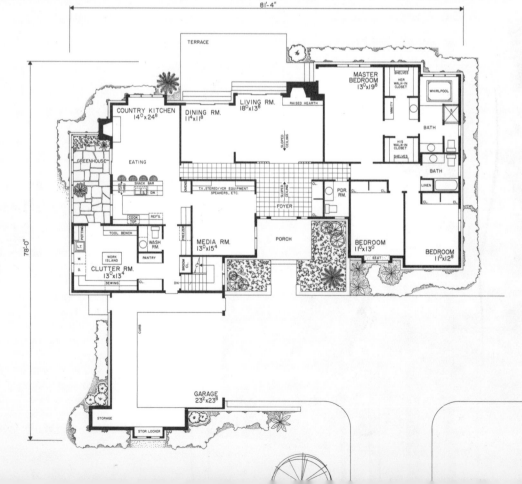

Design T72915 2,758 Sq. Ft.; 60,850 Cu Ft.

● The features of this appealing contemporary design go far beyond the clutter and media rooms. The country kitchen is spacious and caters to the family's informal living and dining activities. While it overlooks the rear yard it is just a step from the delightful greenhouse. Many happy hours will be spent here enjoying to the fullest the outdoors from within. The size of the greenhouse is 8'x18' and contains 149 sq. ft. not included in the square footage quoted above. The formal living and dining areas feature spacious open planning. Sloping ceiling in the living room, plus the sliding glass doors to the outdoor terrace enhance the cheerfulness of this area. The foyer is large and routes traffic efficiently to all areas. Guest coat closets and a powder room are handy. The sleeping zone is well-planned. Two children's bedrooms have fine wall space, good wardrobe facilities and a full bath. The master bedroom is exceptional. It is large enough to accommodate a sitting area and has access to the terrace. Two walk-in closets, a vanity area with lavatory and a compartmented bath are noteworthy features. Observe the stall shower in addition to the dramatic whirlpool installation. The floor plan below is identical with that on the opposite page and shows one of many possible ways to arrange furniture.

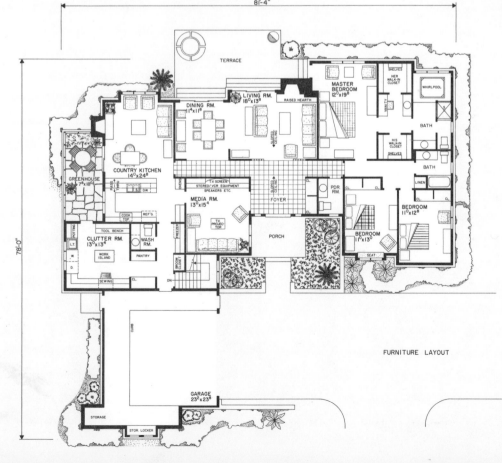

FURNITURE LAYOUT

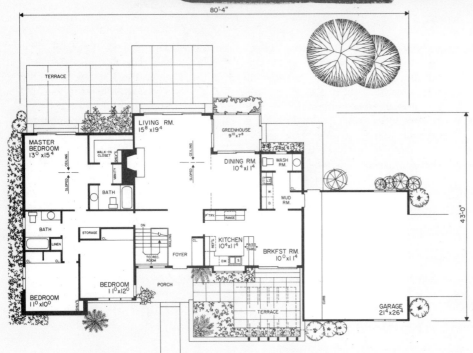

TERRACE

MASTER
BEDROOM
13⁰ x15⁴

WALK-IN
CLOSET

LIVING RM.
15⁸ x19⁴

GREENHOUSE
9¹⁰ x7⁸

DINING RM.
10⁴ x11⁴

WASH
RM.

MUD
RM.

VANITY

BATH

SLOPED CEILING

BATH

STORAGE

DN

TO REC.
ROOM

RANGE

P'TRY

FOYER

KITCHEN
10⁴ x11⁴

PASS
THRU

BRKFST RM.
10⁰ x11⁴

LINEN

BEDROOM
11⁰ x12⁰

PORCH

BEDROOM
11⁰ x10⁰

TERRACE

CURB

GARAGE
21⁴ x26⁴

80'-4"

43'-0"

Design T72871
1,824 Sq. Ft. - Living Area
81 Sq. Ft. - Greenhouse Area
44,590 Cu. Ft.

● A greenhouse area off the dining room and living room provides a cheerful focal point for this comfortable three-bedroom Trend home. The spacious living room features a cozy fireplace and sloped ceiling. In addition to the dining room, there's a less formal breakfast room just off the modern kitchen. Both kitchen and breakfast areas look out into a front terrace. Stairs just off the foyer lead down to a recreation room. Master bedroom suite opens to a terrace. A mud room and washroom off the garage allow rear entry to the house during inclement weather.

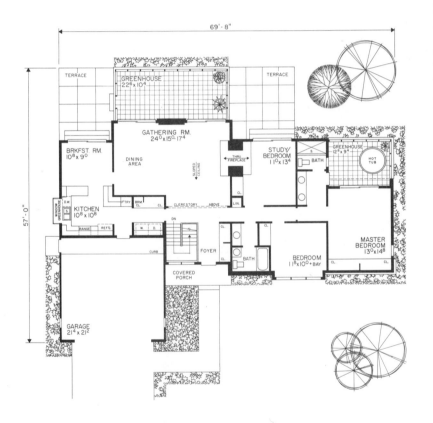

Design T72886
1,733 Sq. Ft.; 34,986 Cu. Ft.

● This one-story house is attractive with its contemporary exterior. It has many excellent features to keep you and your family happy for many years. For example, notice the spacious gathering room with sliding glass doors that allow easy access to the greenhouse. Another exciting feature of this room is that you will receive an abundance of sunshine through the clerestory windows. Also, this plan offers you two nice-sized bedrooms. The master suite is not only roomy but also unique because through both the bedroom and the bath you can enter a greenhouse with a hot tub. The hot tub will be greatly appreciated after a long, hard day at work. Don't forget to note the breakfast room with access to the terrace. You will enjoy the efficient kitchen that will make preparing meals a breeze. A greenhouse window here is charming. An appealing, open staircase leads to the basement. The square and cubic footages of the greenhouses are 394 and 4,070 respectively and are not included in the above figures.

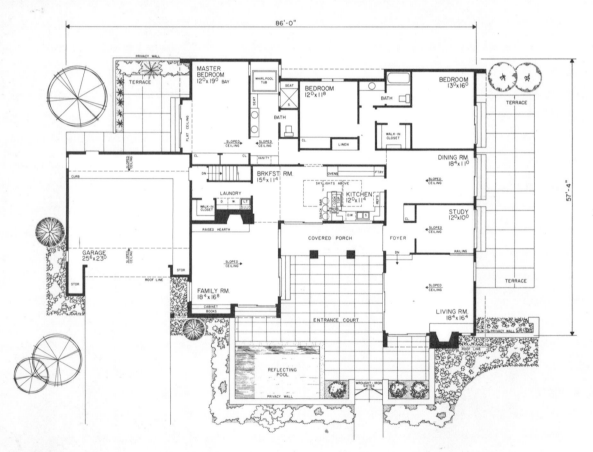

Design T72881 2,346 Sq. Ft.; 60,315 Cu. Ft.

● Energy-efficiency will be obtained in this unique, contemporary design. This plan has been designed for a south facing lot in the temperate zones. There is minimal window exposure on the north side of the house so the interior will be protected. The eastern side of the plan, on the other hand, will allow the morning sunlight to enter. As the sun travels from east to west, the various rooms will have light through windows, sliding glass doors or skylights. The garage acts as a buffer against the hot afternoon sun. The living areas are oriented to the front of the plan. They will benefit from the southern exposure during the cooler months. During the summer months, this area will be shielded from the high, hot summer sun by the overhanging roof. If you plan to build in the south, this house would be ideal for a north facing site. This results in a minimum amount of hot sun for the living areas and a maximum amount of protection from the sun on the rear, southern side of the house.

Design T72858
2,231 Sq. Ft.; 28,150 Cu. Ft.

● This sun oriented design was created to face the south. By doing so, it has minimal northern exposure. It has been designed primarily for the more temperate U.S. latitudes using 2 x 6 wall construction. The morning sun will brighten the living and dining rooms along with the adjacent terrace. Sun enters the garden room by way of the glass roof and walls. In the winter, the solar heat gain from the garden room should provide relief from high energy bills. Solar shades allow you to adjust the amount of light that you want to enter in the warmer months. Interior planning deserves mention, too. The work center is efficient. The kitchen has a snack bar on the garden room side and a serving counter to the dining room. The breakfast room with laundry area is also convenient to the kitchen. Three bedrooms are on the northern wall. The master bedroom has a large tub and a separate shower with a four foot square skylight above. When this design is oriented toward the sun, it should prove to be energy efficient and a joy to live in.

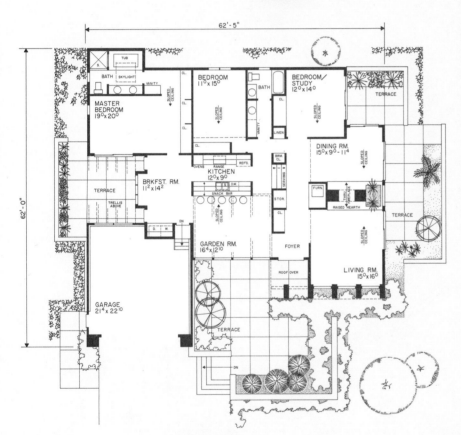

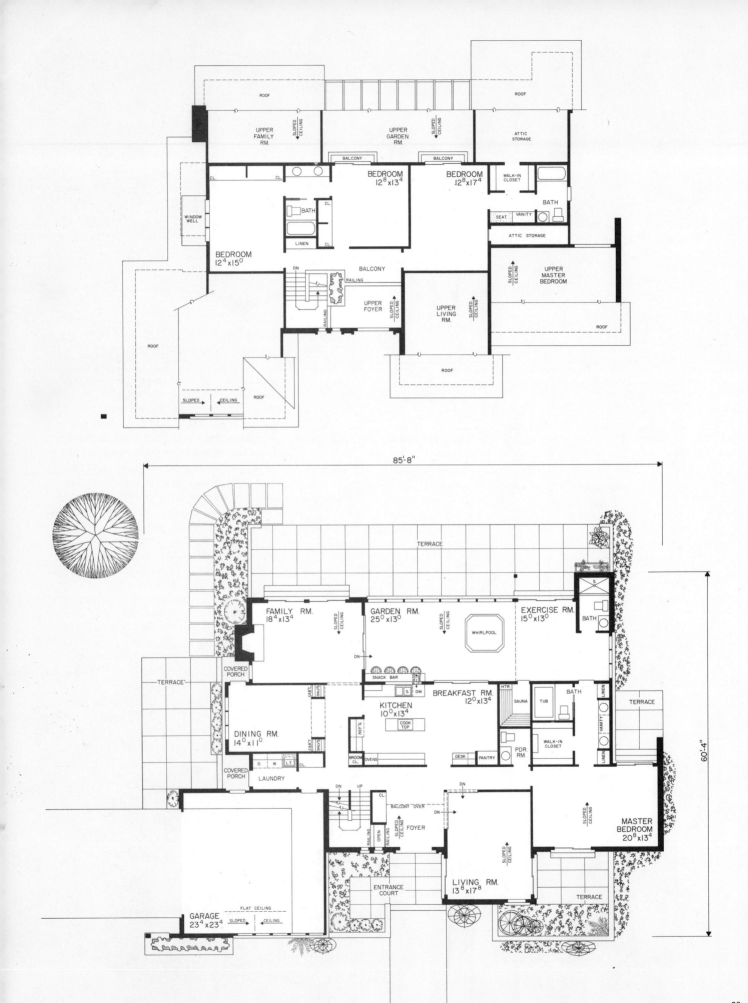

ROOF

ROOF

UPPER FAMILY RM.

SLOPED CEILING

UPPER GARDEN RM.

SLOPED CEILING

ATTIC STORAGE

CL.   CL.

BALCONY

BALCONY

WALK-IN CLOSET

BATH

BEDROOM 12⁸x13⁴

BEDROOM 12⁸x17⁴

WINDOW WELL

CL.

BATH

LINEN   CL.

SEAT   VANITY

ATTIC STORAGE

BEDROOM 12⁴x15⁰

DN

BALCONY

RAILING

UPPER MASTER BEDROOM

SLOPED CEILING

RAILING

UPPER FOYER

SLOPED CEILING

UPPER LIVING RM.

SLOPED CEILING

ROOF

SLOPED   CEILING   ROOF

ROOF

85'-8"

60'-4"

TERRACE

FAMILY RM. 18⁴x13⁴

SLOPED CEILING

GARDEN RM. 25⁰x13⁰

SLOPED CEILING

WHIRLPOOL

EXERCISE RM. 15⁰x13⁰

BATH

TERRACE

COVERED PORCH

SNACK BAR

DN

S.   D.W.

BREAKFAST RM. 12⁰x13⁴

HTR.

SAUNA   TUB   BATH

LINEN

VANITY

TERRACE

TERRACE'

KITCHEN 10⁰x13⁴

REF'G.

COOK TOP

DESK   PANTRY

PDR. RM.

WALK-IN CLOSET

LINEN

DINING RM. 14⁰x11⁰

CAB'T.   SHLVS.

CAB'T.   SHLVS.

BROOM CL.

OVENS

COVERED PORCH

LAUNDRY

D.   W.

LT.

CL.

DN   UP

CL.

BALCONY OVER

DN

DN

SLOPED CEILING

MASTER BEDROOM 20⁸x13⁴

RAILING

OPEN   RAILING

SLOPED CEILING   FOYER

SLOPED CEILING

GARAGE 23⁴x23⁴

FLAT CEILING

SLOPED   CEILING

ENTRANCE COURT

LIVING RM. 13⁸x17⁸

TERRACE

Design T72904 _2,724 Sq. Ft. - First Floor; 1,019 Sq. Ft. - Second Floor; 87,115 Cu. Ft._

● This modern four-bedroom Trend home is loaded with extras that make it an especially comfortable and practical place to live. Extras include a spacious garden room with its own whirlpool, snack bar off the kitchen, sloped ceiling, and view of a backyard terrace. Health-conscious members of the family are certain to appreciate an adjacent exercise room with its own bath and view of a backyard terrace. A modern kitchen is centrally located with a convenient cook-top island and adjacent breakfast room. There's also a more formal dining room downstairs, adjacent to a large family room with its own fireplace and sloped ceiling. A master bedroom suite also is located downstairs with its own view of a front terrace. Adjacent to a master bedroom is a spacious living room with sloped ceiling. Three other bedrooms are located upstairs. Two upstairs rooms have their own balconies. The upstairs area is easily accessible by stairs just off the front foyer. Excellent zoning, traffic patterns, indoor-outdoor relationships, and comforts in this modern design! Study the floor plan of this home carefully.

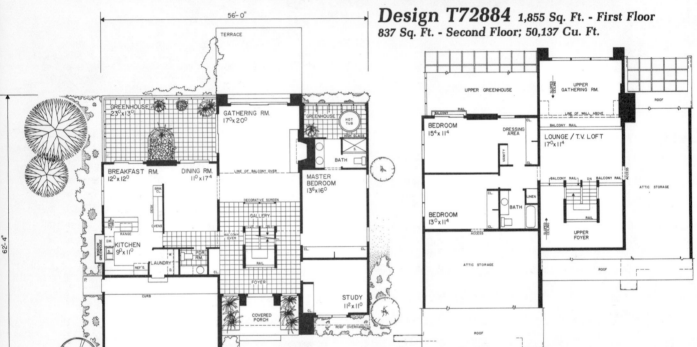

Design T72884 1,855 Sq. Ft. - First Floor
837 Sq. Ft. - Second Floor; 50,137 Cu. Ft.

GREENHOUSE 23⁰x13⁰

GATHERING RM. 17⁰x20⁰

GREENHOUSE

HOT TUB

BATH

BREAKFAST RM. 12⁰x12⁰

DINING RM. 11⁰x17⁴

MASTER BEDROOM 13⁶x16⁰

KITCHEN 9⁰x11⁰

GALLERY

LAUNDRY

PDR. RM.

FOYER

STUDY 11²x11⁰

GARAGE 23⁶x21⁶

TERRACE

COVERED PORCH

56'-0"

62'-4"

UPPER GREENHOUSE

UPPER GATHERING RM.

ROOF

BEDROOM 15⁴x11⁴

DRESSING AREA

LOUNGE / T.V. LOFT 17⁰x11⁴

ATTIC STORAGE

BEDROOM 13⁰x11⁴

BATH

UPPER FOYER

ATTIC STORAGE

ROOF

● The greenhouse in this design enhances its energy-efficiency and allows for spacious and interesting living patterns. Being a one-and-a-half story design, the second floor could be developed at a later date when the space is needed. The greenhouses add an additional 418 sq. ft. and 8,793 cu. ft. to the above quoted figures.

Design T72765 3,365 Sq. Ft.; 59,820 Cu. Ft.

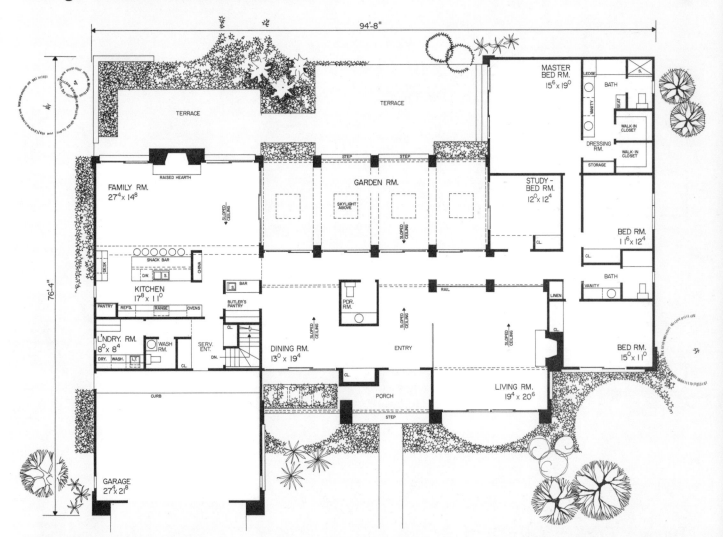

● This three (optional four) bedroom contemporary is a most appealing design. It offers living patterns that will add new dimensions to your everyday routine. The sloped ceilings in the family room, dining room and living room add much spaciousness to this home. The efficient kitchen has many fine features including the island snack bar and work center, built-in desk, china cabinet and wet bar. Adjacent to the kitchen is a laundry room, washroom and stairs to the basement. Formal and informal living will each have its own area. A raised hearth fireplace and sliding glass doors to the rear terrace in the informal family room. Another fireplace in the front formal living room. You will enjoy all that natural light in the garden room from the skylights in the sloped ceiling.

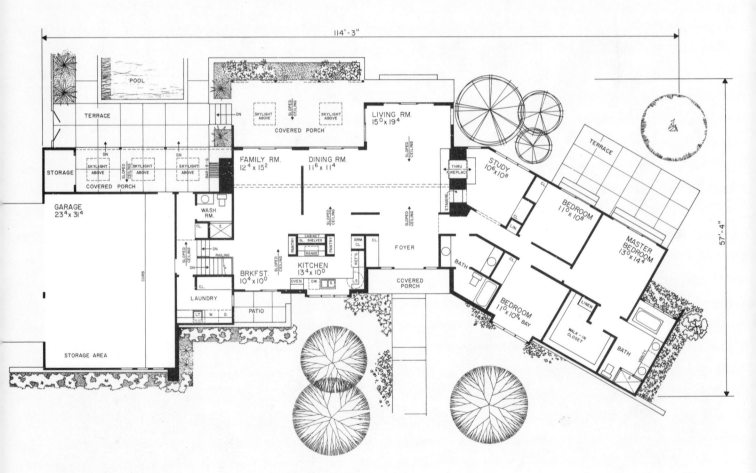

Design T72819 *2,459 Sq. Ft.; 45,380 Cu. Ft.*

● Indoor-outdoor living will be enjoyed to the fullest in this rambling one-story contemporary plan. Each of the rear rooms in this design, excluding the study, has access to a terrace or porch. Even the front breakfast room has access to a private dining patio. The covered porch off the living areas, family, dining and living rooms, has a sloped ceiling and skylights. A built-in barbecue unit and a storage room will be found on the second covered porch. Inside, the plan offers exceptional living patterns for various activities. Notice the thru-fireplace that the living room shares with the study. A built-in etagere is nearby. The three-car garage has an extra storage area.

Design T72866 2,371 Sq. Ft.; 50,120 Cu. Ft.

● An extra living unit has been built into the design of this home. It would make an excellent "mother-in-law" suite. Should you choose not to develop this area as indicated, maybe you might use it as two more bedrooms, a guest suite or even as hobby and game rooms. Whatever its final use, it will compliment the rest of this home. The main house also deserves mention. The focal point will be the large gathering room. Its features include a skylight, sloped ceiling, centered fireplace flanked on both sides by sliding glass doors and adjacent is a dining room on one side, study on the other. The work center is clustered together. Three bedrooms and two baths make up the private area. Note the outdoor areas: court with privacy wall, two covered porches and a large terrace.

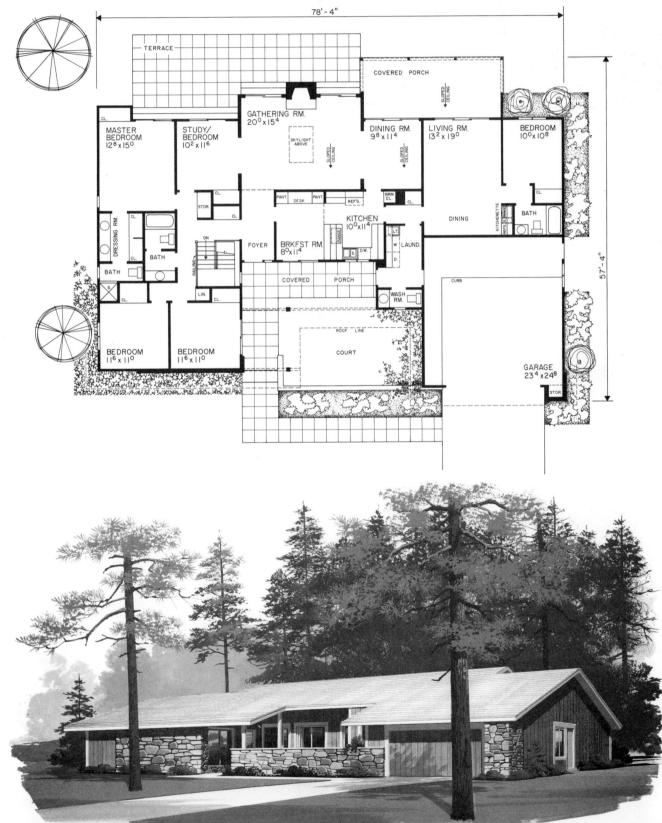

Design T72793 2,065 Sq. Ft.; 48,850 Cu. Ft.

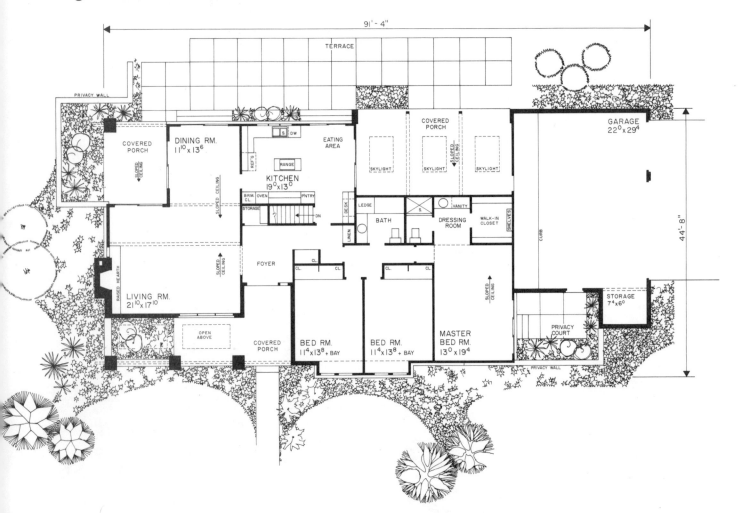

● Privacy will be enjoyed in this home both inside and out. The indoor-outdoor living relationships offered in this plan are outstanding. A covered porch at the entrance. A privacy court off the master bedroom divided from the front yard with a privacy wall. A covered porch serving both the living and dining rooms through sliding glass doors. Also utilizing a privacy wall. Another covered porch off the kitchen eating area. This one is the largest and has skylights above. Also a large rear terrace. The kitchen is efficient with eating space available, an island range and built-in desk. Storage space is abundant. Note storage area in the garage and its overall size. Three front bedrooms. Raised hearth fireplace in the living room.

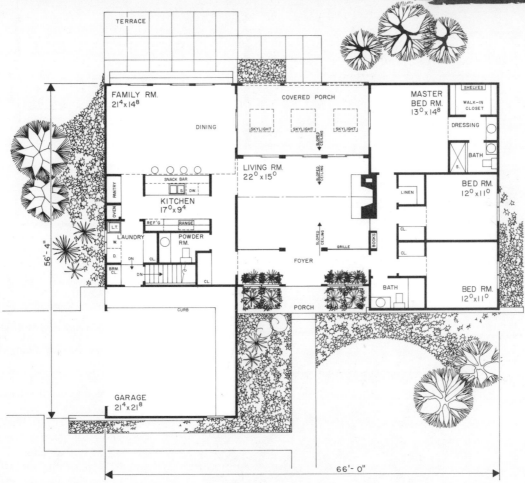

Floor plan labels:

TERRACE

FAMILY RM. 21⁴ x 14⁸

DINING

COVERED PORCH

SKYLIGHT   SKYLIGHT   SKYLIGHT

SLOPED CEILING

MASTER BED RM. 13⁰ x 14⁸

SHELVES   WALK-IN CLOSET

DRESSING   BATH

SNACK BAR   DW.

KITCHEN 17⁰ x 9⁴

PANTRY   OVEN

REF'G   RANGE

LIVING RM. 22⁰ x 15⁰

SLOPED CEILING

LINEN   BED RM. 12⁰ x 11⁰

CL   CL

LT.

LAUNDRY   POWDER RM.

W.   CL

D.   DN

BRM CL.   DN   CL

SLOPED CEILING

BOOKS   GRILLE

FOYER

CL   CL

CURB

PORCH

BATH   BED RM. 12⁰ x 11⁰

GARAGE 21⁴ x 21⁸

56'- 4"

66'- 0"

Design T72790 *2,075 Sq. Ft.; 45,630 Cu. Ft.*

● Enter this contemporary hip-roofed home through the double front doors and immediately view the sloped ceilinged living room with fireplace. This room will be a sheer delight when it comes to formal entertaining. It has easy access to the kitchen and also a powder room nearby. The work area will be convenient. The kitchen has an island work center with snack bar. The laundry is adjacent to the service entrance and stairs leading to the basement. This area is planned to be a real "step saver". The sleeping wing consists of two family bedrooms, bath and master bedroom suite. Maybe the most attractive feature of this design is the rear covered porch with skylights above. It is accessible by way of sliding glass doors in the family/dining area, living room and master bedroom.

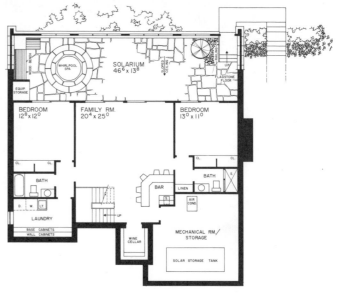

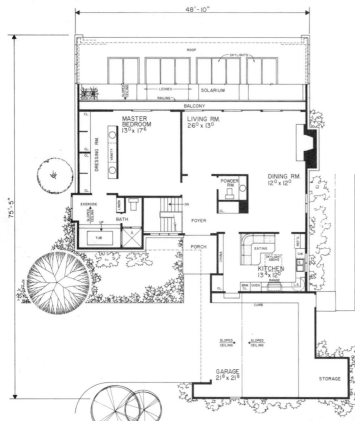

Design T72835 1,626 Sq. Ft. - Main Level
2,038 Sq. Ft. - Lower Level; 50,926 Cu. Ft.

● Passive solar techniques with the help of an active solar component - they can work together or the active solar component can act as a back-up system - heat and cool this striking contemporary design. The lower level solarium is the primary passive element. It admits sunlight during the day for direct-gain heating. The warmth, which was absorbed into the thermal floor, is then radiated into the structure at night. The earth berms on the three sides of the lower level help keep out the winter cold and summer heat. The active system uses collector panels to gather the sun's heat. The heat is transferred via a water pipe system to the lower level storage tank where it is circulated throughout the house by a heat exchanger. Note that where active solar collectors are a design OPTION, which they are in all of our active/passive designs, they must be contracted locally. The collector area must be tailored to the climate and sun angles that characterize your building location.

ATRIUM DESIGNS Accent Modern Homes

. . . Courtyards in the very heart of the home provide color for family members who appreciate nature and excellent indoor-outdoor relationships.

Design T72832
2,805 Sq. Ft. - Excluding Atrium; 52,235 Cu. Ft.

● The advantage of passive solar heating is a significant highlight of this contemporary design. The huge skylight over the atrium provides shelter during inclement weather, while permitting the enjoyment of plenty of natural light to the atrium below and surrounding areas. Whether open to the sky, or sheltered by a glass or translucent covering, the atrium becomes a cheerful spot and provides an abundance of natural light to its adjacent rooms. The stone floor will absorb an abundance of heat from the sun during the day and permit circulation of warm air to other areas at night. During the summer, shades afford protection from the sun without sacrificing the abundance of natural light and the feeling of spaciousness. Sloping ceilings highlight each of the major rooms, three bedrooms, formal living and dining and study. The conversation area between the two formal areas will really be something to talk about. The broad expanses of roof can accommodate solar panels should an active system be desired to supplement the passive features of this design.

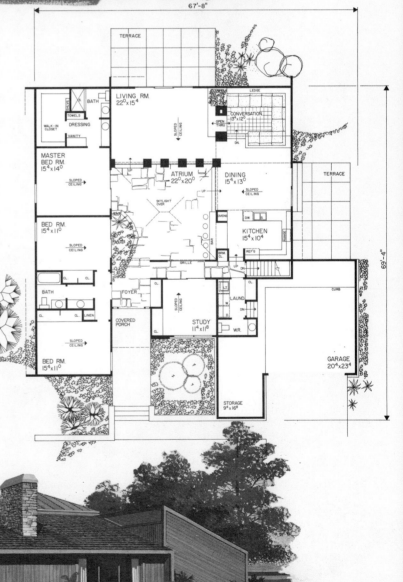

New Living Dimensions - Inside And Out

● Here is an impressive application of the Mansard type roof. Its wide overhang effectively compliments the simplicity of the brick masses. The curving driveway court strikes an appealing note. The entrance, flanked by planting areas, highlights double front doors. To each side, is an attractive glass panel. The breadth of the house is increased by the extension of the front wall. This, in turn, provides privacy for the side living terrace. To the rear, free standing brick walls provide further privacy as well as decorative appeal. The gently sloping roof has plastic domes which permit the interior to enjoy an added measure of natural light. Notice the indoor-outdoor living relationships available from every room in this design. For the active, growing family they are truly outstanding.

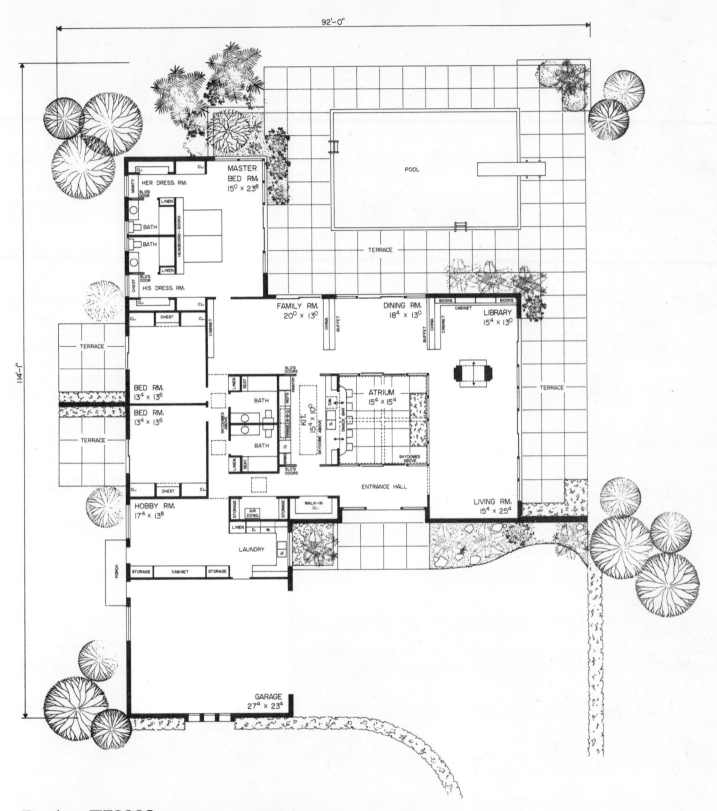

Design T72226 3,340 Sq. Ft. - Excluding Atrium; 41,290 Cu. Ft.

● If anything has been left out of this home it would certainly be difficult to determine just what it is that is missing. Containing over 3,300 square feet, space for living is abundant, indeed. Each of the various rooms is large. Further, each major room has access to the outdoors. The efficient inside kitchen is strategically located in relation to the family and dining rooms. Observe how it functions with the enclosed atrium to provide a snack bar. Functional room dividers separate various areas. Study closely the living area. A two-way fireplace divides the spacious living room and the cozy library highlighted by built-in cabinets and bookshelves. A hobby room with laundry adjacent will be a favorite family activities spot. This home surely has numerous, impressive qualities to recommend it.

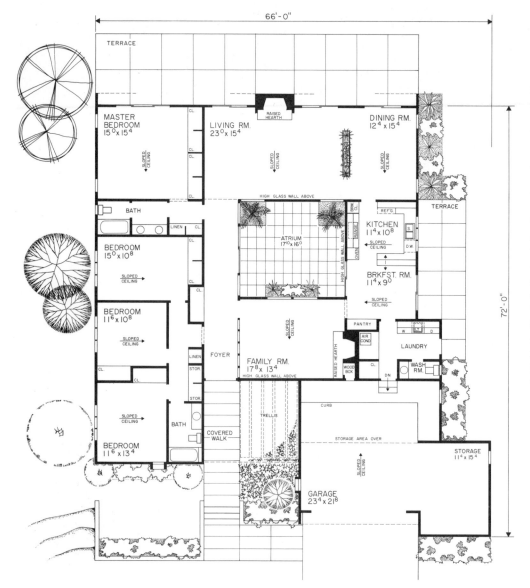

66'-0"

TERRACE

MASTER BEDROOM 15⁰ x 15⁴

LIVING RM. 23⁰ x 15⁴

RAISED HEARTH

DINING RM. 12⁴ x 15⁴

SLOPED CEILING

SLOPED CEILING

SLOPED CEILING

HIGH GLASS WALL ABOVE

BATH

LINEN

ATRIUM 17¹⁰ x 16⁰

TERRACE

KITCHEN 11⁴ x 10⁸

BEDROOM 15⁰ x 10⁸

SLOPED CEILING

REF'G.

SLOPED CEILING

D.W.

HIGH GLASS WALL ABOVE

BRKFST. RM. 11⁴ x 9⁰

BEDROOM 11⁶ x 10⁸

SLOPED CEILING

SLOPED CEILING

PANTRY

LINEN STOR

FOYER

FAMILY RM. 17⁸ x 13⁴

SLOPED CEILING

AIR COND.

LAUNDRY

W D

HIGH GLASS WALL ABOVE

WOOD BOX

WASH RM.

DN

SLOPED CEILING

BATH

TRELLIS

CURB

72'-0"

BEDROOM 11⁶ x 13⁴

COVERED WALK

STORAGE AREA OVER

SLOPED CEILING

STORAGE 11⁴ x 15⁴

GARAGE 23⁴ x 21⁸

Design T72135
2,495 Sq. Ft. - Excluding Atrium
28,928 Cu. Ft.

● For those seeking a new experience in home ownership. The proud occupants of the contemporary home will forever be thrilled at their choice of such a distinguished exterior and such a practical and exciting floor plan. The variety of shed roof planes contrast dramatically with the simplicity of the vertical siding. Inside there is a feeling of spaciousness resulting from the sloping ceilings. The uniqueness of this design is further enhanced by the atrium. Open to the sky, this outdoor area, indoors, can be enjoyed from all parts of the house. The sleeping zone has four bedrooms, two baths and plenty of closets. The informal living zone has a fine kitchen and breakfast room. The formal zone consists of a large living dining area with fireplace.

BRKFST. RM.

FAM. RM.

PANTRY

W D

LAUNDRY

WOOD BOX

DN

W.R.

DN

GARAGE

CURB

OPTIONAL PARTIAL BASEMENT

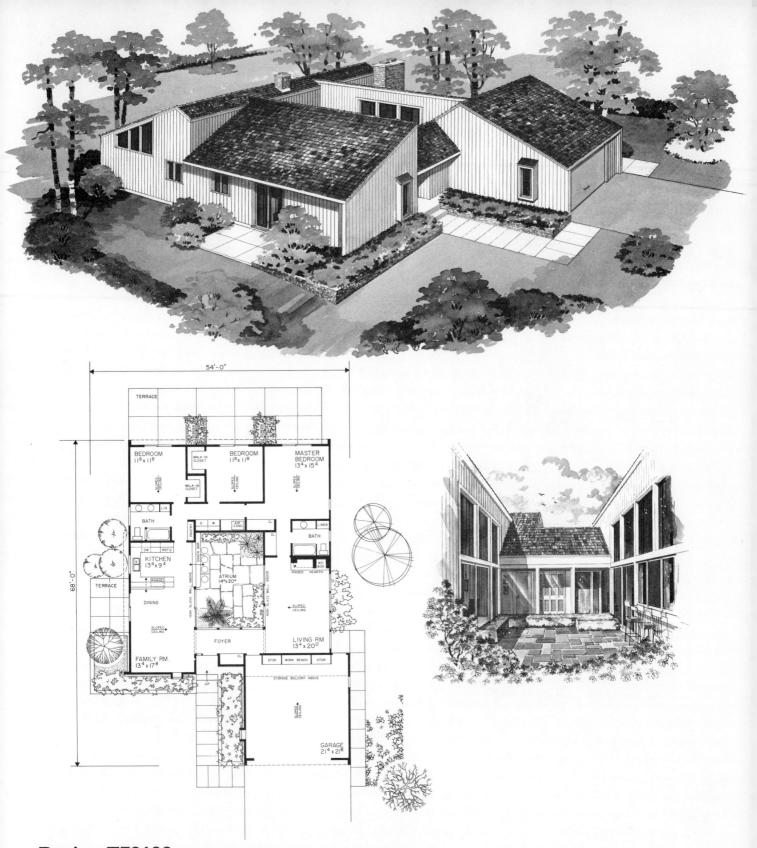

Design T72182 *1,558 Sq. Ft.; 280 Sq. Ft. - Atrium; 18,606 Cu. Ft.*

● What a great new dimension in living is represented by this unique contemporary design! Each of the major zones comprise a separate unit which, along with the garage, clusters around the atrium. High sloped ceilings and plenty of glass areas assure a feeling of spaciousness. The quiet living room will enjoy its privacy, while activities in the informal family room will be great fun functioning with the kitchen. A snack bar opens the kitchen to the atrium. The view, above right, shows portions of snack bar and the front entry looking through the glass wall. There are two full baths strategically located to service all areas conveniently. Storage facilities are excellent, indeed. Don't miss the storage potential found in the garage. There is a workbench and storage balcony above.

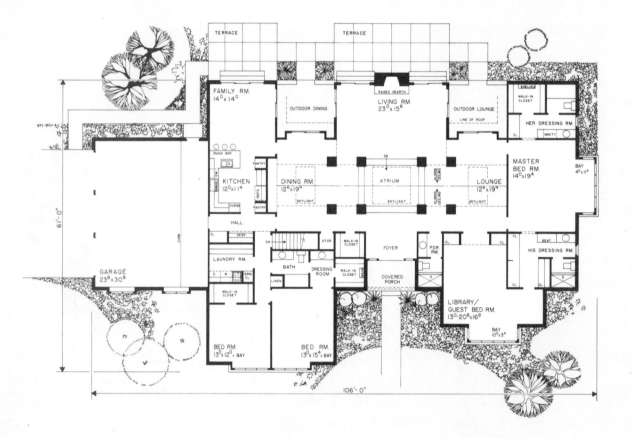

Design T72791 3,809 Sq. Ft.; 64,565 Cu. Ft.

● The use of vertical paned windows and the hipped roof highlight the exterior of this unique design. Upon entrance one will view a charming sunken atrium with skylight above plus a skylight in the dining room and one in the lounge. Formal living will be graciously accommodated in the living room. It features a raised hearth fireplace, two sets of sliding glass doors to the rear terrace plus two more sliding doors, one to an outdoor dining terrace and the other to an outdoor lounge. Informal living will be enjoyed in the family room with snack bar and in the large library. All will praise the fine planning of the master suite. It features a bay window, "his" and "her" dressing room with private baths and an abundance of closet space.

Design T71283 1,904 Sq. Ft. - Excluding Atrium; 18,659 Cu. Ft.

● Here is a unique home whose livable area is basically a perfect square. Completely adaptable to a narrow building site, the presence of the interior atrium permits the enjoyment of private outdoor living "indoors". Glass sliding doors open onto this delightful area with its attractive planting areas. In colder climates the atrium may be adapted to function as the formal living room, thus permitting the present living room to function as a study/guest room. In addition to the formal dining room, there is the informal snack bar in the family room accessible from the kitchen via the pass-thru. Three bedrooms, two baths, a fireplace and excellent storage facilities also are highlights of this plan. Don't miss the planting areas.

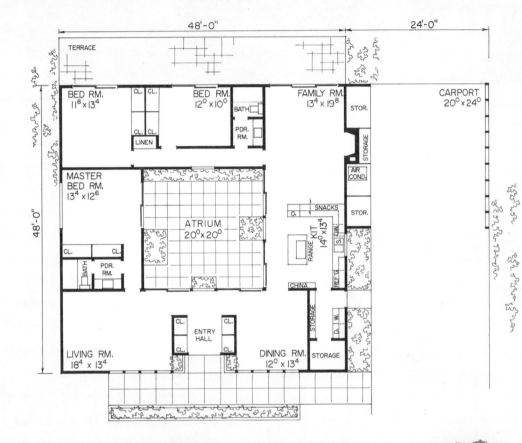

134490

45

Design T71841
1,920 Sq. Ft. - Excluding Atrium
19,806 Cu. Ft.

● Atrium living is wonderfully illustrated by this attractive design. You forever will be aware of its delightful presence and it will offer pleasingly different patterns of living to your family. It may be in constant use since the skylight provides protection during inclement weather. Clever planning results in excellent zoning of the basic area of the plan. The formal living room and master bedroom are located to the front and enjoy plenty of peace and quiet. The children's rooms are by themselves and are but a few steps from the informal family room. The efficient kitchen has eating space and functions ideally with the dining and family rooms. A mud room is accessible from the garage and the rear terrace.

Design T71837 2,016 Sq. Ft. - Excluding Atrium; 27,280 Cu. Ft.

Design T71867
1,692 Sq. Ft. - Excluding Atrium
21,383 Cu. Ft.

● Looking for a new house involves a number of varied considerations. One that is most basic involves what you would like your family's living patterns to be. If you would like to introduce your family to something that is different and is sure to be fun for all, consider this dramatic atrium house. Parents and children alike will be thrilled by the experience and the environment engendered by this outdoor living area indoors. A skylight provides for the protection during inclement weather without restricting the flood of natural light. Notice how this atrium functions with the various areas. Observe relationships between children's rooms and family room between master bedroom and the quiet living room.

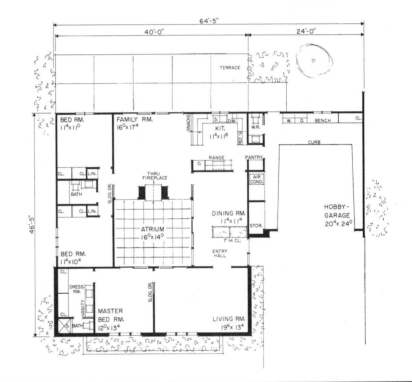

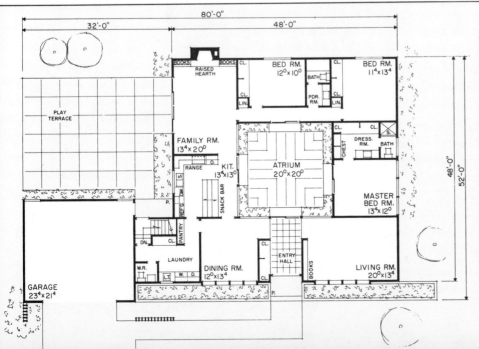

● Picture yourself and your family enjoying this new home. Sheltered from the weather, whatever the season, the atrium will be favorite spot for eating, reading, playing games or just plain sitting. Amidst all that natural light and those attractive planting areas, you'll enjoy the informality of outdoor living under controlled conditions. Four pairs of sliding glass doors make the atrium accessible from all areas of the house. Observe how the formal living room is located from the informal family room. Note kitchen snack bar and the separate dining room. Don't miss the laundry, pantry and extra wash room. The family room will also be a favorite spot. Its focal point is the raised hearth fireplace.

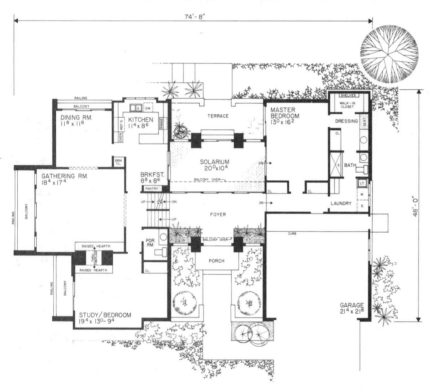

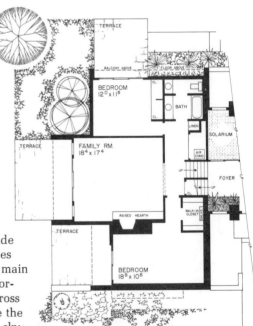

Design T72836 998 Sq. Ft. - Foyer Level; 1,146 Sq. Ft. - Main Level
1,090 Sq. Ft. - Lower Level; 241 Sq. Ft. - Studio Level; 39,705 Cu. Ft.

● Here is a dramatic, hip-roofed contemporary with exciting living patterns. Inside the double front doors, flanked by planting areas, is the foyer level which includes the solarium, master bedroom and laundry. Up seven steps from the foyer is the main level comprised of a gathering room with a thru-fireplace opening to the study, formal dining and informal breakfast rooms and an efficient, U-shaped kitchen. Across from the gathering room is the short flight of stairs to the upper level studio. Like the breakfast room immediately below, the studio looks down into the solarium. The skylight provides both studio and solarium with an abundance of natural light. Heat is absorbed and stored in the thermal brick floor of this centrally located solarium. The floor will then radiate heat into the living areas to stabilize the temperature when necessary. The lower sleeping level is down a few steps from the foyer. It functions well with its terrace and the children's bedrooms. Don't miss the three main level balconies and the three lower level terraces. They will create wonderful indoor-outdoor living relationships for the entire family to enjoy.

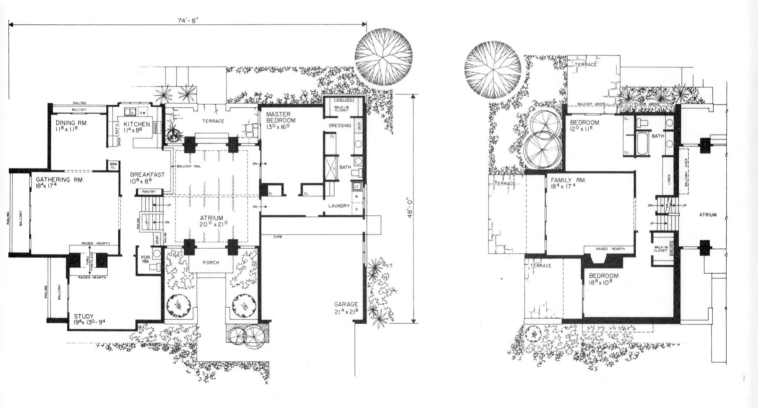

Design T72837 *1,165 Sq. Ft. - Main Level; 998 Sq. Ft. - Atrium Level; 1,090 Sq. Ft. - Lower Level; 43,760 Cu. Ft.*

● This atrium plan is housed in the same dramatic exterior as the solarium plan on the opposite page. The exterior remains exactly the same but the floor plan has been altered to house an atrium. Enclosed in glass, the atrium admits daytime solar warmth, which radiates into the other rooms for direct-gain heating. Seeing that this plan includes a basement underneath the atrium, it lacks the thick, heat-storing thermal floor which is featured in the solarium version. For this reason, the plan calls for a furnace in the basement as the primary heat source. The floor plan of this atrium version is similar to its solarium counterpart except that the studio level has been omitted. As a result it has three living levels instead of four, plus a basement.

The master suite is outstanding. It is complete with dressing room, two large closets, bathroom and access to the laundry. The rear terrace is accessible by way of sliding glass doors. Fireplaces can be enjoyed in three rooms, gathering, study and lower level family room. Continue to study this unique design and its solarium counterpart for their many features.

49

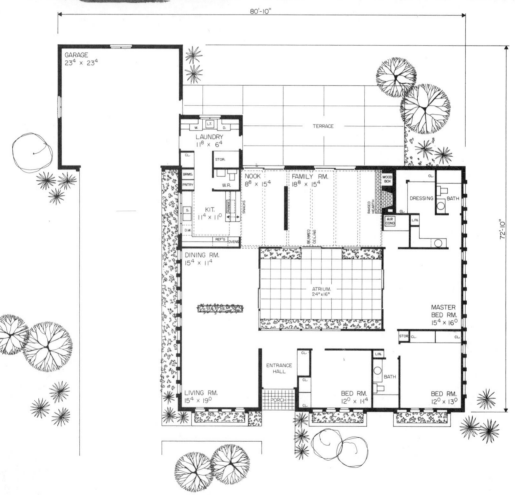

GARAGE
23⁴ x 23⁴

LAUNDRY
11⁸ x 6⁴

TERRACE

NOOK
8⁸ x 15⁴

FAMILY RM.
18⁸ x 15⁴

DRESSING   BATH

KIT.
11⁴ x 11⁰

DINING RM.
15⁴ x 11⁴

ATRIUM
24⁰ x 16⁰

MASTER
BED RM.
15⁴ x 16⁰

ENTRANCE
HALL

BATH

LIVING RM.
15⁴ x 19⁰

PORCH

BED RM.
12⁰ x 14⁰

BED RM.
12⁰ x 13⁰

Design T72298 2,489 Sq. Ft. - Excluding Atrium; 27,700 Cu. Ft.

● If you've ever wanted to enjoy outdoor living indoors, this distinctive and refreshing design comes close to providing that opportunity. All the tremendous livability offered the basic rectangular plan is wrapped around a breathtaking 24 x 16 foot atrium which

is open to the sky. Sliding glass doors provide direct access to this unique area from the family room, the dining room and the master bedroom. Also noteworthy is the functioning of other areas such as: the living and dining rooms; the kitchen and laundry; the

master bedroom and its dressing/bath area. The two front bedrooms are serviced by a second full bath. That's a four foot, six inch high planter with storage below separating the living and dining rooms. This will be just a great area for formal entertaining.

Design T72383 1,984 Sq. Ft. – Excluding Atrium; 20,470 Cu. Ft.

● Design your home around an atrium and you will enjoy living patterns unlike any you have experienced in the past. This interior area is assured complete outdoor privacy. Five sets of sliding glass doors enhance the accessibility of this unique area. With the two-car garage projecting from the front of the house, this design will not require a large piece of property. Worthy of particular note is the separation of the master bedroom from the other three bedrooms - a fine feature to assure peace and quiet. Side-by-side are the formal and informal living rooms. Both function with the rear terrace. Separating the two rooms is the thru-fireplace and double access wood box.

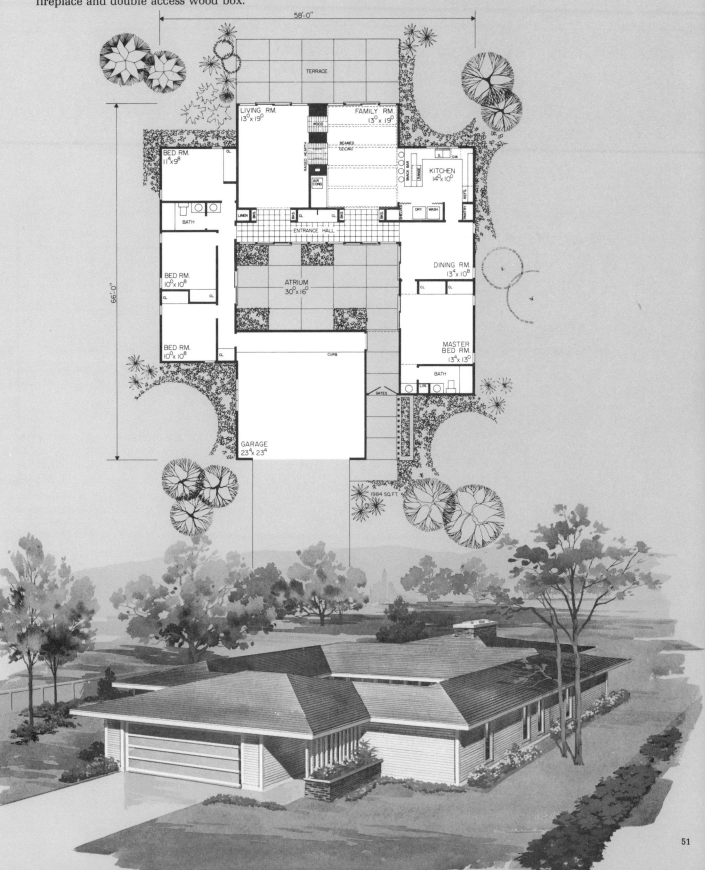

Design T72831
1,758 Sq. Ft. - First Floor
1,247 Sq. Ft. - Second Floor
44,265 Cu. Ft.

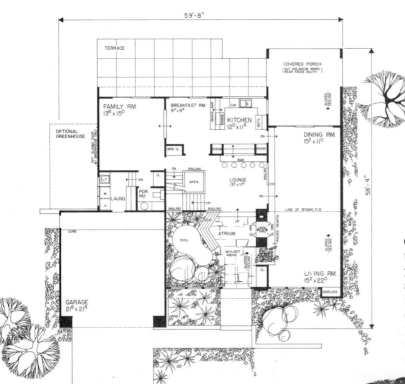

● You can incorporate energy-saving features into the elevation of this passive solar design to enable you to receive the most sunlight on your particular site. Multiple plot plans (included with the blueprints) illustrate which elevations should be solarized for different sites and which extra features can be incorporated. The features can include a greenhouse added to the family room, the back porch turned into a solarium or skylights installed over the entry.

EARTH-SHELTERED HOUSES

... A Unique Living Experience! So-called underground homes and earth-berm designs are energy-efficient approaches to modern home building well worth consideration.

Design T72863 2,955 Sq. Ft.; 30,387 Cu. Ft.

● Livability is outstanding in this earth-shelter design. Each of the three bedrooms has access to the terrace, along with the gathering and dining rooms. All of the sliding glass doors, along with the atrium, will brighten the interior nicely. The atrium will be enjoyed from the lounge, kitchen and gathering/dining rooms. Efficient work space will be found in the kitchen. It has easy access to the atrium and dining room.

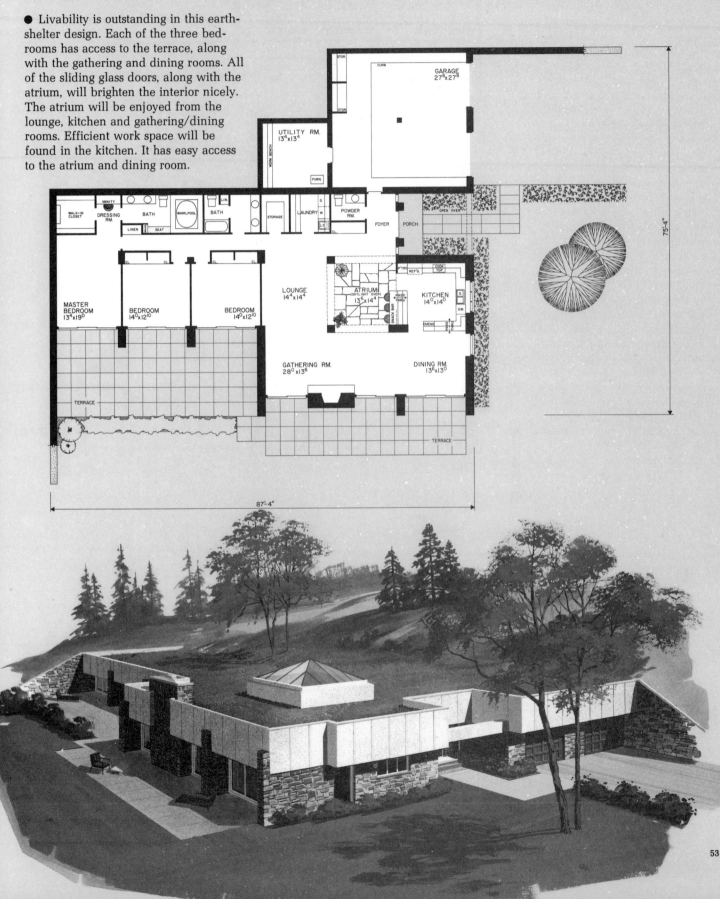

Design T72860

2,240 Sq. Ft.; 27,685 Cu. Ft.

● Here is truly a unique home to satisfy your family's desires for something appealing and refreshing. This three bedroom home is also, the very embodiment of what's new and efficient in planning and technology. This is an excellent example of outstanding coordination of house structure, site, interior livability and the sun. Orienting this earth sheltered house toward the south assures a warm, bright and cheerful interior. Major contributions to energy-efficiency result from the earth covered roof, the absence of northern wall exposure and the lack of windows on either end of the house. This means a retention of heat in the winter and cool air in the summer. An effective use of skylights provide the important extra measure of natural light to the interior. Sliding glass doors in the living and dining rooms also help bring the light to the indoors. This earth sheltered house makes no sacrifice of good planning and excellent, all 'round livability. The section is cut through the living room and the skylit hall looking toward the bedrooms.

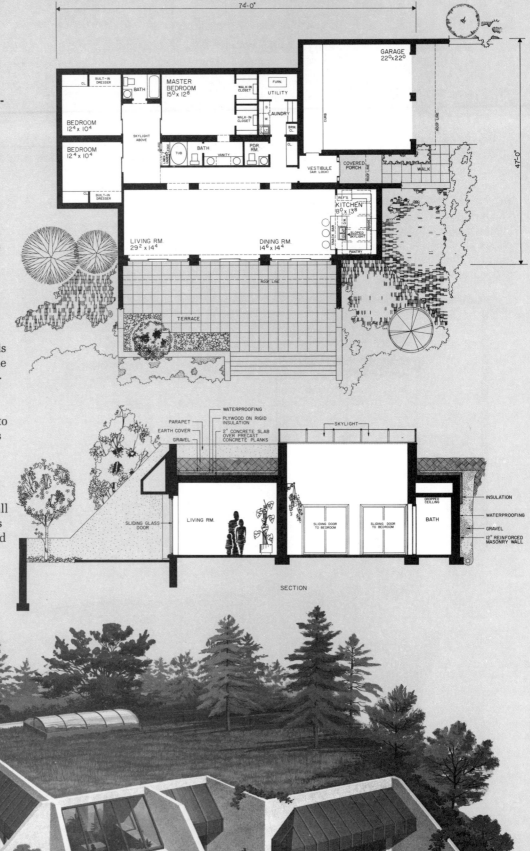

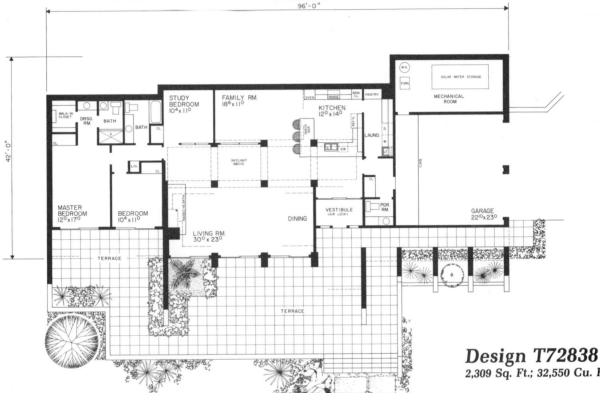

96'-0"

42'-0"

WALK-IN CLOSET | DRSG. RM. | BATH | BATH | CL
STUDY BEDROOM 10⁴ x 11⁰ | FAMILY RM. 18⁶ x 11⁰ | OVEN | RANGE | BRM CL. | PANTRY
KITCHEN 12⁰ x 14⁰ | SNACK BAR | REF'G. | MECHANICAL ROOM | SOLAR WATER STORAGE | WH | FURN
LAUND.
SKYLIGHT ABOVE
LIN. | CL
MASTER BEDROOM 12⁰ x 17⁰ | BEDROOM 10⁴ x 11⁰ | RAISED HEARTH | LIVING RM. 30⁰ x 23⁰ | DINING | VESTIBULE (AIR LOCK) | PDR. RM. | CURB | GARAGE 22¹⁰ x 23⁰
TERRACE
TERRACE

Design T72838
2,309 Sq. Ft.; 32,550 Cu. Ft.

● Here is another dramatic earth sheltered home which will function with the sun like Design 22860. The spaciousness of the living area in this design is enhanced by the central location of the dramatic skylight. In addition to the passive solar heating gain for the living and bedroom areas, the impressively designed "mansard" roof effect lends itself to the installation of active solar heating panels. The illustration above shows panels only on the garage wing. Consultation with local solar heating experts will determine the effectiveness in your area of additional panels. A special room adjacent to the garage will accommodate mechanical equipment.

SKYLIGHT
PARAPET
EARTH COVER
GRAVEL
WATERPROOFING
PLYWOOD ON RIGID INSULATION
2" CONCRETE SLAB OVER PRECAST CONCRETE PLANKS
MIRRORS
FAMILY ROOM
SLDG. GLASS DOOR
LIVING / DINING ROOM
INSULATION
DRYWALL
WATERPROOFING
12" REINFORCED MASONRY WALL

● Earth berms are banked against all four exterior walls of this design to effectively reduce heating and cooling demands. The berming is cost-efficient during both hot and cold seasons. In the winter, berming reduces heat loss through the exterior walls and shields the structure from cold winds. It helps keep warm air out during the summer. The two most dramatic interior highlights are the atrium and thru-fireplace. Topped with a large skylight, the atrium floods the interior with natural light. Shades are used to cover the atrium in the summer to prevent solar heat gain. Three bedrooms are featured in this plan and they each open via sliding glass doors to the atrium. This would eliminate any feeling of being closed in. An island with range and oven is featured in the kitchen. Informal dining will be enjoyed at the snack bar. The family/dining room can house those more formal dining occasions. The section at the right is cut through the study, atrium and rear bedroom looking toward master bedroom.

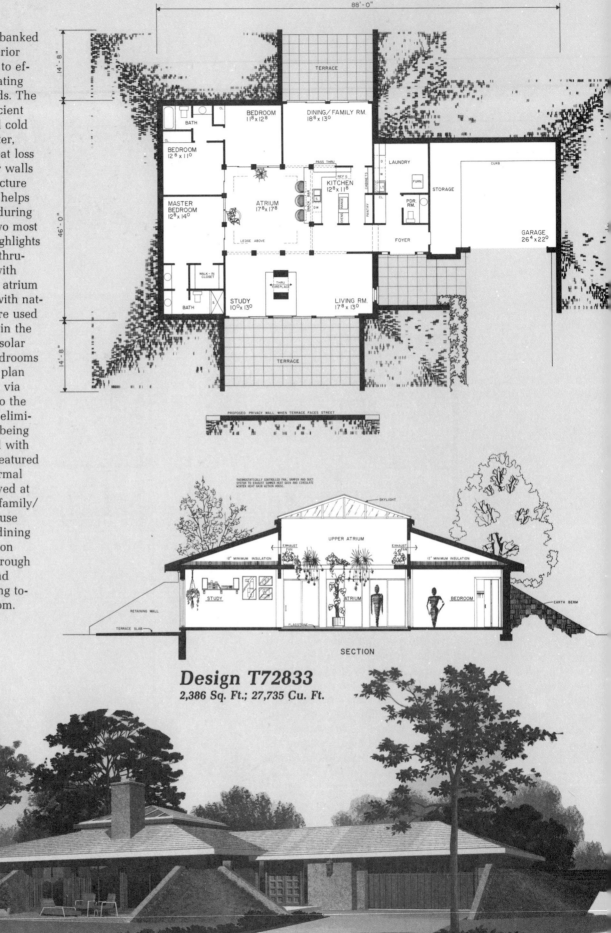

Design T72833
2,386 Sq. Ft.; 27,735 Cu. Ft.

SECTION

Design T72861
2,499 Sq. Ft.; 29,100 Cu. Ft.

● Berming the earth against the walls of a structure prove to be very energy efficient. The earth protects the interior from the cold of the winter and the heat of the summer. Interior lighting will come from the large skylight over the garden room. Every room will benefit from this exposed area. The garden room will function as a multi-purpose area for the entire family. The living/dining room will receive light from two areas, the garden room and the wall of sliding glass doors to the outside. Family living will be served by the efficient floor plan. Three bedrooms and two full baths are clustered together. The kitchen is adjacent to the air-locked vestibule where the laundry and utility rooms are housed. The section is cut through the dining, garden and master bedroom facing the kitchen.

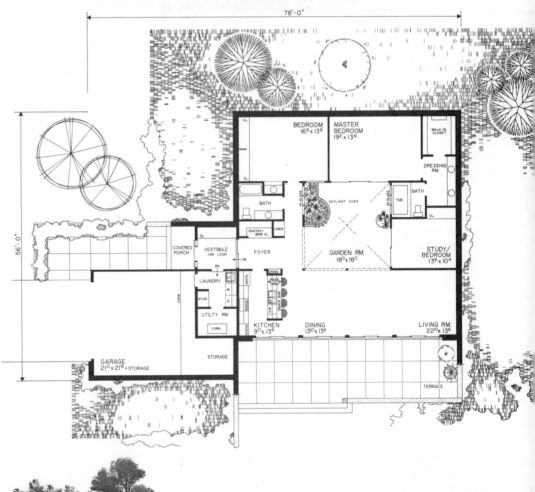

SECTION

● Earth shelters the interior of this house from both the cold of the winter and the heat of the summer. This three bedroom design has passive solar capabilities. The sun room, south facing for light, has a stone floor which will absorb heat. When needed, the heat will be circulated to the interior by opening the sliding glass doors or by mechanical means. Entrance to this home will be obtained through the vestibule or the garage. Both have a western exposure. A large, centrally located, skylight creates an open feeling and lights up the interior of this plan where the formal and informal living areas are located. The sun room contains 425 sq. ft. and 5,228 cu. ft. not included in totals to the right.

95'-4"

51'-0"

BEDROOM 12⁰ x 11⁰

BEDROOM 12⁰ x 11⁰

BATH

CL

LINEN

CL

BRM CL

PANTRY

AIR COND.

STORAGE

BATH

DRESSING RM.

WALK-IN CLOSET

COVERED ENTRANCE

VESTIBULE (AIR LOCK)

SKYLIGHT ABOVE

STORAGE

CURB

OVENS

COOK

REFG.

SNACK BAR

BOOKS

BOOKS

OPEN THRU FIREPLACE

KITCHEN 9⁰ x 15⁰

DINING RM. 15⁴ x 11⁰

LIVING RM. 14⁰ x 16⁸

STUDY 11⁰ x 14⁸

MASTER BEDROOM 12⁰ x 16⁸

GARAGE 22⁰ x 24⁰+ STOR.

FAMILY RM. 14⁰ x 13⁸

SUN RM. 31⁰ x 12⁸

ROOF LINE

TERRACE

Design T72862
2,808 Sq. Ft.; 37,219 Cu. Ft.

Floor plan labels:

80'-8"

TERRACE

COVERED TERRACE
ROOF LINE

GARDEN RM.
11⁴x11⁸

ROOF LINE

LIVING RM.
18⁶x16⁰

DINING RM.
12²x10⁰

MASTER BEDROOM
12²x18⁰

BEDROOM
11⁰x12⁰

BEDROOM
11⁰x12⁰

FAMILY RM.
11⁸x18⁸

RAISED HEARTH

KITCHEN
12²x14⁴

TERRACE

CL   CL   CL   CL

FOYER

PTRY   REF'G.   DESK

WALK-IN CLOSET

LINEN

BATH   BATH

WALK-IN CLOSET   VESTIBULE (AIR LOCK)   PDR. RM.   AIR COND.   CL   LT   W   D

MUD RM.   LAUNDRY

VANITY

EARTH BERM

ENTRANCE COURT

EARTH BERM

STUDY
12¹⁰x11⁸

GATE

PRIVACY WALL

GARAGE
24⁸x21⁸

ROOF LINE

61'-0"

Design T72903
2,555 Sq. Ft.; 32,044 Cu. Ft.

● Earth berms on the sides of this house help it achieve energy-efficiency. The maximum amount of light enters this home by way of the many glass areas on the southern exposure. Every room in this plan, except the study, has the benefit of the southern sun. A garden room, tucked between the family and dining rooms, can be used for passive solar capabilities. A front privacy wall and the entrance court will shield the interior from the harsh northern winds. The air-locked vestibule also will be an energy saver. Summer heat gain will be reduced by the wide overhanging roof. The occupants of this home will appreciate the excellent interior planning. Garden room contains 144 sq. ft. and 1,195 cu. ft. not included in above totals.

SECOND-FLOOR LOUNGES

... and Other Amenities of Contemporary Living

The upstairs lounge is one popular comfort of many homes designed for contemporary lifestyle. Designs on the following pages offer many such features.

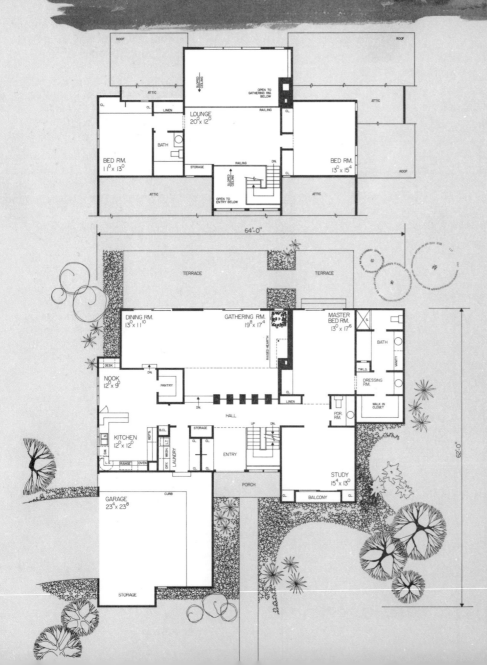

Design T72708

2,108 Sq. Ft. - First Floor
824 Sq. Ft. - Second Floor
52,170 Cu. Ft.

● Here is a one-and-a-half story home whose exterior is distinctive. It has a contemporary feeling, yet it retains some of the fine design features and proportions of traditional exteriors. Inside the appealing double front doors there is livability galore. The sunken rear living-dining area is delightfully spacious and is looked down into from the second floor lounge. The open end fireplace, with its raised hearth and planter, is another focal point. The master bedroom features a fine compartmented bath with both shower and tub. The study is just a couple steps away. The U-shaped kitchen is outstanding. Notice the pantry and laundry. Upstairs provides children with their own sleeping, studying and TV quarters. Absolutely a great design! Study all the fine details closely with your family.

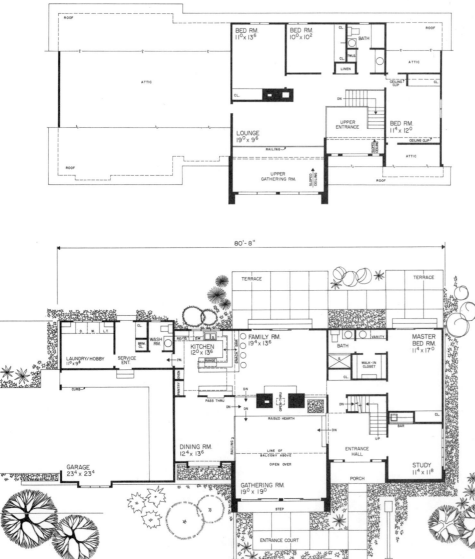

Design T72782
2,060 Sq. Ft. - First Floor
897 Sq. Ft. - Second Floor
47,750 Cu. Ft.

● What makes this such a distinctive four bedroom design? Let's list some of the features. This plan includes great formal and informal living for the family at home or when entertaining guests. The formal gathering room and informal family room share a dramatic raised hearth fireplace. Other features of the sunken gathering room include: high, sloped ceilings, built-in planter and sliding glass doors to the front entrance court. The kitchen has a snack bar, many built-ins, a pass-thru to dining room and easy access to the large laundry/washroom. The master bedroom suite is located on the main level for added privacy and convenience. There's even a study with a built-in bar. The upper level has three more bedrooms, a bath and a lounge looking down into the gathering room.

Design T72821
1,363 Sq. Ft. - First Floor
351 Sq. Ft. - Second Floor
37,145 Cu. Ft.

Mansard Roof
Adaptation

A Trend House . . .

● Here is a truly unique house whose interior was designed with the current decade's economies, life-styles and demographics in mind. While functioning as a one-story home, the second floor provides an extra measure of livability when required. In addition, this two-story section adds to the dramatic appeal of both the exterior and the interior. Within only 1,363 square feet, this contemporary delivers refreshing and outstanding living patterns for those who are buying their first home, those who have raised their family and are looking for a smaller home and those in search of a retirement home. The center entrance routes traffic effectively to each area. The great room with its raised hearth fireplace, two-story arching and delightful glass areas is most distinctive. The kitchen is efficient and but a step from the dining room. The covered porch will provide an ideal spot for warm-weather, outdoor dining. The separate laundry room is strategically located. The sleeping area may consist of one bedroom and a study, or two bedrooms. Each room functions with the sheltered wood deck - a perfect location for a hot tub.

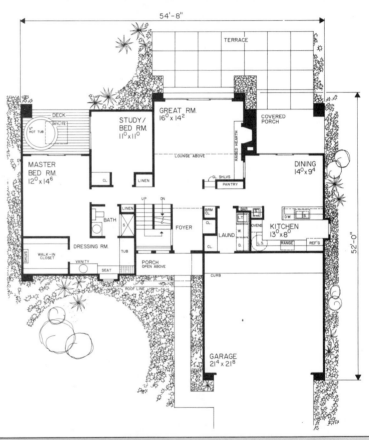

Design T72822
1,363 Sq. Ft. - First Floor
351 Sq. Ft. - Second Floor
36,704 Cu. Ft.

Gable Roof
Version

UPPER GREAT RM.

RAILING

CL.

LOUNGE / HOBBIES
16⁰ x 9²

SKYLITE

CL.

DN

RAILING

UPPER FOYER

STOR./ BATH

RAILING

BALCONY

LOUNGE /GUEST RM./
GRANDCHILDREN'S RM.
16⁰ x 19²

CL.

DN

RAILING

UPPER FOYER

BATH

RAILING

ALTERNATE SECOND FLOOR

...For the 80's and Decades to Come

● The full bath is planned to have easy access to the master bedroom and living areas. Note the stall shower, tub, seat and vanity. The second floor offers two optional layouts. It may serve as a lounge, studio or hobby area overlooking the great room. Or, it may be built to function as a complete private guest room. It would be a great place for the visiting grandchildren. Don't miss the outdoor balcony. Additional livability and storage facilities may be developed in the basement. Then, of course, there are two exteriors to choose from. Design T72821, with its horizontal frame siding and deep, attractive cornice detail, is an eye-catcher. For those with a preference for a contemporary fashioned gable roof and vertical siding, there is Design T72822. With the living areas facing the south, these designs will enjoy benefits of passive solar exposure. The overhanging roofs will help provide relief from the high summer sun. This is surely a modest-sized floor plan which will deliver new dimensions in small-family livability.

Design T72771

2,087 Sq. Ft. - First Floor
816 Sq. Ft. - Second Floor; 53,285 Cu. Ft.

● This design will provide an abundance of livability for your family. The second floor is highlighted by an open lounge which overlooks both the entry and the gathering room below.

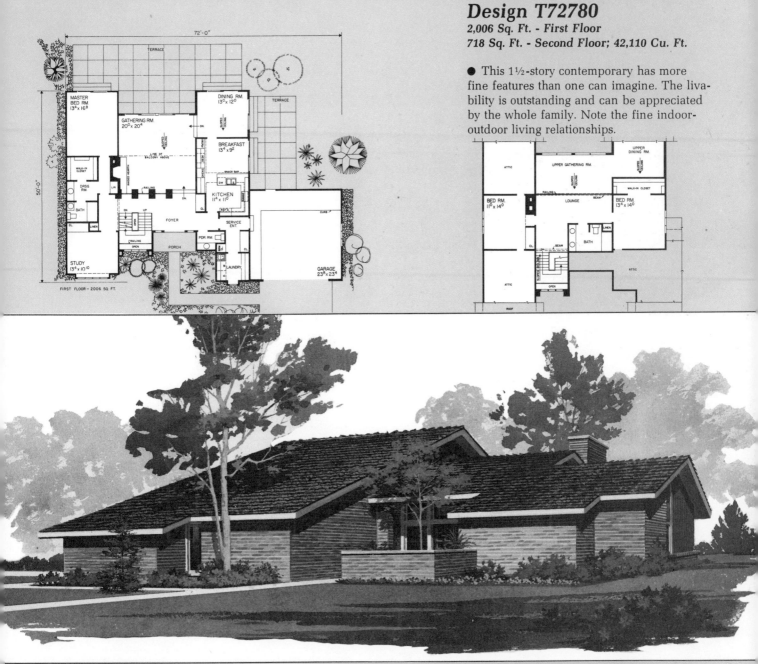

Design T72780
2,006 Sq. Ft. - First Floor
718 Sq. Ft. - Second Floor; 42,110 Cu. Ft.

● This 1½-story contemporary has more fine features than one can imagine. The livability is outstanding and can be appreciated by the whole family. Note the fine indoor-outdoor living relationships.

Design T72701 1,909 Sq. Ft. - First Floor
891 Sq. Ft. - Second Floor; 50,830 Cu. Ft.

● A snack bar in the kitchen! Plus a breakfast nook and formal dining room. Whether it's an elegant dinner party or a quick lunch, this home provides the right spot. There's a wet bar in the gathering room. Built-in bookcases in the study. And between these two rooms, a gracious fireplace. Three large bedrooms. Including a luxury master suite. Plus a balcony lounge overlooking gathering room below.

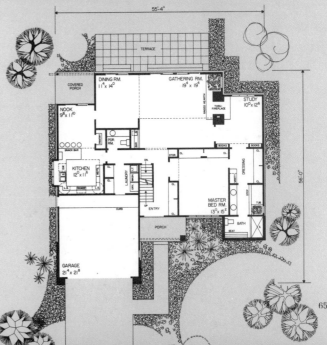

Design T72879 3,173 Sq. Ft. - Living Area Including Atrium
267 Sq. Ft. - Upper Lounge/Balcony; 61,219 Cu. Ft.

● This plush modern design seems to have it all, including an upper lounge, upper family room, and upper foyer. There's also an atrium with skylight centrally located downstairs. A modern kitchen with snack bar service to a breakfast room also enjoys its own greenhouse window. A deluxe master bedroom includes its own whirlpool and bay window. Three other bedrooms also are isolated at one end of the house downstairs to allow privacy and quiet. A spacious family room in the rear enjoys its own raised-hearth fireplace and view of a rear covered terrace. A front living room with its own fireplace looks out upon a side garden court and the central atrium. There's also a formal dining room situated between the kitchen and living room, plus a three-car garage, covered porches, and sizable laundry with washroom just off the garage.

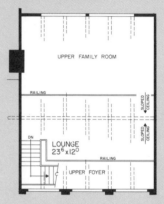

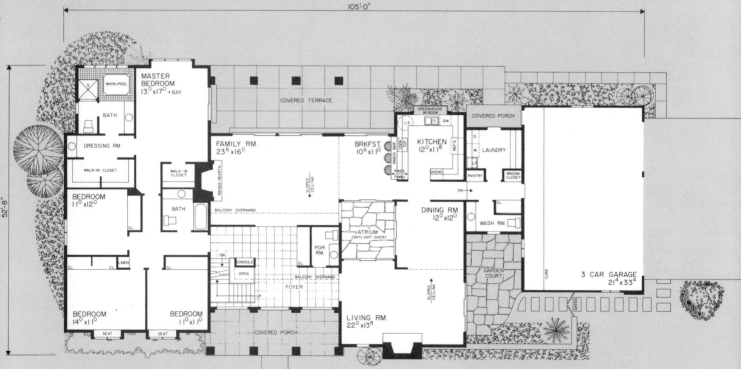

Design T72906 2,121 Sq. Ft. - First Floor
913 Sq. Ft. - Second Floor; 45,180 Cu. Ft.

● This striking Contemporary with Spanish good looks offers outstanding living for life-styles of today. A three-car garage opens to a mudroom, laundry, and washroom to keep the rest of the house clean. An efficient, spacious kitchen opens to a spacious dining room, with pass-thru also leading to a family room. The family room and adjoining master bedroom suite overlook a backyard terrace. Just off the master bedroom is a sizable study that opens to a foyer. Steps just off the foyer make up-stairs access quick and easy. The center point of this modern Contemporary is a living room that faces a front courtyard and a lounge above the living room. Three second-story bedrooms and an upper foyer join the upstairs lounge.

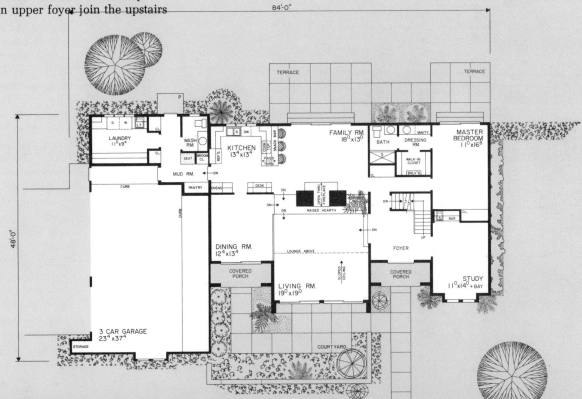

Design T72781

2,132 Sq. Ft. - First Floor
1,156 Sq. Ft. - Second Floor
47,365 Cu. Ft.

● This beautifully designed two-story could be considered a dream house of a lifetime. The exterior is sure to catch the eye of anyone who takes sight of its unique construction. The front kitchen features an island range, adjacent breakfast nook and pass-thru to formal dining room. The master bedroom suite with its privacy and convenience on the first floor has a spacious walk-in closet and dressing room. The side terrace is accessible through sliding glass doors from the master bedroom, gathering room and study. The second floor has three bedrooms and storage space galore. Also notice the lounge which has a sloped ceiling and a skylight above. This delightful area looks down into the gathering room. The outdoor balconies overlook the wrap-around terrace. Surely an outstanding trend house for decades to come.

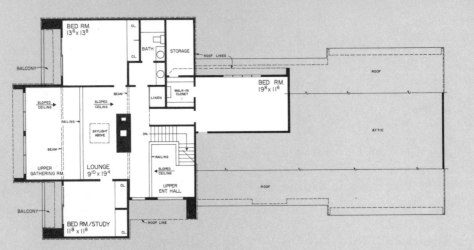

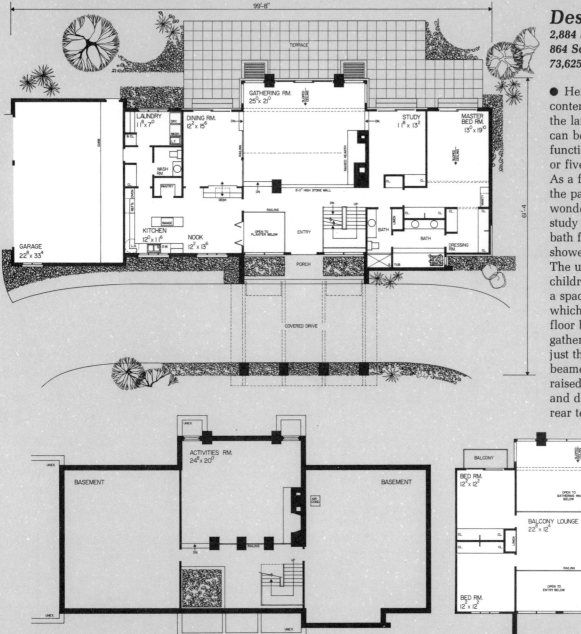

Design T72562

2,884 Sq. Ft. - First Floor
864 Sq. Ft. - Second Floor
73,625 Cu. Ft.

● Here is an exciting contemporary design for the large, active family. It can be called upon to function as either a four or five bedroom home. As a four bedroom home the parents will enjoy a wonderful suite with study and exceptional bath facilities. Note stall shower, plus sunken tub. The upstairs features the children's bedrooms and a spacious balcony lounge which looks down to the floor below. The sunken gathering room will be just that with its sloped beamed ceiling, dramatic raised hearth fireplace and direct access to the rear terrace.

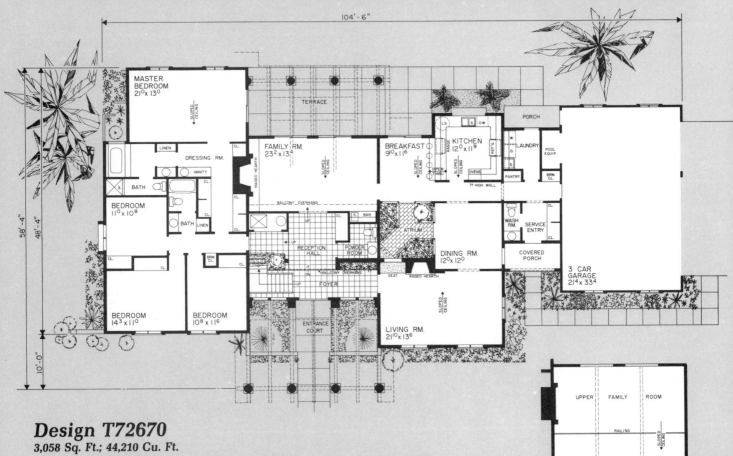

Design T72670

3,058 Sq. Ft.; 44,210 Cu. Ft.

● A centrally located interior atrium is one of the most interesting features of this Spanish design. The atrium has a built-in seat and will bring light to its adjacent rooms; living, dining and breakfast. Beyond the foyer, sunken one step, is a tiled reception hall that includes a powder room. This area leads to the sleeping wing and up one step to the family room. Overlooking the family room is a railed lounge, 279 square feet, which can be used for various activities. The work center area will be convenient to work in.

Design T72887 1,338 Sq. Ft. - First Floor; 661 Sq. Ft. - Second Floor; 36,307 Cu. Ft.

● This attractive, contemporary one-and-a-half story will be the envy of many. First, examine the efficient kitchen. Not only does it offer a snack bar for those quick meals but also a large dining room. Notice the adjacent dining porch. The laundry and garage access are also adjacent to the kitchen.

An exciting feature is the gathering room with fireplace. The first floor also offers a study with a wet bar and sliding glass doors that open to a private porch. This will make those quiet times cherishable. Adjacent to the study is a full bath followed by a bedroom. Upstairs a large master bedroom suite oc-

cupies the entire floor. It features a bath with an oversized tub and shower, a large walk-in closet with built-ins and an open lounge with fireplace. Both the lounge and master bedroom, along with the gathering room, have sloped ceilings. Develop the lower level for additional space.

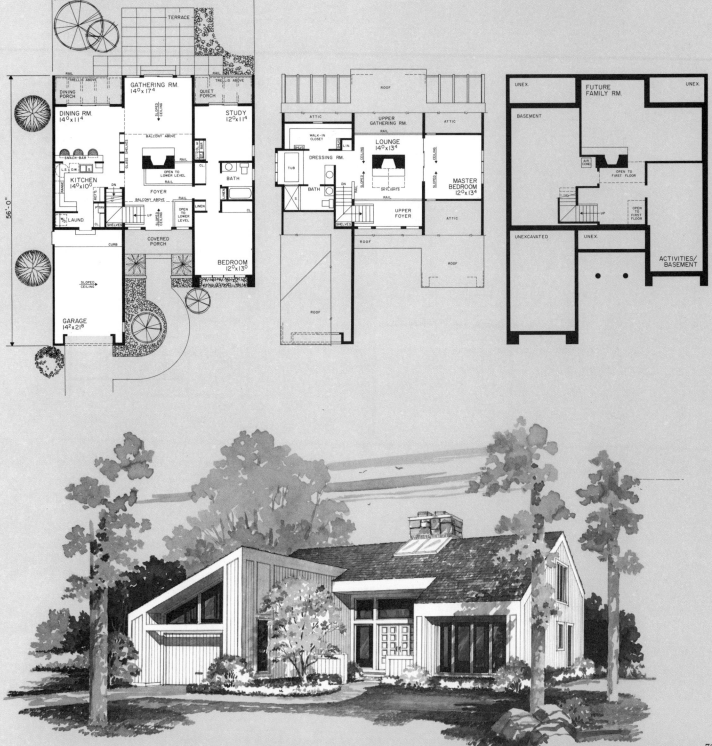

Design T72905 *1,342 Sq. Ft. - First Floor; 619 Sq. Ft. - Second Floor; 33,655 Cu. Ft.*

● All of the livability in this plan is in the back! Each first floor room, except the kitchen, has access to the rear terrace via sliding glass doors. A great way to capture an excellent view. This plan is also ideal for a narrow lot seeing that its width is less than 50 feet. Two bedrooms and a lounge, overlooking the gathering room, are on the second floor.

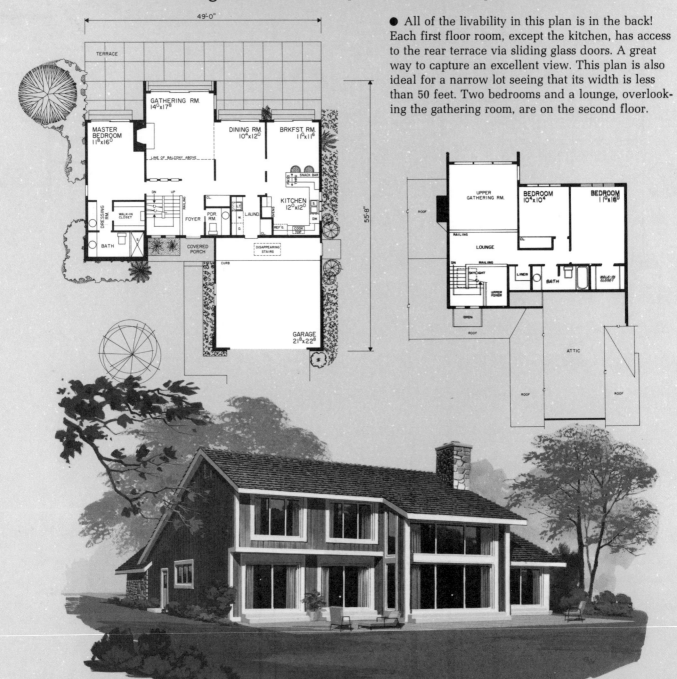

Design T71783

2,412 Sq. Ft. - First Floor
640 Sq. Ft. - Second Floor
36,026 Cu. Ft.

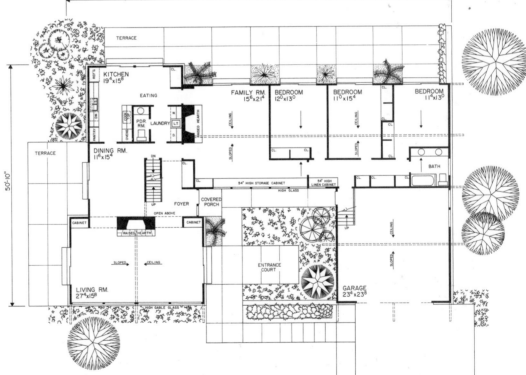

● This U-shaped home design features a central entrance court and an upper-story lounge with a balcony. There are four bedrooms in all, including a master bedroom with its own balcony on the second floor. There's a spacious front living room with its own raised-hearth fireplace, in addition to a rear family room with its own raised-hearth fireplace. A modern L-shaped kitchen features a casual eatery area and handy access to a laundry room nearby. In addition to the casual eatery area in the kitchen, there's a more formal dining room just off the kitchen area. Stairs to the upper lounge and master bedroom are located just off the foyer. A two-car garage allows extra storage room. This elegant Contemporary design with stylish stone exterior and overhanging gable roof lines provides the modern family with excellent traffic patterns and indoor-outdoor relationships. Study this fine floor plan carefully.

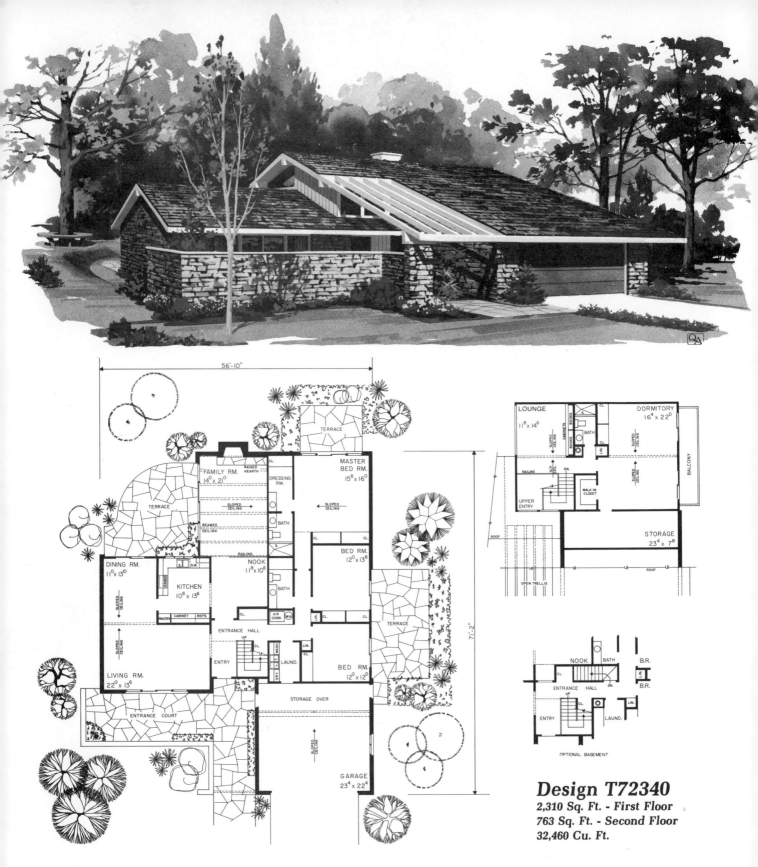

Design T72340

2,310 Sq. Ft. - First Floor
763 Sq. Ft. - Second Floor
32,460 Cu. Ft.

● If you have a flair for the extraordinary and wish to introduce your family to living patterns that will be delightfully different, then this design should fill the bill. Whether you build with quarried stone, brick veneer or some other exterior material of your choice, you'll surely experience pride of ownership here. However, inside is where your family's fun really begins. This is a highly integrated plan which allows for the full expression of a family's diverse activities. Study the effective zoning of the first floor.

There are the formal, the informal and the sleeping areas. Then, upstairs there is a lounge which can look down on the entrance hall. Also, the dormitory with its own bath, balcony and fine closet facilities. Note optional basement. Laundry remains upstairs.

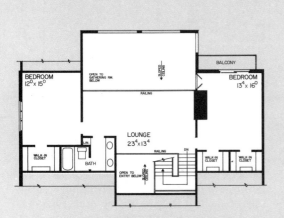

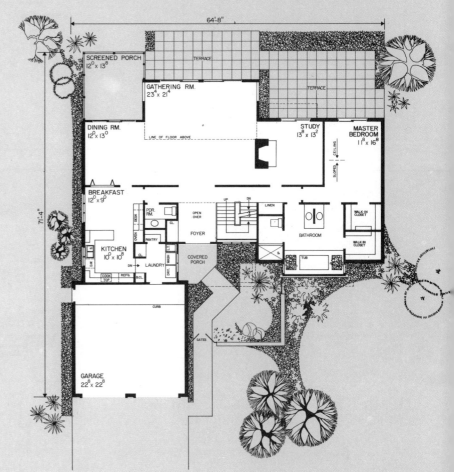

Design T72581

2,125 Sq. Ft. - First Floor
903 Sq. Ft. - Second Floor
54,476 Cu. Ft.

● A study with a fireplace! What a fine attraction to find in this lovely three-bedroom home. And the fine features certainly do not stop there. The gathering room has a sloped ceiling and two sliding glass doors to the rear terrace. The study and master bedroom (which has first floor privacy and convenience) also have glass doors to the wrap-around terrace. Adajacent to the gathering room is a formal dining room and screened-in porch. The efficient kitchen with its many built-ins has easy access to the first floor laundry. The separate breakfast nook has a built-in desk. The second floor has two bedrooms each having at least one walk-in closet. Also, a lounge overlooking the gathering room below and a balcony. Note the oversized two-car garage for storing bikes and lawn mowers. The front courtyard adds a measure of privacy to the covered porch entrance.

● This exciting contemporary has dramatic roof lines and appealing glass areas. The interior planning is, indeed, unique. The spaciousness of the dining/family room will make entertaining a memorable occasion. Note the privacy of the master bedroom. The second floor is devoted to the activities of the younger generation. The lounge looks down into the gathering room.

Design T72530 1,616 Sq. Ft. - First Floor
997 Sq. Ft. - Second Floor; 41,925 Cu. Ft.

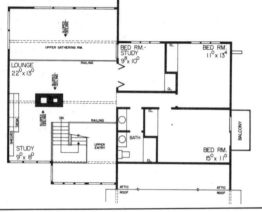

● This is a refeshingly dramatic contemporary. The use of the vertical paned windows highlight the exterior. Upon entrance to this home, one will enjoy the openness. An indoor-outdoor living relationship is present throughout this design. Note the lounge on the second floor. It is open on two sides so you can look down into the gathering room and entry hall below.

Design T72749 1,716 Sq. Ft. - First Floor
1,377 Sq. Ft. - Second Floor; 72,885 Cu. Ft.

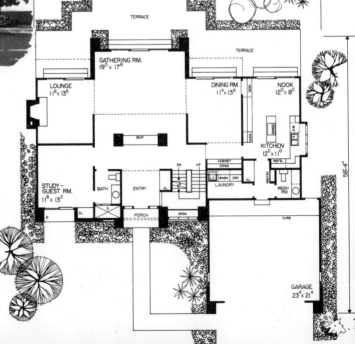

CONTEMPORARY CONFIGURATIONS

... Striking Modern Building Shapes

Many bold new designs for Contemporary lifestyles lead to interesting new building configurations. When homes are shaped for actual living patterns with attention to zoning and traffic patterns, interesting new building configurations result.

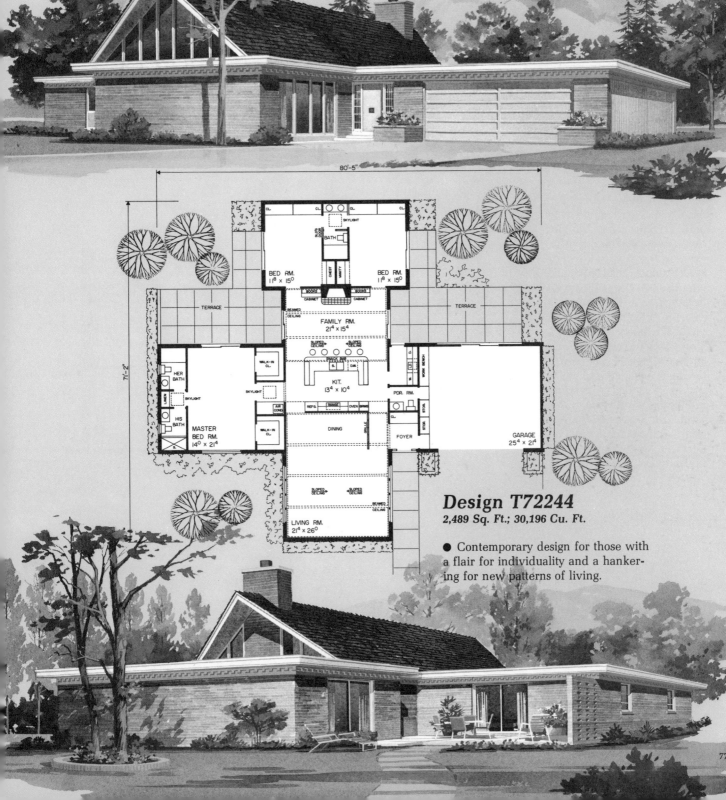

Design T72244
2,489 Sq. Ft.; 30,196 Cu. Ft.

● Contemporary design for those with a flair for individuality and a hankering for new patterns of living.

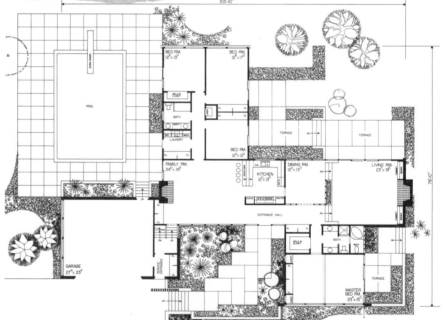

Design T72251
3,112 Sq. Ft.; 36,453 Cu. Ft.

● It will not matter at all where this distinctive ranch home is built. Whether located in the south, east, north or west the exterior design appeal will be breathtakingly distinctive and the interior livability will be delightfully different. The irregular shape is enhanced by the low-pitched, wide overhanging roof. Two wings project to help form an appealing entrance court from the main living area of the house. Variations in grade result in the garage being on a lower level. The plan reflects an interesting study in zoning and a fine indoor-outdoor relationship of the various areas.

Design T72343 3,110 Sq. Ft.; 51,758 Cu. Ft.

● If yours is a growing active family the chances are good that they will want their new home to relate to the outdoors. This distinctive design puts a premium on private outdoor living. And you don't have to install a swim- ming pool to get the most enjoyment from this home. Developing this area as a garden court will provide the in- door living areas with a breathtaking awareness of nature's beauty. Notice the fine zoning of the plan and how each area has its sliding glass doors to provide an unrestricted view. Three bedrooms plus study are serviced by three baths. The family and gathering rooms provide two great living areas. The kitchen is most efficient.

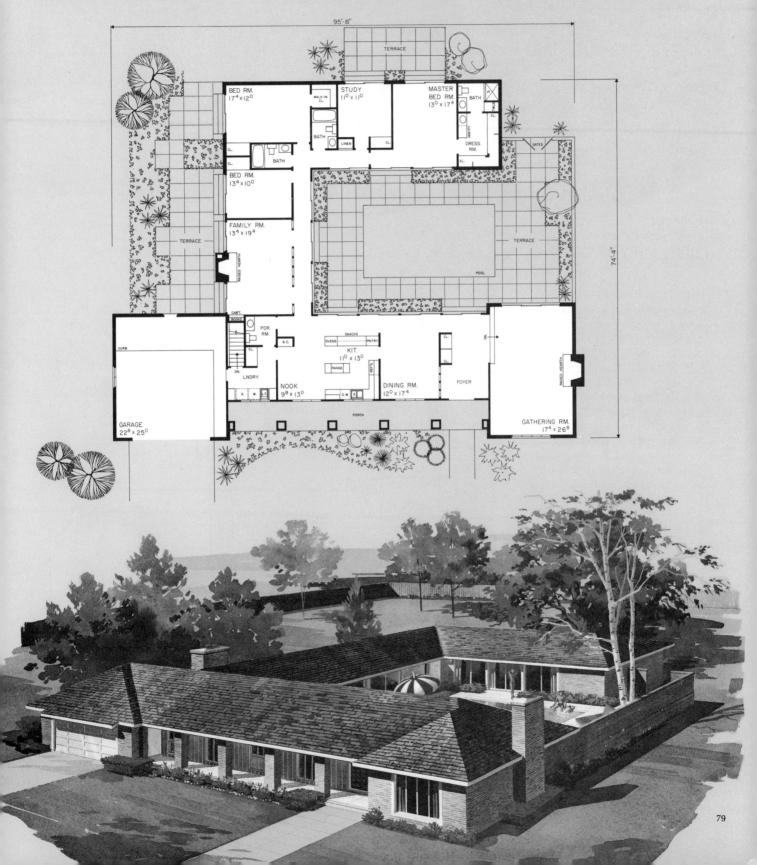

Design T72747 3,211 Sq. Ft.; 50,930 Cu. Ft.

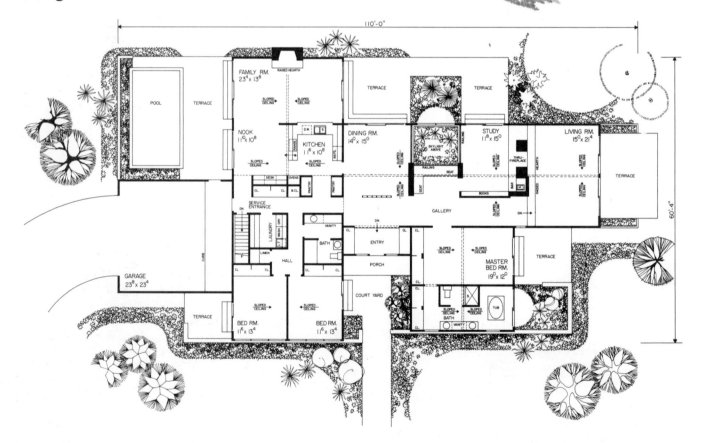

● This home will provide its occupants with a glorious adventure in contemporary living. Its impressive exterior seems to foretell that great things are in store for even the most casual visitor. A study of the plan reveals a careful zoning for both the younger and older family members. The quiet area consists of the exceptional master bedroom suite with private terrace, the study and the isolated living room. For the younger generation, there is a zone with two bedrooms, family room and nearby pool. The kitchen is handy and serves the nook and family rooms with ease. Be sure not to miss the sloping ceilings, the dramatic planter and the functional terrace.

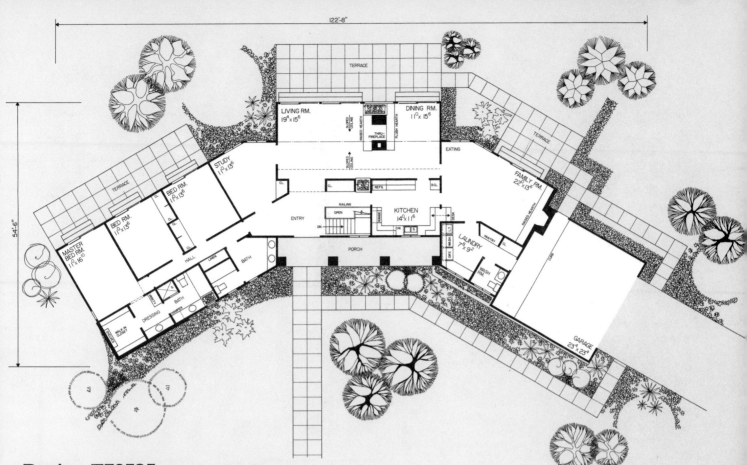

Design T72595 2,653 Sq. Ft.; 40,600 Cu. Ft.

● A winged design puts everything in the right place! At the center, formal living and dining rooms with sloped ceiling share one fireplace for added charm. Sliding glass doors in both rooms open onto the main terrace. In the right wing, there is a spacious family room with another raised hearth fireplace, built-in desk, dining area and adjoining smaller terrace. Also, a first floor laundry with pantry and half bath. A study, the master suite and family bedrooms (all bedrooms having access to a third terrace) plus baths are in the left wing. This home has a floor plan that helps you organize your life. Notice the open staircase leading to the basement.

Design T72857
2,982 Sq. Ft.; 60,930 Cu. Ft.

● Imagine yourself occupying this home! Study the outstanding master bedroom. You will be forever pleased by its many features. It has "his" and "her" baths each with a large walk-in closet, sliding glass doors to a private, side terrace (a great place to enjoy a morning cup of coffee) and an adjacent study. Notice that the two family bedrooms are separated from the master bedroom. This allows for total privacy both for the parents and the children. Continue to observe this plan. You will have no problem at all entertaining in the gathering room. Your party can flow to the adjacent balcony on a warm summer evening. The work center has been designed in an orderly fashion. The U-shaped kitchen utilizes the triangular work pattern, said to be the most efficient. Only a few steps away, you will be in the breakfast room, formal dining room, laundry or washroom. Take your time and study every last detail in this home plan.

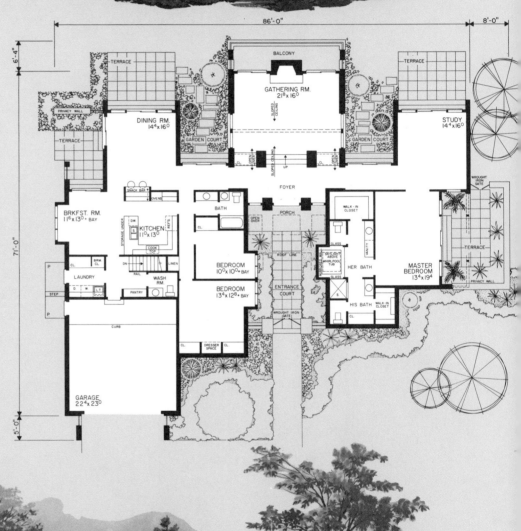

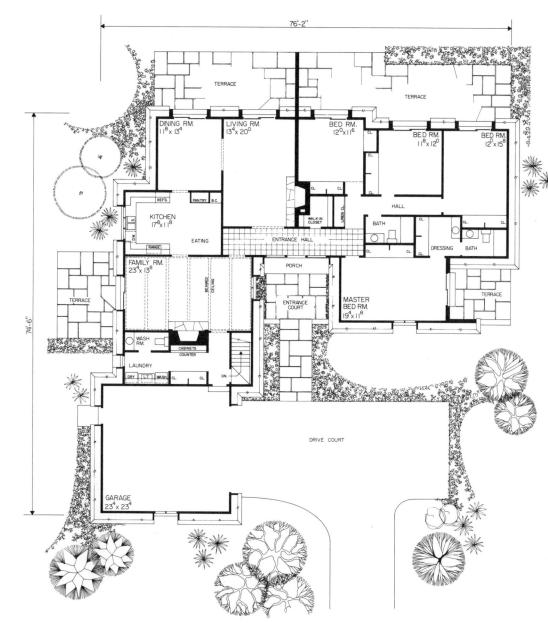

TERRACE

DINING RM.
11⁸ x 13⁴

LIVING RM.
13⁴ x 20⁰

TERRACE

BED RM.
12⁰ x 11⁶

BED RM.
11⁸ x 12⁰

BED RM.
12⁰ x 15⁰

76'-2"

74'-6"

REF'G.   PANTRY   B.C.

KITCHEN
17⁶ x 11⁸

EATING

ENTRANCE HALL

HALL

CL.

LINEN

CL.

WALK-IN
CLOSET

BATH

DRESSING   BATH

RANGE

FAMILY RM.
23⁴ x 13⁸

TERRACE

BEAMED CEILING

PORCH

ENTRANCE
COURT

MASTER
BED RM.
19⁴ x 11⁸

TERRACE

WASH
RM.

CABINETS

COUNTER

LAUNDRY

DRY   CL.T   WASH   CL.   CL.

DN.

DRIVE COURT

GARAGE
23⁴ x 23⁴

Design T72384
2,545 Sq. Ft.; 44,041 Cu. Ft.

● A dramatic Mansard roof with a contemporary adaption. The various overhanging and sloping roof planes give this L-shaped ranch home a unique appeal. Extended brick wing walls help create an entrance court leading to the attractively detailed front entry. The well-lighted entrance hall is spacious and effectively controls the traffic patterns to the major areas. Observe that each of the major rooms (kitchen excepted) enjoys direct access to outdoor living. The large master bedroom will have a full measure of privacy. On the other hand, the efficient kitchen is strategically located between dining and family rooms. A practical mud room area, adjacent to the entry from the garage, features washroom, laundry, closet and cabinet space. This home has a partial basement.

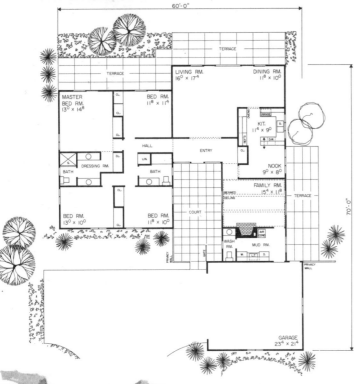

Design T72293
2,010 Sq. Ft.; 23,014 Cu. Ft.

● This is an L-shaped design which gives the interesting appearance of a group of cluster units. A front court is shielded from the street by a privacy wall. Three terraces will serve many other outdoor family activities. The various hipped-roof planes have a wide overhang and an appealing raised cap. The sleeping area is a unit by itself and contains four bedrooms and two full baths. Formal living and dining rooms represent a delightfully spacious area with plenty of glass looking out on the rear terrace. Functioning through sliding glass doors with both the court and the side terrace, the family room with beamed ceiling has a fireplace. The front, projecting garage appears to be a unit by itself, yet it is attached to the mud room with the extra washroom nearby.

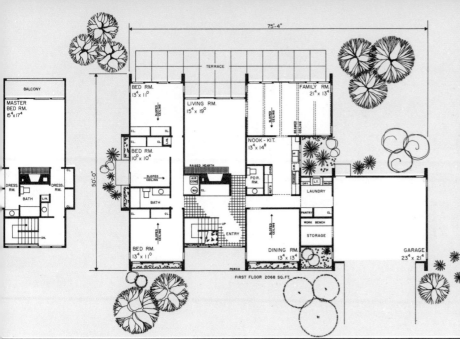

Design T72339 2,068 Sq. Ft. - First Floor
589 Sq. Ft. - Second Floor; 27,950 Cu. Ft.

● This modern Spanish design offers excellent indoor-outdoor relationships and creature comforts. Second-floor windows draw sunlight into a master bedroom suite, complete with its own fireplace and his and her dressing rooms. Three other bedrooms are located downstairs. A living room in the rear of the downstairs area enjoys its own fireplace and a functional relationship with a rear terrace. There's also a spacious family room adjacent to the living room. An L-shaped kitchen includes a nook for breakfasts. There's also a dining room adjacent to the kitchen, plus a storage room with workbench and a laundry area. Notice also the side courtyard wedged between the kitchen nook and family room. The interesting modern configuration of this home allows plenty of indoor-outdoor relationships.

Design T72386
1,994 Sq. Ft.; 22,160 Cu. Ft.

● This distinctive home may look like the Far West, but don't let that inhibit you from enjoying the great livability it has to offer. Wherever built, you will experience a satisfying pride of ownership. Imagine, an entrance court in addition to a large side courtyard! A central core is made up of the living, dining and family rooms, plus the kitchen. Each functions with an outdoor living area. The younger generation has its sleeping zone divorced from the master bedroom. The location of the attractive, attached garage provides direct access to the front entry. Don't miss the vanity, the utility room with laundry equipment, the snack bar and the raised hearth fireplace. Note three pass-throughs from the kitchen. Observe the beamed and sloping ceilings of the living areas.

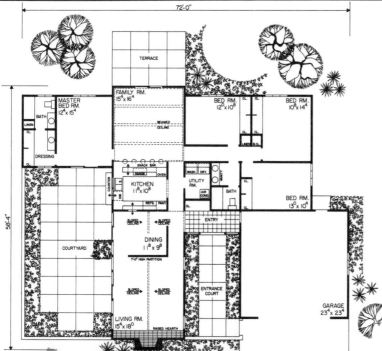

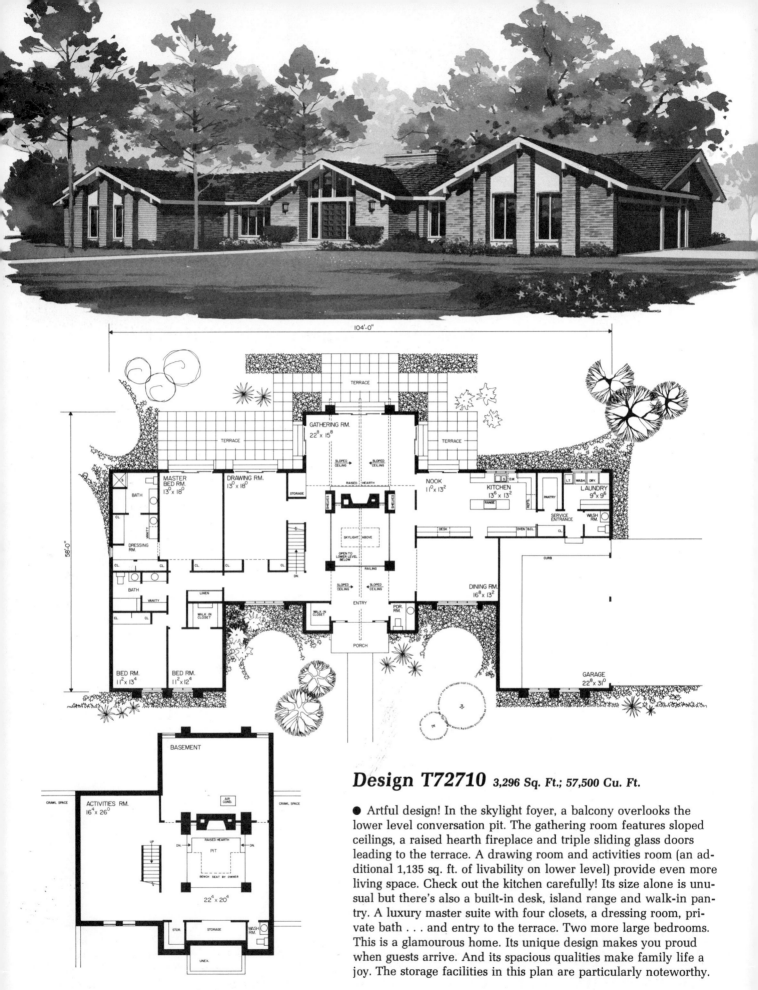

TERRACE

GATHERING RM.
22⁸ x 15⁸

SLOPED CEILING   SLOPED CEILING

TERRACE   TERRACE

RAISED HEARTH

MASTER BED RM.
13⁰ x 18⁰

DRAWING RM.
13⁰ x 18⁰

STORAGE

BATH

DRESSING RM.

NOOK
11⁰ x 13²

KITCHEN
13⁶ x 13²

RANGE

PANTRY

LT WASH DRY

LAUNDRY
9⁴ x 9⁶

SERVICE ENTRANCE

WASH RM.

SHELVES   SHELVES

SKYLIGHT ABOVE

OPEN TO LOWER LEVEL BELOW

RAILING

DESK

OVEN B.CL.

DN.

CL.

BATH

VANITY

CL.   CL.

SLOPED CEILING   SLOPED CEILING

CURB

DINING RM.
16⁸ x 13²

LINEN

LLL

WALK-IN CLOSET

WALK-IN CLOSET

ENTRY

PDR. RM.

BED RM.
11² x 13⁴

BED RM.
11² x 12⁴

PORCH

GARAGE
22⁸ x 31⁰

104'-0"

58'-0"

BASEMENT

CRAWL SPACE   CRAWL SPACE

ACTIVITIES RM.
16⁴ x 26⁰

AIR COND.

UP

DN.   RAISED HEARTH   DN.

PIT

BENCH SEAT BY OWNER

22⁴ x 20⁴

STOR.   STORAGE   WASH RM.

UNEX.

Design T72710 3,296 Sq. Ft.; 57,500 Cu. Ft.

● Artful design! In the skylight foyer, a balcony overlooks the
lower level conversation pit. The gathering room features sloped
ceilings, a raised hearth fireplace and triple sliding glass doors
leading to the terrace. A drawing room and activities room (an additional 1,135 sq. ft. of livability on lower level) provide even more
living space. Check out the kitchen carefully! Its size alone is unusual but there's also a built-in desk, island range and walk-in pantry. A luxury master suite with four closets, a dressing room, private bath . . . and entry to the terrace. Two more large bedrooms.
This is a glamourous home. Its unique design makes you proud
when guests arrive. And its spacious qualities make family life a
joy. The storage facilities in this plan are particularly noteworthy.

COVERED PORCH

TERRACE

GATHERING RM.
21⁰ x 21⁶

DINING RM.
14² x 11¹⁰

STUDY
11⁸ x 13⁴

MASTER
BED RM.
13⁰ x 18⁸

THRU
FIREPLACE

SHLVS   SHLVS

WALK-IN CLOSET

BREAKFAST
14⁰ x 11⁰

DESK   BAR

BOOKS

CABINET

POWDER
RM.

DRESSING / BATH

VANITY

SEAT

PANTRY

CL.

FOYER

SHELVES   TUB

LINEN   WALK-IN
CLOSET

BATH

KITCHEN
13⁰ x 10⁰

RANGE   OVEN

REF'G.

W.

DN

CL.

COVERED
PORCH

BED RM.
11⁰ x 12⁰

BATH

BED RM.
11⁶ x 12⁰

STEP-UP

PATIO

CURB

GARAGE
31⁴ x 21⁸

SLOPED
CEILING   TUB

72'-4"

85'-10"

Design T72789 *2,732 Sq. Ft.; 54,935 Cu. Ft.*

● An attached three car garage! What a fantastic feature of this three bedroom contemporary design. And there's more. As one walks up the steps to the covered porch and through the double front doors the charm of this design will be overwhelming. Inside, a large foyer greets all visitors and leads them to each of the three areas, each down a few steps. The living area has a large gathering room with fireplace and a study adjacent on one side and the for-mal dining room on the other. The work center has an efficient kitchen with island range, breakfast room, laundry and built-in desk and bar. Then there is the sleeping area. Note the raised tub with sloped ceiling.

Design T72534 3,262 Sq. Ft.; 58,640 Cu. Ft.

● The angular wings of this ranch home surely contribute to the unique character of the exterior. These wings effectively balance what is truly a dramatic and inviting front entrance. Massive masonry walls support the wide overhanging roof with its exposed wood beams. The patterned double front doors are surrounded by delightful expanses of glass. The raised planters and the masses of quarried stone (make it brick if you prefer) enhance the exterior appeal. Inside, a distinctive and practical floor plan stands ready to shape and serve the living patterns of the active family. The spacious entrance hall highlights sloped ceiling and an attractive open stairway to the lower level recreation area. An impressive fireplace and an abundance of glass are features of the big gathering room. Interestingly shaped dining room and study flank this main living area. The large kitchen offers many of the charming aspects of the family-kitchen of yesteryear. The bedroom wing has a sunken master suite.

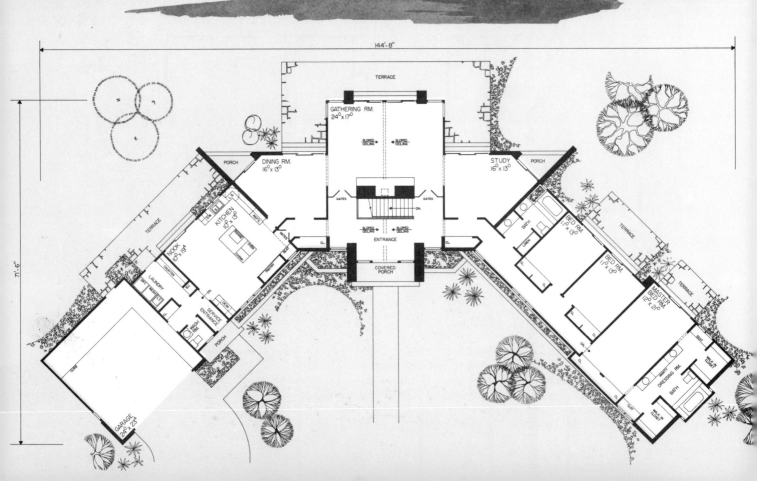

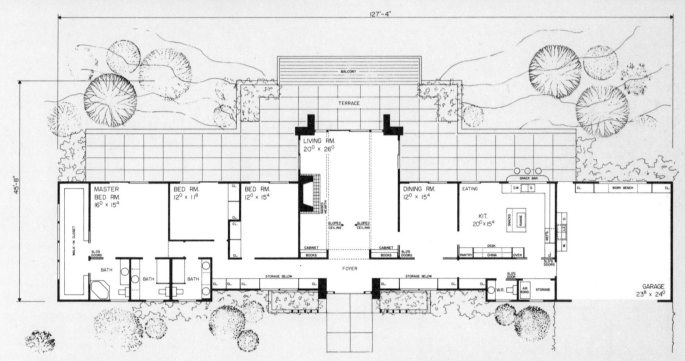

Design T72256 2,632 Sq. Ft.; 35,023 Cu. Ft.

● A dream home for those with young ideas. A refreshing, contemporary exterior with a unique, highly individualized interior. What are your favorite features.

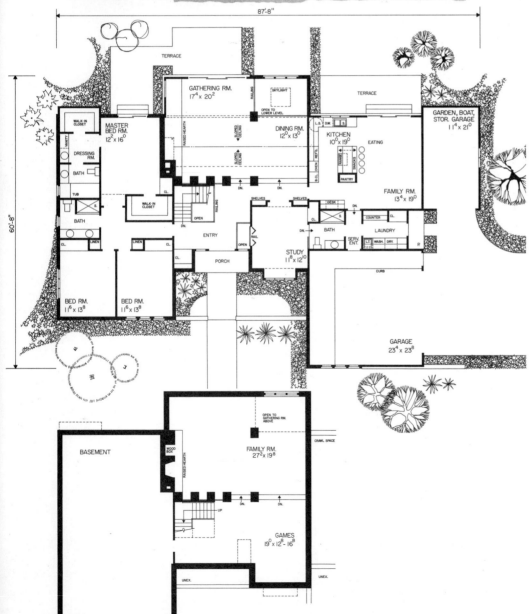

Design T72721
2,667 Sq. Ft.; 53,150 Cu. Ft.

● Visually exciting! A sunken gathering room with a sloped ceiling, raised hearth fireplace, corner balcony and skylight . . . the last two features shared by the formal dining room. There's more. Two family rooms . . . one on the lower level (1,153 sq. ft.) with a raised hearth fireplace, another adjacent to the kitchen with a snack bar! Plus a study and game room. A lavish master suite and two large bedrooms. A first floor laundry and reams of storage space, including a special garage for a boat, sports equipment, garden tools etc. There's plenty of space for family activities in this home. From chic dinner parties for friends to birthday gatherings for kids, there's always the right setting . . . and so much room that adults and children can entertain at the same time.

Design T72730

2,490 Sq. Ft.; 50,340 Cu. Ft.

● Here is a basic one-story home that is really loaded with livability on the first floor and has a bonus of an extra 1,086 sq. ft. of planned livability on a lower level. What makes this so livable is that the first floor, adjacent to the stairs leading below, is open and forms a balcony looking down into a dramatic planting area. The first floor traffic patterns flow around this impressive and distinctive feature. In addition to the gathering room, study and family room, there is the lounge and activity room. Notice the second balcony open to the activity room below. The master bedroom is outstanding with two baths and two walk-in closets. The attached three-car garage has a bulk storage area and is accessible through the service area.

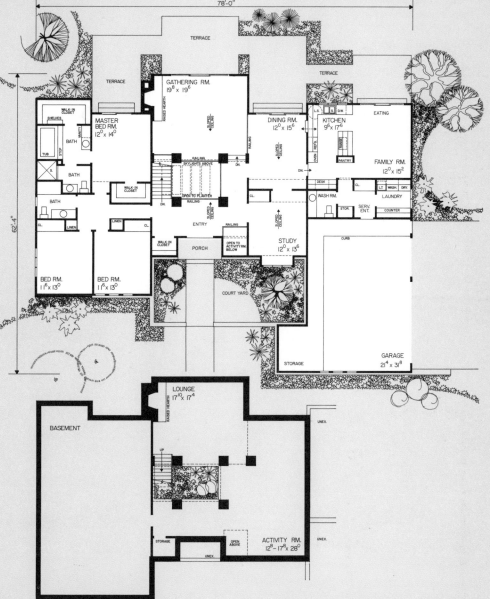

Design T72304

2,313 Sq. Ft.; 26,110 Cu. Ft.

● What an appealing home! And what a list of reasons why it is so eye-catching. First of all, there is the irregular shape and the low-pitched, wide-overhanging roof. Then, there is the interesting use of exterior materials, including vertical glass window treatment. Further, there are the raised planters flanking the porch of the recessed entrance. Inside, the traffic patterns are excellent. Among the focal points is the 33 foot, beam ceilinged living area. This will surely be fun to plan and furnish for the family's living and dining pursuits. Among other highlights is the layout of the laundry-kitchen-nook area. The extra washroom is strategically located. The sleeping wing has much to offer with its privacy, its convenient bath facilities, and its fine storage.

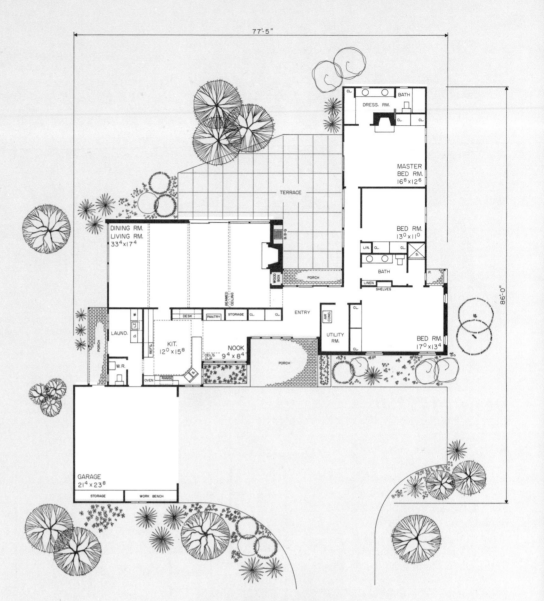

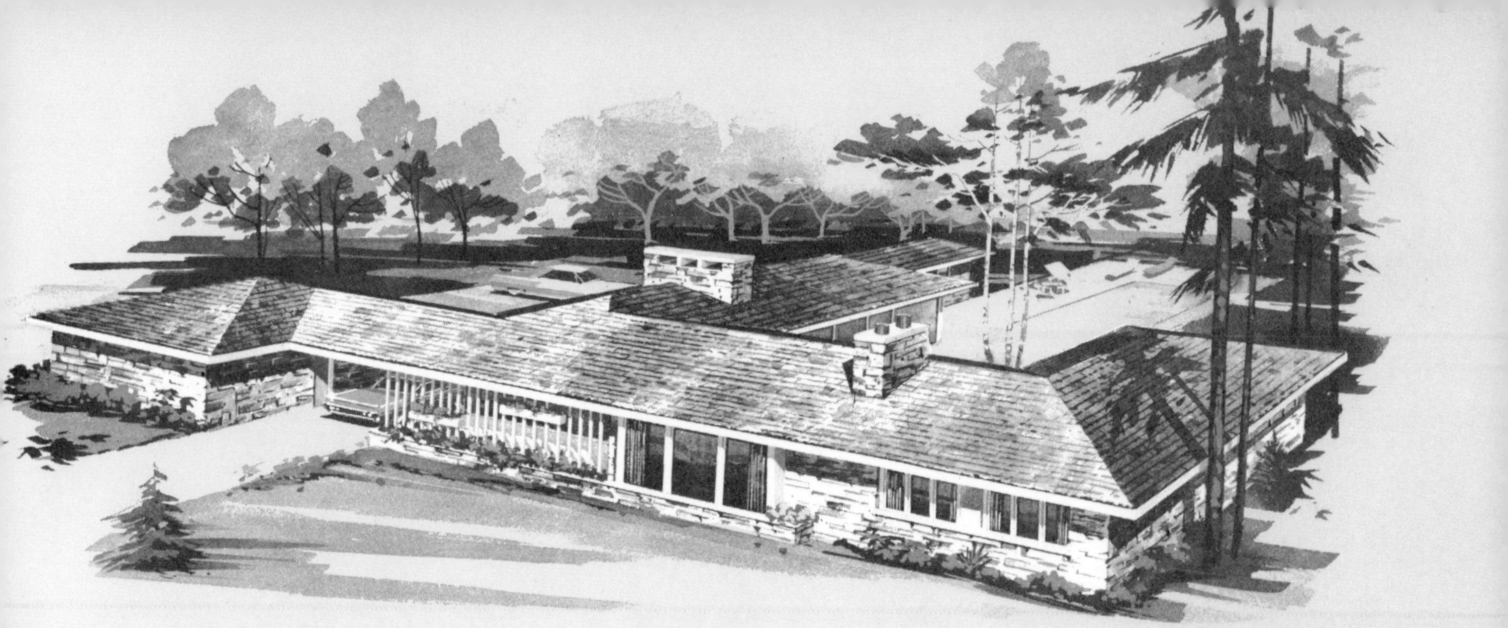

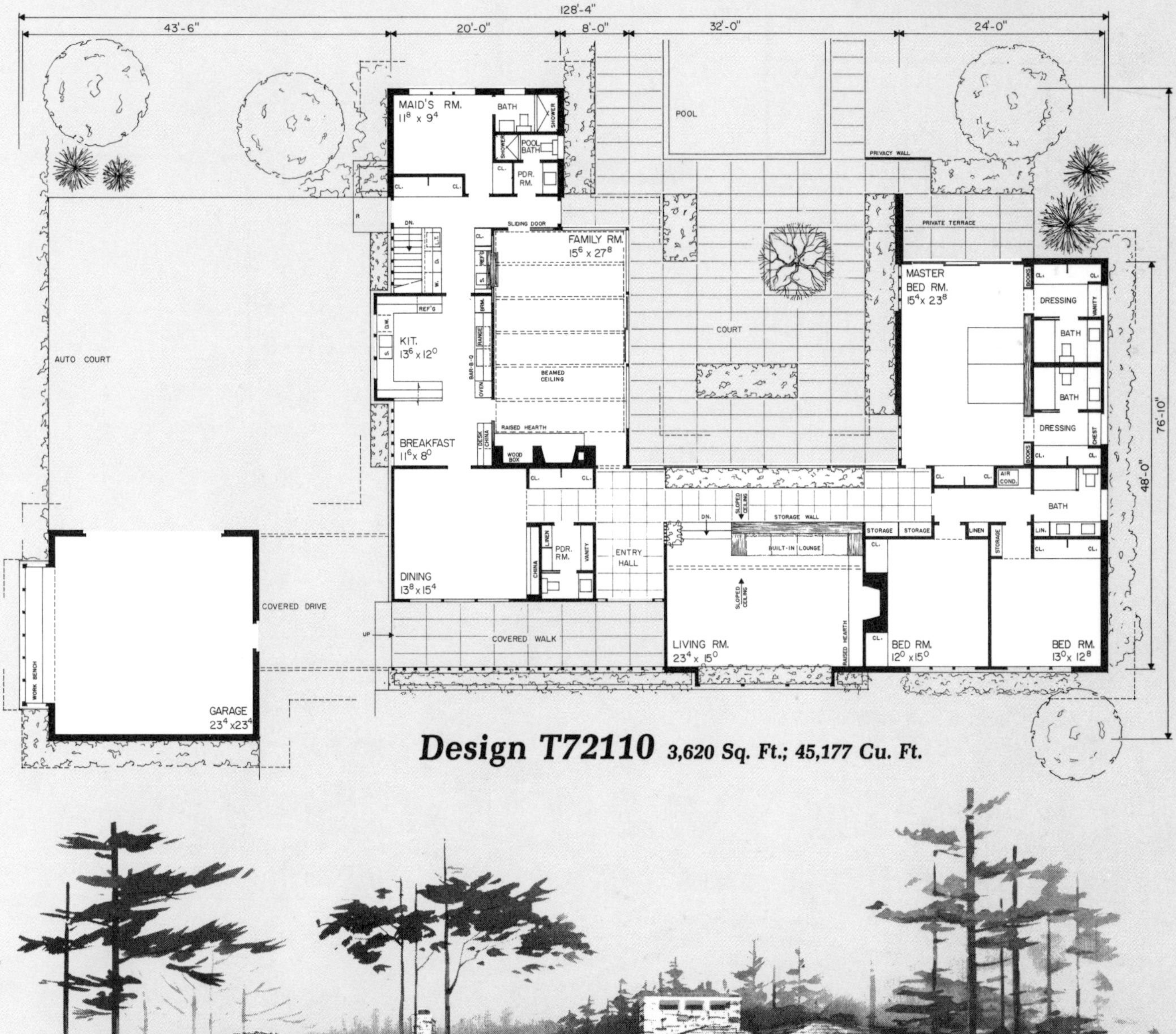
128'-4"
43'-6"
20'-0"
8'-0"
32'-0"
24'-0"
76'-10"
48'-0"
MAID'S RM. 11⁸ x 9⁴
BATH
SHOWER
POOL BATH
PDR. RM.
CL.
POOL
PRIVACY WALL
PRIVATE TERRACE
DN.
SLIDING DOOR
FAMILY RM. 15⁶ x 27⁸
BEAMED CEILING
RAISED HEARTH
WOOD BOX
REF'G
KIT. 13⁶ x 12⁰
BAR-B-Q
RANGE
OVEN
DESK
CHINA
BREAKFAST 11⁶ x 8⁰
AUTO COURT
COURT
MASTER BED RM. 15⁴ x 23⁸
DRESSING
BATH
VANITY
BOOKS
CHEST
AIR COND.
SLOPED CEILING
STORAGE WALL
BUILT-IN LOUNGE
STORAGE
LINEN
LIN.
ENTRY HALL
PDR. RM.
DINING 13⁸ x 15⁴
COVERED DRIVE
COVERED WALK
UP
LIVING RM. 23⁴ x 15⁰
RAISED HEARTH
BED RM. 12⁰ x 15⁰
BED RM. 13⁰ x 12⁸
WORK BENCH
GARAGE 23⁴ x 23⁴

Design T72110 3,620 Sq. Ft.; 45,177 Cu. Ft.

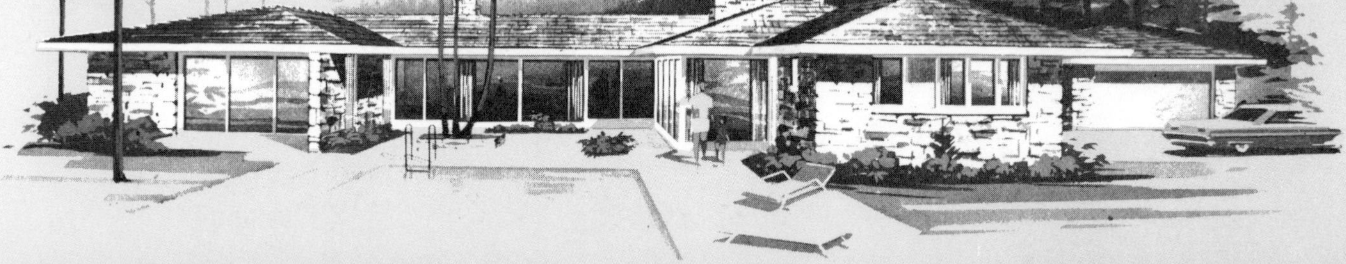

Design T71928 3,272 Sq. Ft.; 46,294 Cu. Ft.

● You'll find this contemporary home is worthy of your consideration if you're looking for a house of distinction. The dramatic exterior is a sure-fire stopper. Even the most casual passer-by will take a second look. In-teresting roof surfaces, massive brick chimney wall, recessed entrance, raised planters and garden wall are among the features that spell design distinction. And yet, the exterior is only part of the story this home has to tell. Its interior is no less unique. Con-sider the sunken living room, sloping, beamed ceiling of the family room, wonderful kitchen/laundry area, four-bedroom sleeping area with all those closets, bath facilities and sliding doors.

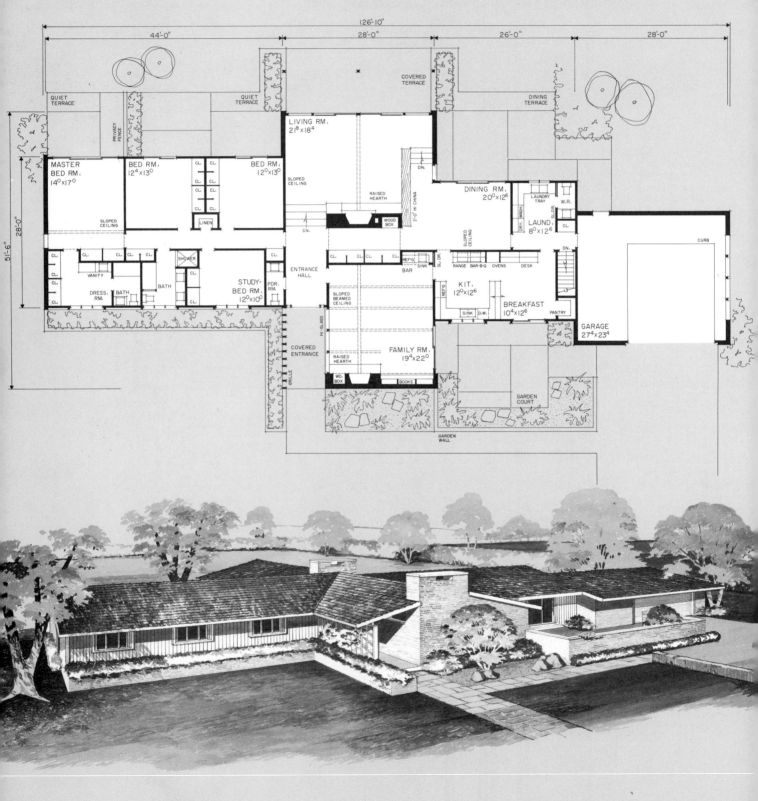

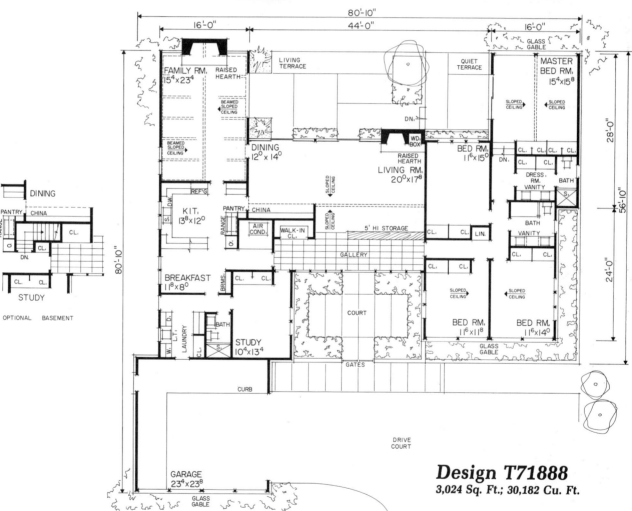

Design T71888
3,024 Sq. Ft.; 30,182 Cu. Ft.

● If you have an active family that needs plenty of well-defined space to move around, then this modified H-shaped, contemporary house may be perfect for your family. With all that space, you should be happy to know that you won't have to buy the biggest piece of property in town. The shape of the house keeps the overall dimension small enough to fit a modest sized lot. However, there is nothing modest about the inside. The list of features will be king size, indeed. Which features will be at the top of your list? The court, gallery or 32 foot living/dining area? How about the study, family room or master bedroom? Note details for an optional basement plan.

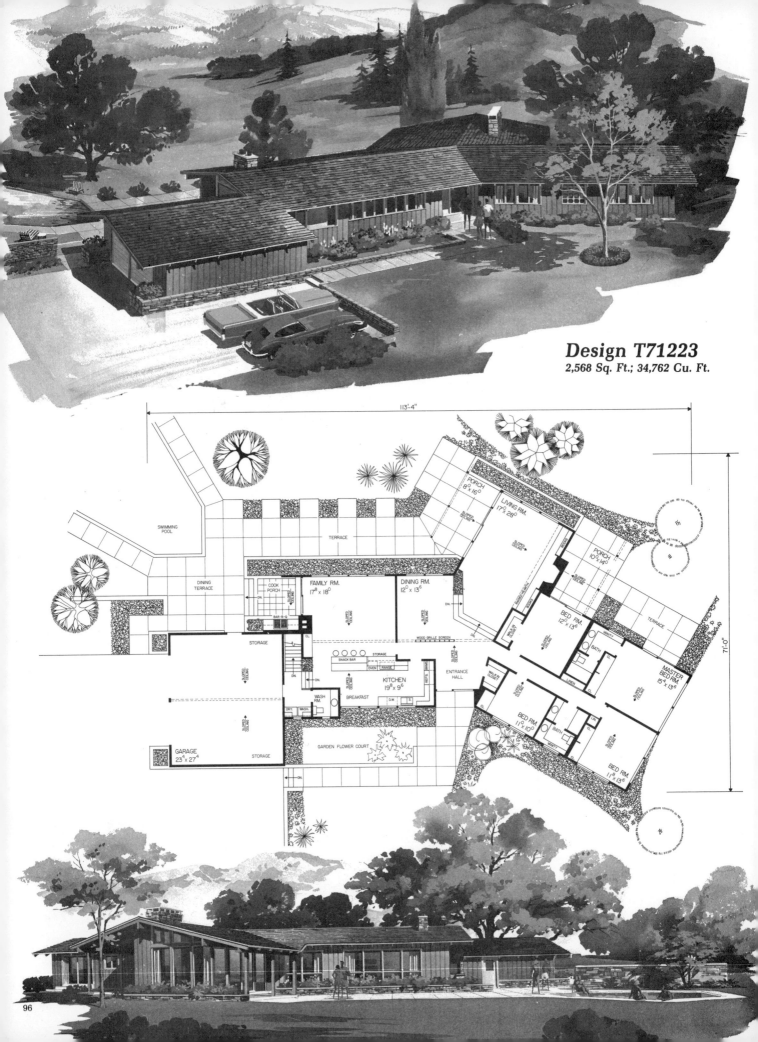

Design T71223
2,568 Sq. Ft.; 34,762 Cu. Ft.

113'-4"

71'-0"

SWIMMING POOL

TERRACE

DINING TERRACE

STORAGE

COOK PORCH

FAMILY RM.
17⁸ x 18⁰

DINING RM.
12⁰ x 13⁶

PORCH
8⁰ x 16⁰

LIVING RM.
17⁰ x 28⁰

PORCH
10⁰ x 14⁰

TERRACE

BED RM.
12 x 13⁶

MASTER BED RM.
15⁴ x 13⁶

BATH

SNACK BAR

STORAGE

OVEN   RANGE

KITCHEN
19⁸ x 9⁶

BREAKFAST

WASH RM.

BAR-B-Q

ENTRANCE HALL

WOOD GRILLE SCREEN

BATH

BED RM.
11⁹ x 10⁶

GARAGE
23⁴ x 27⁴

STORAGE

GARDEN FLOWER COURT

BED RM.
11⁸ x 13⁶

FRONT COURTYARDS For Modern Lifestyles

... Designs for Contemporary homes on the following pages incorporate courtyards in the front of the home for people who appreciate indoor-outdoor relationships in modern living patterns.

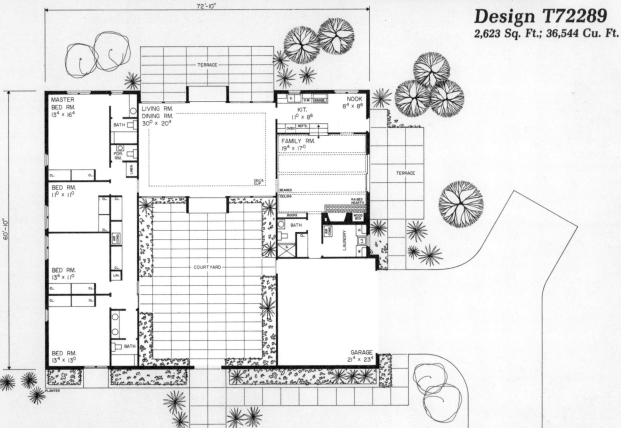

Design T72289
2,623 Sq. Ft.; 36,544 Cu. Ft.

● Impressive? You bet it is! And, as a matter of fact, it looks almost palatial. It is easy to guess that there will be as much fun (and maybe more) in that huge courtyard as in any other part of the unique plan. The formality of the exterior is derived from the trim plant-ing areas and the contemporary ad-aptation of the French Mansard roof. The two-story effect of the front en-trance is, indeed, dramatic. Separating the peaceful sleeping wing is the for-mal living-dining area. Measuring 30 x 20 feet, this will be a real joy to fur-nish. With all that glass and the 17 foot ceiling, spaciousness will be the by-word. The kitchen — family room — laundry area functions well. Don't miss the three full baths, the raised hearth fireplace or the breakfast nook. Note the pass-thru from kitchen to family room.

Design T71825

2,170 Sq. Ft.; 21,417 Cu. Ft.

● Five wonderful outdoor living areas headed by the front private court are highlights of this impressive U-shaped, four bedroom home. The low-pitched, wide overhanging roof, the exposed rafters, the grille work and the attractive gate are all features which remind one of the Spanish Southwest.

OPTIONAL BASEMENT

Design T72590

2,380 Sq. Ft.; 26,680 Cu. Ft.

● A large enclosed garden courtyard. A rear terrace. Formal living and dining rooms, plus a family room with a raised hearth fireplace. Three large bedrooms, including a master suite with a dressing room and private bath. These are just some of the outstanding features of this design. This home is designed for easy living, whether you're entertaining with a summer barbecue or a formal dinner party. And it's got the extras you want to help ensure life-long convenience . . . an island range and built-in desk in the kitchen, a first-floor laundry, lots of convenient storage. You will like the strategically placed walk-in closet adjacent to the kitchen.

Design T71754
2,080 Sq. Ft.; 21,426 Cu. Ft.

● Boasting a traditional Western flavor, this rugged U-shaped ranch home has all the features to assure grand living. The low-pitched, wide-overhanging roof with exposed rafters, the masses of brick, and the panelled doors with their carriage lamps above are among the exterior highlights which create this design's unique character. The private front flower court, inside the high brick wall, fosters a delightfully dramatic atmosphere which carries inside. The floor plan is positively unique and exceptionally livable. Wonderfully zoned, the three bedrooms enjoy their full measure of privacy. Observe the dressing room, walk-in closet and linen storage. The formal living and dining rooms function together in a most pleasing fashion. An attractive open railing separates the dining room from the sunken living room.

Design T71932

1,678 Sq. Ft.; 17,115 Cu. Ft.

● Here is a unique contemporary design whose projecting wings reach out to enclose a spacious, front court. The high privacy wall helps support the covering for the walkway inside. This enchanting area will be enjoyed the year-round. Windows in the living room permit a fine view of this area and the undisturbed beauty of its landscaping, whatever the season. A study of the basic, L-shaped floor plan reveals convenient living patterns. The informal family room and the formal living/dining area feature sloping ceilings for a feeling of sspaciousness. Study the plan's other areas.

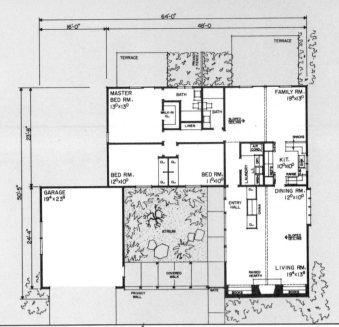

Design T71940

2,400 Sq. Ft.; 40,260 Cu. Ft.

● This hip-roofed, U-shaped ranch home features a large front court plus plenty of other extras. These include four large bedrooms, two full baths, exceptional storage facilities, two fireplaces, spacious living and dining areas, a breakfast room, partial basement, large family room, built-in desk and china units, oversized two-car garage, outdoor window planters, built-in barbecue, and stone privacy wall.

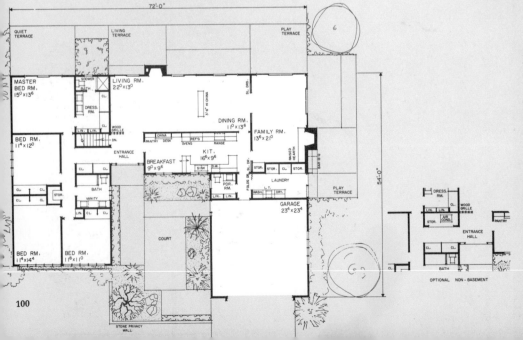

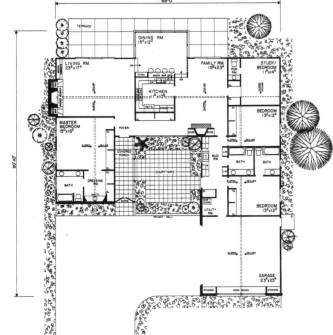

Design T72229 2,728 Sq. Ft.; 29,482 Cu. Ft.

● The irregular shape of this rustic ranch home creates an enclosed front entrance court. Twin gates open to a covered walk that looks out upon the delightful private court on way to the front door. The house also is specially zoned to provide maximum privacy in the living room and master bedroom. At the other end of the house are children's rooms and an informal family room. The kitchen is strategically located. A dining room projects outward into a terrace with an abundance of glass for full enjoyment of the outdoors during meals. This one-story design also enjoys two fireplaces and sloped ceilings.

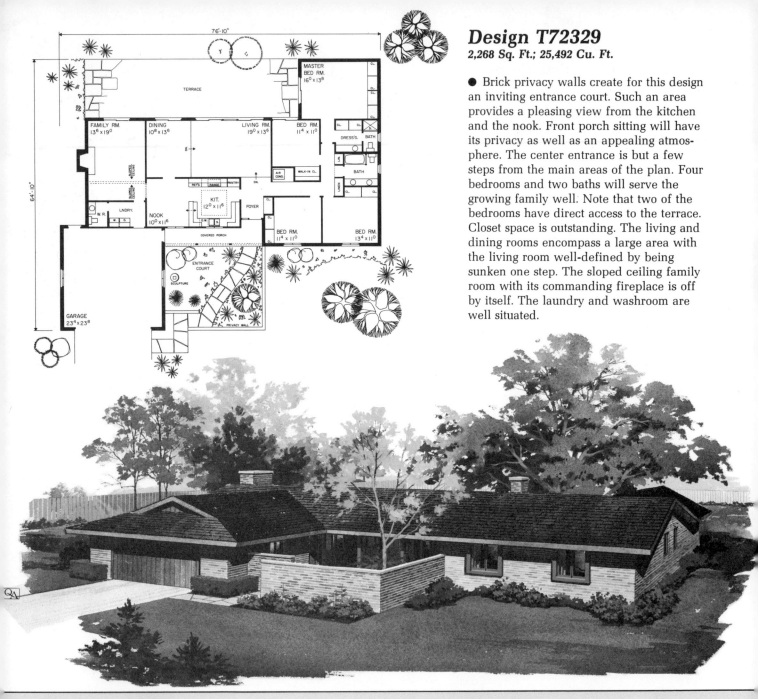

Design T72329
2,268 Sq. Ft.; 25,492 Cu. Ft.

● Brick privacy walls create for this design an inviting entrance court. Such an area provides a pleasing view from the kitchen and the nook. Front porch sitting will have its privacy as well as an appealing atmosphere. The center entrance is but a few steps from the main areas of the plan. Four bedrooms and two baths will serve the growing family well. Note that two of the bedrooms have direct access to the terrace. Closet space is outstanding. The living and dining rooms encompass a large area with the living room well-defined by being sunken one step. The sloped ceiling family room with its commanding fireplace is off by itself. The laundry and washroom are well situated.

Design T72529
2,326 Sq. Ft.; 47,012 Cu. Ft.

● The front entrance court with its plant areas and surrounding accents of colorful quarried stone (make it brick, if you prefer), provides a delightful introduction to this interesting contemporary home. The spacious entry hall leads directly to a generous L-shaped living and dining area. Sliding glass doors provide direct access to the outdoor terrace. An efficient, interior kitchen will be fun in which to work. It could hardly be more strategically located — merely a step or two from the formal dining area, the breakfast nook, and the family room. Although this home has a basement, there is a convenient first floor laundry and an extra washroom. The four bedroom sleeping wing has two full baths. Two of the rooms have access to the outdoor terraces. Notice garage storage.

Design T72311
2,205 Sq. Ft.; 19,880 Cu. Ft.

● You could really have fun if you were to ask the various members of your family what they liked best about this contemporary design. Somebody, of course, would say the entrance court and how it functioned through sliding glass doors with the beamed ceilinged family room. Another, perhaps, would say the efficient rear kitchen flanked by the dining room and breakfast nook and overlooking the terrace. Others would chime in with the privacy of the front living room, the laundry/washroom, all those closets and the large shop room behind the garage. Naturally, sooner or later, the list of favorite features would include the raised hearth fireplace in the family room, the snack bar and pass-thru to kitchen and the isolation of the master bedroom and its private bath.

Design T72795
1,952 Sq. Ft.; 43,500 Cu. Ft.

● This three-bedroom design leaves no room for improvement. Any size family will find it difficult to surpass the fine qualities that this home offers. Begin with the exterior. This fine contemporary design has open trellis work above the front, covered private court. This area is sheltered by a privacy wall extending from the projecting garage. Inside, the floor plan will be just as breathtaking. Begin at the foyer and choose a direction. To the right is the sleeping wing equipped with three bedrooms and two baths. Straight ahead from the foyer is the gathering room with thru-fireplace to the dining room. To the right is the work center. This area includes a breakfast room, a U-shaped kitchen and laundry.

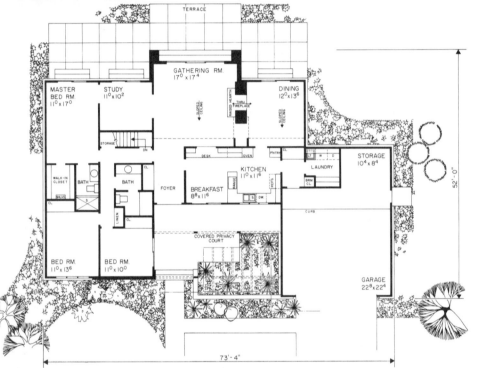

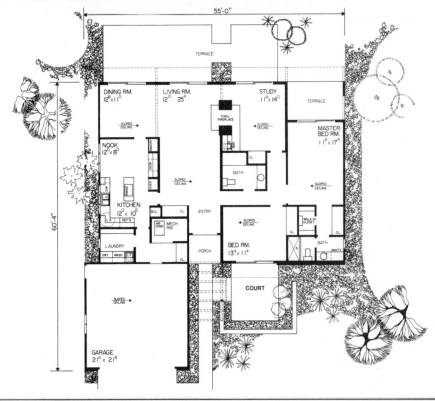

Design T72754
1,844 Sq. Ft.; 26,615 Cu. Ft.

● This really is a most dramatic and refreshing contemporary home. The slope of its wide overhanging roofs is carried right indoors to provide an extra measure of spaciousness. The U-shaped privacy wall of the front entrance area provides an appealing outdoor living spot accessible from the front bedroom. The rectangular floor plan will be economical to build. Notice the efficient use of space and how it all makes its contribution to outstanding livability. The small family will find its living patterns delightful, indeed. Two bedrooms and two full baths comprise the sleeping zone. The open planning of the L-shaped living and dining rooms is most desirable. The thru-fireplace is just a great room divider. The kitchen and breakfast nook function well together. There is laundry and mechanical room nearby.

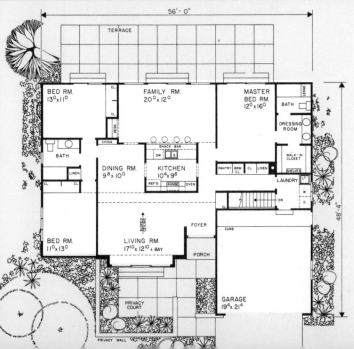

Design T72796
1,828 Sq. Ft.; 39,990 Cu. Ft.

● This home features a front living room with sloped ceiling and sliding glass doors which lead to a front private court. What a delightful way to introduce this design. This bi-nuclear design has a great deal to offer. First - the children's and parent's sleeping quarters are on opposite ends of this house to assure the utmost in privacy. Each area has its own full bath. The interior kitchen is a great idea. It frees up valuable wall space for the living areas exclusive use. There is a snack bar in the kitchen/family room for those very informal meals. Also, a planning desk is in the family room. The dining room is conveniently located near the kitchen plus it has a built-in china cabinet. The laundry area has plenty of storage closets plus the stairs to the basement. This home will surely be a welcome addition to any setting.

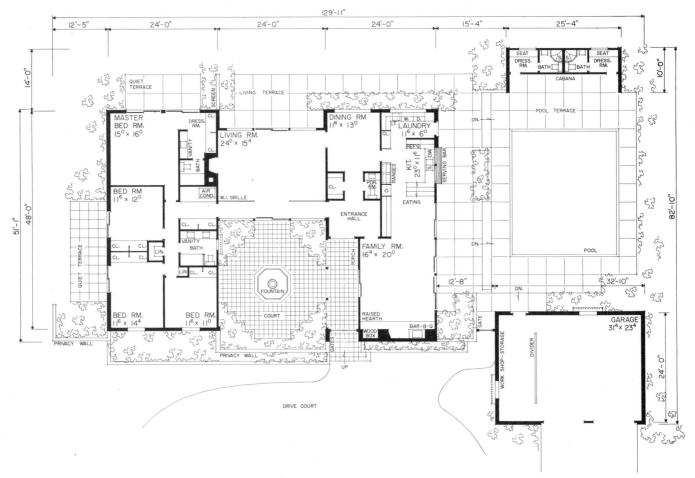

Design T71756 2,736 Sq. Ft.; 29,139 Cu. Ft.

● Reminiscent of the West and impressive, indeed. If you are after something that is luxurious in both its appearance and its livability this design should receive your consideration. This rambling ranch house, which encloses a spacious and dramatic flower court, is designed for comfort and privacy indoors and out. Study the outdoor areas. Notice the seclusion each of them provides. Three bedrooms, plus a master suite with dressing room and bath form a private bedroom wing. Formal and informal living areas serve ideally for various types of entertaining. There is excellent circulation of traffic throughout the house. The kitchen is handy to the formal dining room and the informal family room. Don't miss raised hearth fireplace.

CONTEMPORARY HILLSIDE LIVING
. . . and the Exposed Lower Level
These designs are planned to take full advantage of hillside sites and sloped terrain. A hillside house can be one-story, two-story, bi-level, or split-level. Often the lower level is exposed with the added advantage of private terraces or patios created below.

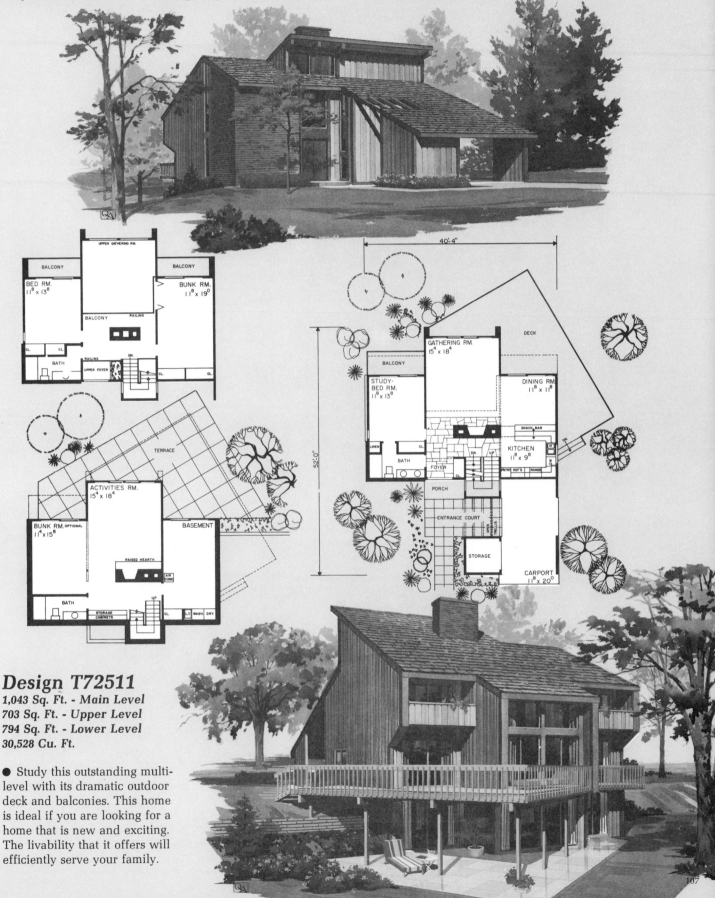

Design T72511
1,043 Sq. Ft. - Main Level
703 Sq. Ft. - Upper Level
794 Sq. Ft. - Lower Level
30,528 Cu. Ft.

● Study this outstanding multilevel with its dramatic outdoor deck and balconies. This home is ideal if you are looking for a home that is new and exciting. The livability that it offers will efficiently serve your family.

107

A Lifetime of Exciting, Contemporary Living Patterns

● Here is a home for those with a bold, contemporary living bent. The exciting exteriors give notice of an admirable flair for something delightfully different. The varying roof planes and textured blank wall masses are distinctive. Two sets of panelled front doors permit access to either level. The inclined ramp to the upper main level is dramatic, indeed. The rear exterior highlights a veritable battery of projecting balconies. This affords direct access to outdoor living for each of the major rooms in the house. Certainly an invaluable feature should your view be particularly noteworthy. Notice two covered outdoor balconies plus a covered terrace. Indoor-outdoor living at its greatest.

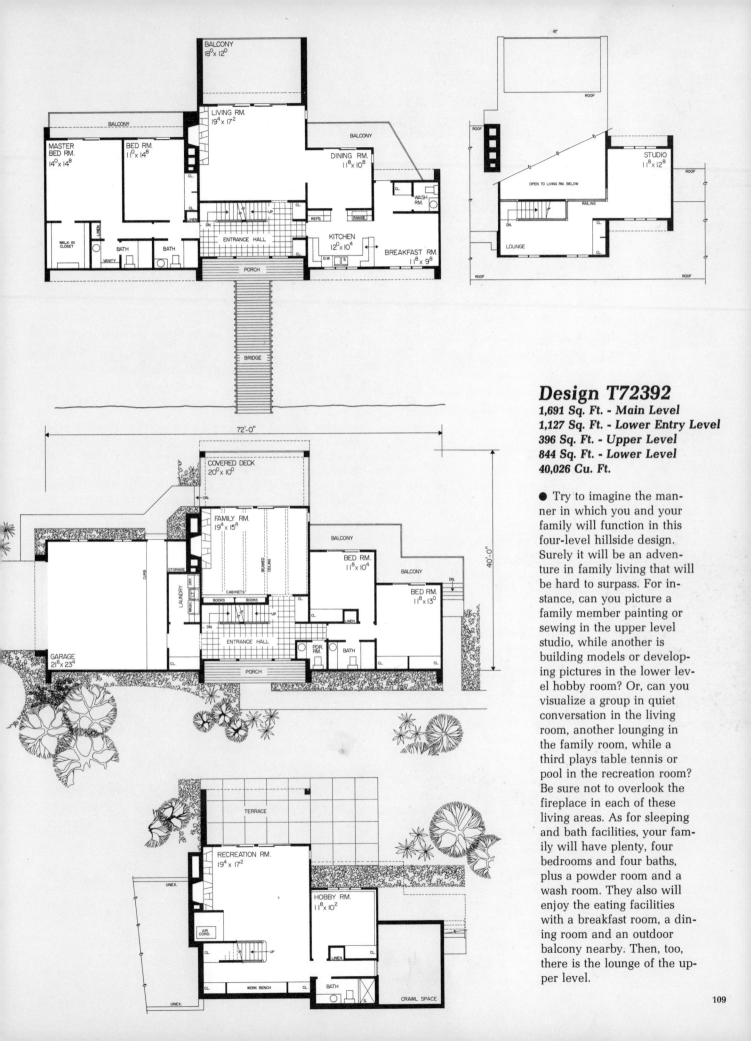

Upper Level Plan

STUDIO
11⁸ x 12⁸

OPEN TO LIVING RM. BELOW

RAILING

LOUNGE

ROOF

Main Level Plan

BALCONY
18⁰ x 12⁰

LIVING RM.
19⁴ x 17²

BALCONY

DINING RM.
11⁸ x 10⁸

WASH RM.

MASTER BED RM.
14⁰ x 14⁸

BED RM.
11⁸ x 14⁸

BALCONY

CL.

CL.

CL.

LINEN

REFG.

RANGE

CL.

WALK-IN CLOSET

LINEN

BATH

BATH

ENTRANCE HALL

DN.

UP

KITCHEN
12⁰ x 10⁴

VANITY

D.W.

S

BREAKFAST RM.
11⁸ x 9⁸

PORCH

BRIDGE

Lower Entry Level Plan

72'-0"

40'-0"

COVERED DECK
20⁰ x 10⁰

DN.

FAMILY RM.
19⁴ x 15⁸

BEAMED CEILING

BALCONY

BED RM.
11⁸ x 10⁴

BALCONY

BED RM.
11⁸ x 13⁰

CL.

STORAGE

WASH

DRY.

CABINETS

BOOKS

BOOKS

LAUNDRY

GARAGE
21⁸ x 23⁴

CURB

UP

DN.

LINEN

CL.

DN.

ENTRANCE HALL

PDR. RM.

BATH

CL.

CL.

PORCH

Lower Level Plan

TERRACE

RECREATION RM.
19⁴ x 17²

UNEX.

AIR COND.

HOBBY RM.
11⁸ x 10²

CL.

UP

LINEN

BATH

CL.

WORK BENCH

UNEX.

CRAWL SPACE

Design T72392

1,691 Sq. Ft. - Main Level
1,127 Sq. Ft. - Lower Entry Level
396 Sq. Ft. - Upper Level
844 Sq. Ft. - Lower Level
40,026 Cu. Ft.

● Try to imagine the manner in which you and your family will function in this four-level hillside design. Surely it will be an adventure in family living that will be hard to surpass. For instance, can you picture a family member painting or sewing in the upper level studio, while another is building models or developing pictures in the lower level hobby room? Or, can you visualize a group in quiet conversation in the living room, another lounging in the family room, while a third plays table tennis or pool in the recreation room? Be sure not to overlook the fireplace in each of these living areas. As for sleeping and bath facilities, your family will have plenty, four bedrooms and four baths, plus a powder room and a wash room. They also will enjoy the eating facilities with a breakfast room, a dining room and an outdoor balcony nearby. Then, too, there is the lounge of the upper level.

109

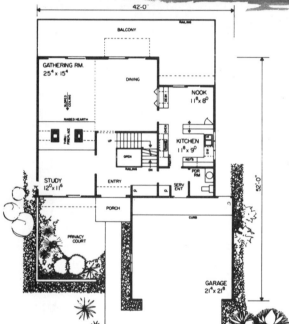

Design T72716 1,013 Sq. Ft. - Main Level

885 Sq. Ft. - Upper Level; 1,074 Sq. Ft. - Lower Level; 32,100 Cu. Ft.

● A genuine master suite! It overlooks the gathering room through shuttered windows and includes a private balcony, a 9'x 9' sitting/dressing room and a full bath. There's more, a two-story gathering room with a raised hearth fireplace, sloped ceiling and sliding glass doors onto the main balcony. Plus, a family room and a study both having a fireplace. A kitchen with lots of built-ins and a separate dining nook.

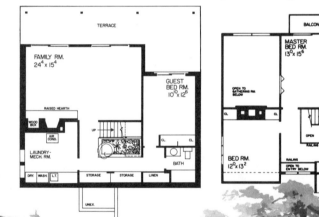

Design T72552 1,437 Sq. Ft. - Main Level; 1,158 Sq. Ft. - Upper Level; 1,056 Sq. Ft. - Lower Level; 43,000 Cu. Ft.

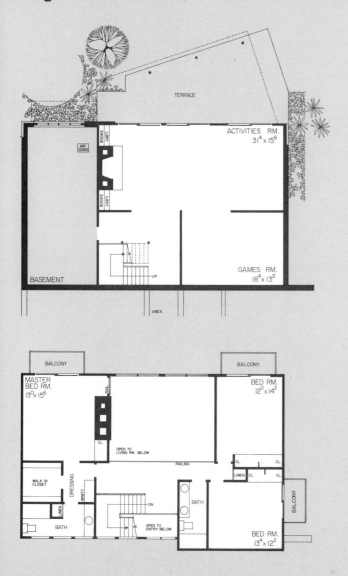

TERRACE

AIR COND.

BOOKS CAB'T.

ACTIVITIES RM.
31⁴ x 15⁶

BOOKS CAB'T.

BASEMENT

GAMES RM.
18⁴ x 13²

UP

UNEX.

BALCONY

BALCONY

MASTER BED RM.
13⁰ x 15⁶

BED RM.
12⁰ x 14²

OPEN TO LIVING RM. BELOW

CL.

RAILING

CL.
CL.

WALK-IN CLOSET

DRESSING

VANITY

LINEN

CL.
LINEN

BATH

DN.

BATH

OPEN TO ENTRY BELOW

BED RM.
13⁴ x 12²

BALCONY

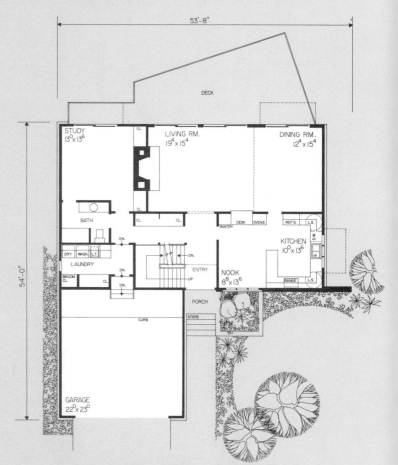

53'-8"

DECK

STUDY
13⁰ x 13⁶

LIVING RM.
19⁴ x 15⁴

DINING RM.
12⁴ x 15⁴

54'-0"

BATH

CL.

CL.

CL.

PANTRY

DESK

OVENS

REF'G.

L.S.

KITCHEN
10⁰ x 13⁶

DRY.

WASH

LT.

LAUNDRY

DN.

DN.

ENTRY

NOOK
8⁸ x 13⁶

BROOM

CL.

DN.

UP

RANGE

L.S.

PORCH

CURB

STEPS

GARAGE
22⁰ x 23⁰

● Whatever you call this design - a hillside home or a two-story with an exposed basement - it will deliver an abundance of family livability. Study the three levels carefully. Notice how the upper level hall and master bedroom look down into the living room. Observe the study with access to a full bath.

Design T72761 1,242 Sq. Ft. - Main Level
1,242 Sq. Ft. - Lower Level; 25,045 Cu. Ft.

● Here is another one-story that doubles its livability by exposing the lowest level at the rear. Formal living on the main level and informal living, the activity room and study, on the lower level. Observe the wonderful outdoor living facilities. The deck acts as a cover for the terrace.

TERRACE

ACTIVITIES RM.
14⁰ x 17⁶

STUDY
15¹⁰ x 10⁰

CL.

STORAGE
UP

BED RM.
10¹⁰ x 13¹⁰

BED RM.
11² x 12⁸

LINEN

BATH

CL. VANITY CL.

MECH. RM.

AIR COND.

WALK IN CLOSET

UNEX.

UNEX.

50'-0"

DECK

LIVING RM.
14⁴ x 17⁶

DINING RM.
10⁰ x 10⁰

NOOK
8⁸ x 10⁰

BALCONY

RAILING

KITCHEN
12⁰ x 13⁰

MASTER
BED RM.
11⁸ x 15⁰

DN

BCL OVEN RANGE

BATH

LIN. CL.

CL. LT WASH DRY

WASH RM.

ENTRY

SERVICE ENTRANCE

LAUNDRY

PORCH

CURB

52'-0"

GARAGE
21⁴ x 21⁸

STORAGE

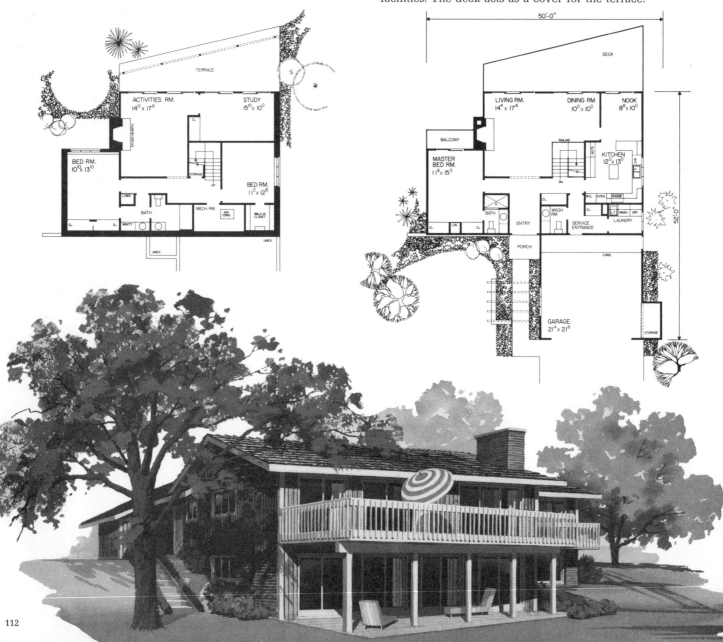

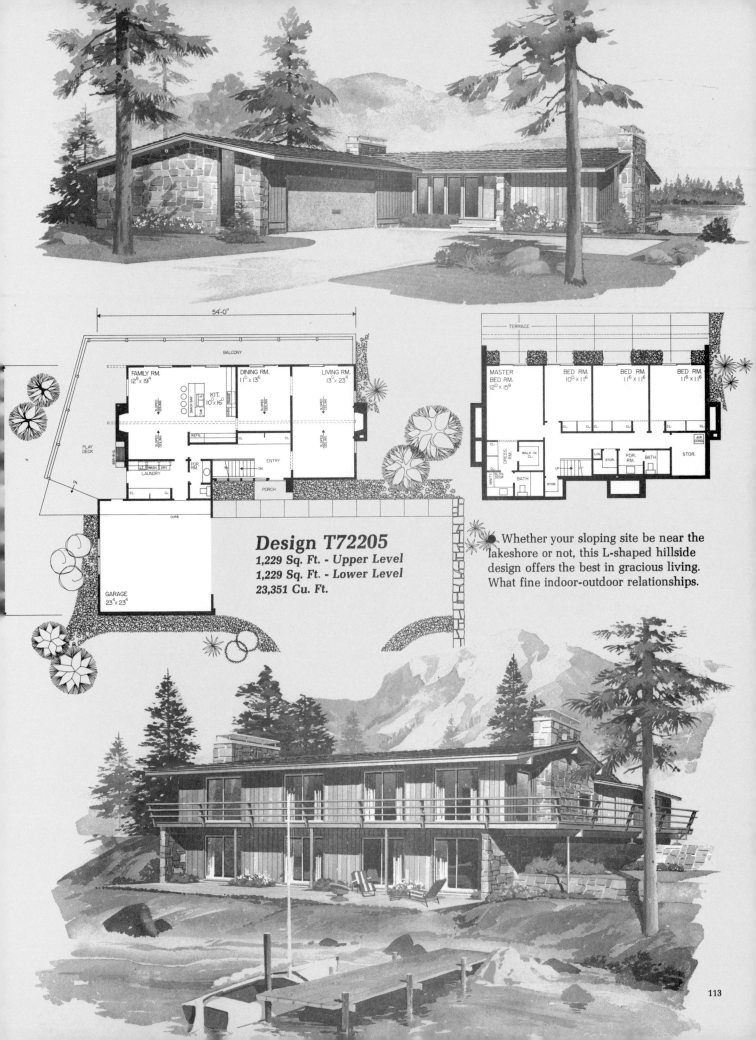

54'-0"

FAMILY RM.
12⁸ x 19⁴

KIT.
10⁰ x 16⁰

DINING RM.
11⁰ x 13⁶

LIVING RM.
13⁰ x 23⁴

BALCONY

SNACK BAR

SLOPED CEILING

SLOPED CEILING

SLOPED CEILING

SLOPED CEILING

REF'S.

CL.

ENTRY

PLAY DECK

WASH. DRY.

LAUNDRY

POR. RM.

DN.

CL.

CL.

PORCH

CURB

GARAGE
23⁴ x 23⁴

TERRACE

MASTER BED RM.
12⁰ x 15⁸

BED RM.
10⁰ x 11⁶

BED RM.
11⁶ x 11⁶

BED RM.
11⁶ x 11⁶

CL.

CL. CL.

CL.

CL.

DRESS.

WALK-IN CL.

SLD. DOOR

BATH

STOR.

LIN.

STOR.

UP

POR. RM.

BATH

STOR.

AIR COND.

Design T72205
1,229 Sq. Ft. - Upper Level
1,229 Sq. Ft. - Lower Level
23,351 Cu. Ft.

● Whether your sloping site be near the lakeshore or not, this L-shaped hillside design offers the best in gracious living. What fine indoor-outdoor relationships.

113

Design T72502

2,606 Sq. Ft. - Main Level
1,243 Sq. Ft. - Lower Level; 45,000 Cu. Ft.

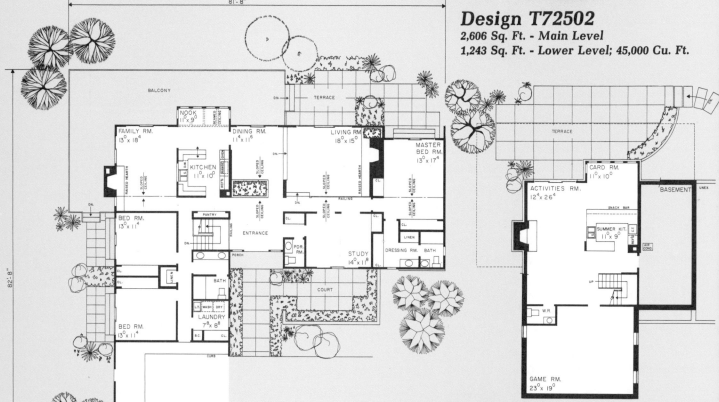

● A home with two faces. From the street this design gives all the appearances of being a one-story, L-shaped home. One can only guess at the character of the rear elevation as dictated by the sloping terrain. A study of the interior reveals tremendous convenient living potential.

Design T72504
1,918 Sq. Ft. - Main Level
1,910 Sq. Ft. - Lower Level; 39,800 Cu. Ft.

● A front court area welcomes guests on their way to the double front doors. These doors, flanked by floor-to-ceiling glass panels, are sheltered by the porch. Adjacent to this area is the sliding glass doors of the breakfast nook which can enjoy to the fullest the beauty of the front yard. This design has taken the advantage of the sloping site to open up the lower level. In this case, the lower level has virtually the same glass treatment as its corresponding room above.

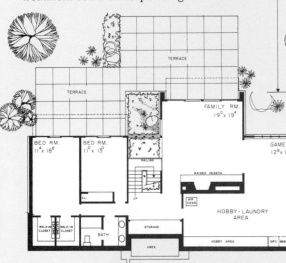

Design T72546 1,143 Sq. Ft. - Main Level; 746 Sq. Ft. - Upper Level
1,143 Sq. Ft. - Lower Level; 31,128 Cu. Ft.

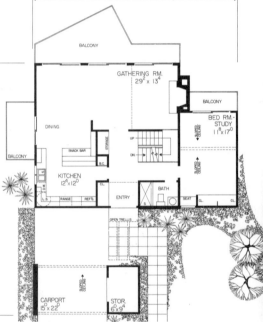

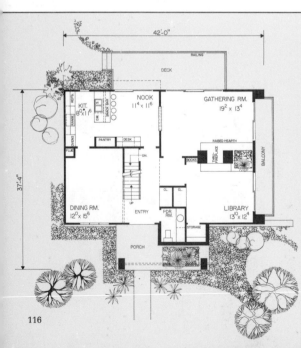

Design T72770
**1,182 Sq. Ft. - Main Level
998 Sq. Ft. - Upper Level
25,830 Cu. Ft.**

● If you are looking for a home with loads of livability, then consider these two-story contemporary homes which have an exposed lower level.

Design T72548 1,109 Sq. Ft. - Main Level; 739 Sq. Ft. - Upper Level
869 Sq. Ft. - Lower Level; 31,370 Cu. Ft.

DECK

39'-8"

48'-0"

BED RM.-
STUDY
12⁴x13⁰

GATHERING RM.
26⁰x15⁴

LINEN

BATH

UP DN.

PANTRY BROOMS

KITCHEN
9⁶x11⁶

ENTRY

DINING RM.
10⁰x11⁶

TERRACE

PORCH

CARPORT
20⁰x20⁰

STORAGE

BALCONY

BED RM.
12⁴x13⁰

OPEN TO GATHERING RM. BELOW

SLOPED CEILING

RAILING

CL.

LINEN CLERESTORY
ABOVE

BATH

DN.

RAILING

SLOPED CEILING

BALCONY

STORAGE CL.

OPEN TO
ENTRY BELOW

SLEEPING
LOFT
26⁰x13⁶

TERRACE

BED RM.
12⁰x13⁰

ACTIVITIES RM.
25⁴x15⁴

CL.

LINEN

BATH

UP

AIR
COND.

LT WASH. DRY.

LAUNDRY
19⁰x11²

Design T72895
2,700 Sq. Ft. - Main Level
1,503 Sq. Ft. - Lower Level; 54,645 Cu. Ft.

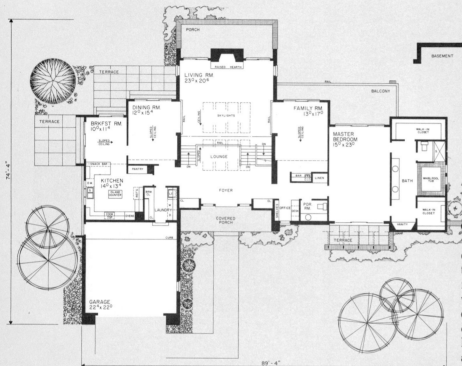

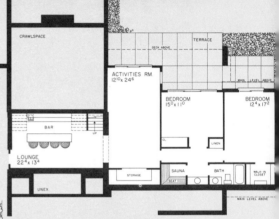

This contemporary design is ideal for those with a sloping site. A large kitchen with adjacent breakfast room offers easy access to the terraces as does the dining room. Other main floor areas include: a master bedroom suite with private terrace and access to the rear balcony, a family room, powder room and a sunken living room. Special features include a skylight in the living room, wet bar in family room and sloped ceilings. The lower level has two more bedrooms, activity room and lounge with built-in bar. Note the special bath facilities on both levels.

Design T72896
1,856 Sq. Ft. - Main Level; 1,454 Sq. Ft. - Lower Level; 43,390 Cu. Ft.

● This design is very inviting with its contemporary appeal. A large kitchen with an adjacent snack bar makes light meals a breeze. The adjoining breakfast room offers a scenic view through sliding glass doors. Notice the sloped ceiling in the dining and gathering rooms. A fireplace in the gathering room adds a cozy air. An interesting feature is the master bedroom's easy access to the study. Also, take note of the sliding doors in the master bedroom which lead to a private balcony. On the lower level, a large activities room will be a frequently used spot by family members. The fireplace and wet bar add a nice touch for entertaining friends. Also, notice the sliding glass doors which lead to the terrace. Take note of the two or optional three bedrooms - the choice is yours.

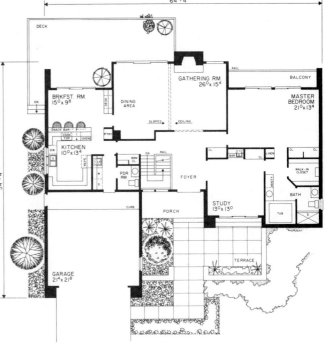

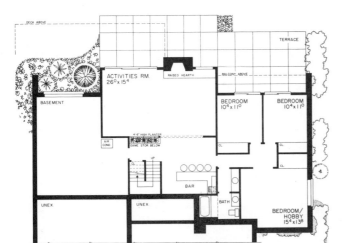

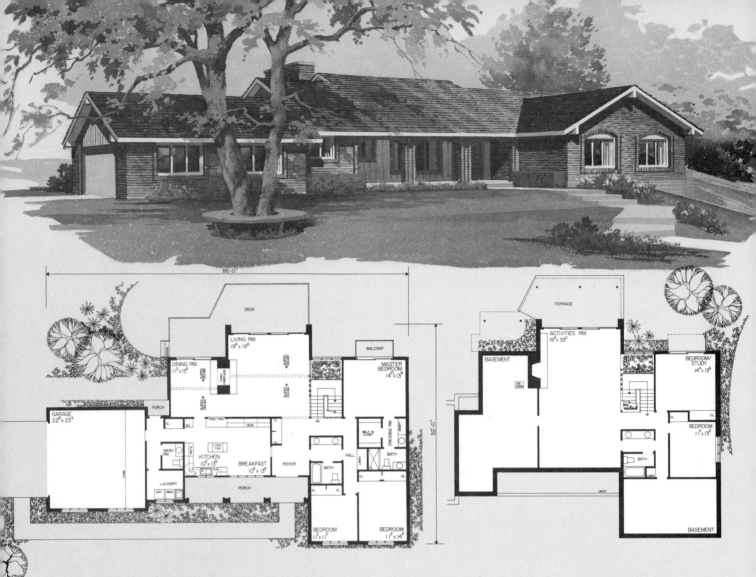

● This hillside home gives all the appearances of being a one-story ranch home; and what a delightful one at that! Should the contours of your property slope to the rear, this plan permits the exposing of the lower level. This results in the activities room and bedroom/study gaining direct access to outdoor living. Certainly a most desirable aspect for active, outdoor family living. The large and growing family will be admirably served with five bedrooms and three baths. An extra washroom and separate laundry add to the convenient living potential.

Design T72549
2,260 Sq. Ft. - Main Level
1,406 Sq. Ft. - Lower Level; 51,857 Cu. Ft.

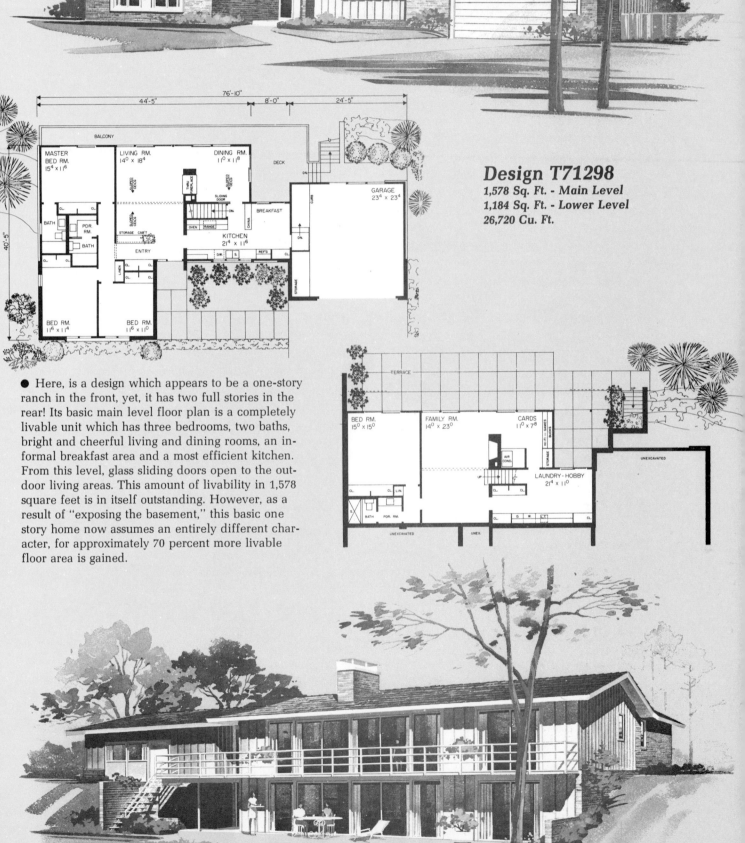

Design T71298
1,578 Sq. Ft. - Main Level
1,184 Sq. Ft. - Lower Level
26,720 Cu. Ft.

● Here, is a design which appears to be a one-story ranch in the front, yet, it has two full stories in the rear! Its basic main level floor plan is a completely livable unit which has three bedrooms, two baths, bright and cheerful living and dining rooms, an informal breakfast area and a most efficient kitchen. From this level, glass sliding doors open to the outdoor living areas. This amount of livability in 1,578 square feet is in itself outstanding. However, as a result of "exposing the basement," this basic one story home now assumes an entirely different character, for approximately 70 percent more livable floor area is gained.

● Four bedrooms! Or three plus a study, it's your choice. A fireplace in the study/bedroom guarantees a cozy atmosphere. The warmth of a fireplace also will be enjoyed in the gathering room and activities room. Lots of living space, too. An exceptionally large gathering room with sliding glass doors that open onto the main terrace to enjoy the scenic outdoors. A formal dining room, too. And a kitchen that promises to turn a novice cook into a pro. Check out the counter space, the pantry and the island range. This house is designed to make living pleasant.

Design T72583 1,838 Sq. Ft. - Main Level
1,558 Sq. Ft. - Lower Level; 29,400 Cu. Ft.

Design T71976
1,616 Sq. Ft. - Upper Level
1,472 Sq. Ft. - Lower Level
29,909 Cu. Ft.

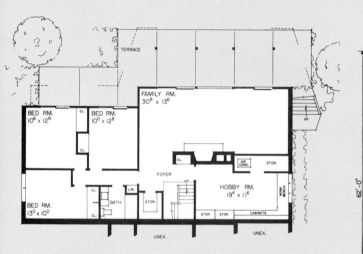

● Here's a hillside design just patterned for the large, active family. Whatever the pursuits and interests of the various members, you'd have to guess there would be more than enough space to service one and all with plenty of room to spare. If the children were teenagers, just imagine the fun they would have with their bedrooms, their family room and their hobby room on the lower level. The parents would be equally thrilled with their more formal facilities on the upper level.

Rear Living Enjoys Maximum View

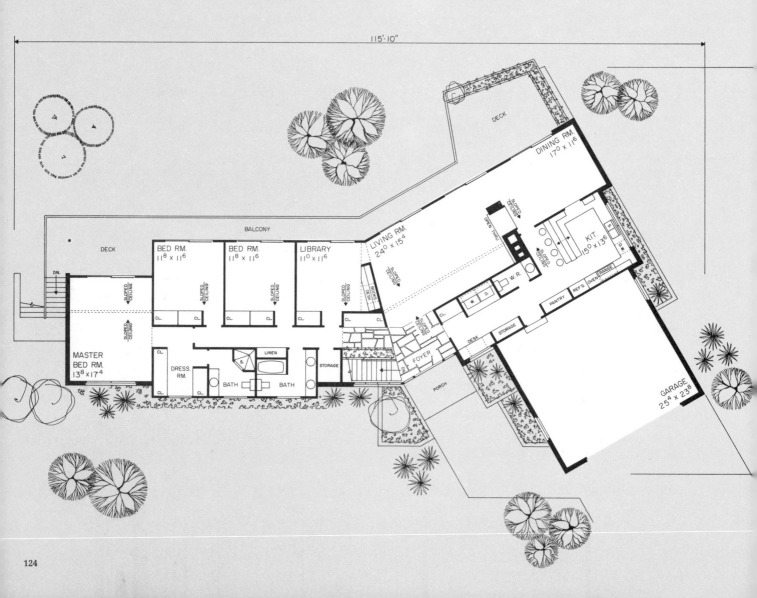

115'-10"

DECK

BALCONY

DECK

DN.

BED RM.
11⁸ x 11⁶

BED RM.
11⁸ x 11⁶

LIBRARY
11⁰ x 11⁶

LIVING RM.
24⁰ x 15⁴

DINING RM.
17⁰ x 11⁶

KIT.
15⁰ x 13⁶

SLOPED CEILING

SLOPED CEILING

SLOPED CEILING

SLOPED CEILING

CL.

CL.

CL.

CL.

CL.

CL.

CL.

CL.

MASTER
BED RM.
13⁸ x 17⁴

DRESS.
RM.

BATH

BATH

LINEN

STORAGE

W.R.

PANTRY

REF'G

OVEN

RANGE

DESK

STORAGE

FOYER

PORCH

GARAGE
25⁴ x 23⁸

124

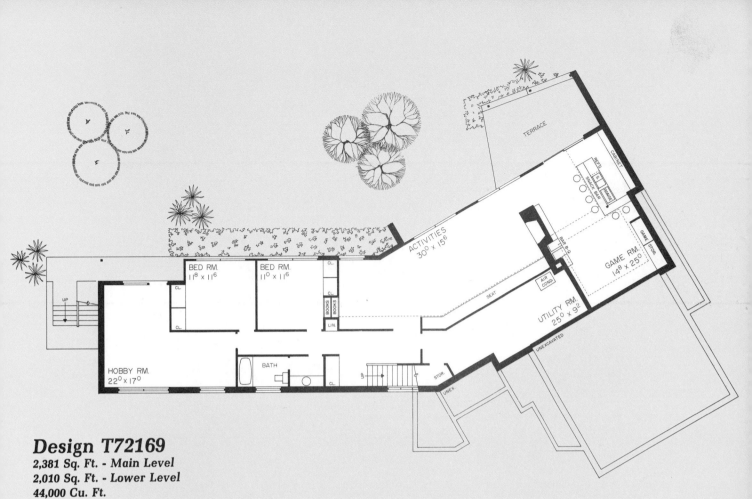

BED RM.
11⁸ x 11⁶

BED RM.
11⁰ x 11⁶

HOBBY RM.
22⁰ x 17⁰

BATH

UP

ACTIVITIES
30⁰ x 15⁶

GAME RM.
14⁸ x 25⁰

UTILITY RM.
25⁰ x 9²

TERRACE

SEAT

AIR COND.

UNEXCAVATED

STOR.

UNEX.

Design T72169

2,381 Sq. Ft. - Main Level
2,010 Sq. Ft. - Lower Level
44,000 Cu. Ft.

● Behold, the view! If, when looking toward the rear of your site, nature's scene is breathtaking or in any way inspiring, you may wish to maximize your enjoyment by orienting your living areas to the rear of your plan. In addition to greater enjoyment of the landscape, such floor planning will provide extra privacy from the street. The angular configuration can enhance the enjoyment of a particular scene, plus it adds appeal to the exterior of the design. A study of both levels reveals that the major living areas look out upon the rear yard. Further, the upper level rooms have direct access to the decks and balcony. The kitchen with its large window over the sink is not without its view. With five bedrooms, plus a library, a game, activities and hobby room, the active family will have an abundance of space to enjoy individualized pursuits. Can't you envision your family living in this house?

Design T72848 2,028 Sq. Ft. - Main Level; 1,122 Sq. Ft. - Lower Level; 45,695 Cu. Ft.

● This contemporary design is characterized by the contrast in diagonal and vertical wood siding. The private front court adjacent to the covered porch is a nice area for evening relaxation and creates an impressive entry. Once inside the house, the livability begins to unfold. Three bedrooms are arranged to one side of the entry with two baths sharing back-to-back plumbing. The master bedroom has a balcony. A view of the front court will be enjoyed from the kitchen and breakfast room. Along with the breakfast room, both the formal dining room and the screened porch will have easy access to the kitchen. A formal living room will be enjoyed on many occasions. It is detailed by a sloped ceiling and the warmth of a fireplace. A fourth bedroom is on the lower level. This level is opened to the outdoors by three sets of sliding glass doors. A second fireplace, this one with a raised hearth, is in the family room. A full bath and two work rooms also are located on the lower level.

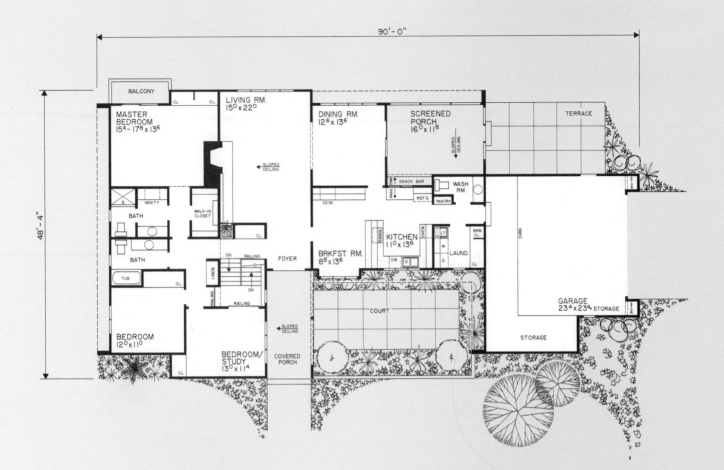

Contemporary Hillside Living

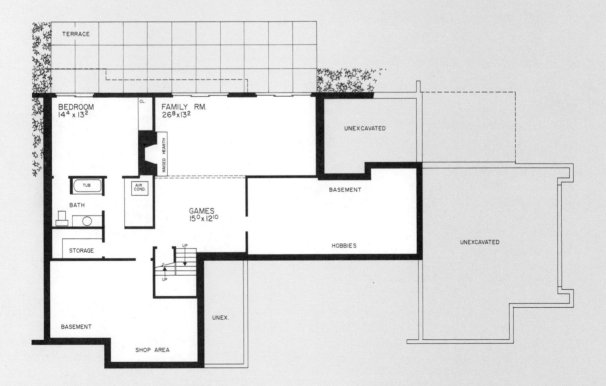

Elegance And Grandeur On Two Levels

● The above illustrations of the front and rear views of this hillside contemporary design are impressive. And indeed rightly so! For the varied design features are so numerous and they are so delightfully incorporated under the wide overhanging roofs that the result is almost breathtaking at first glance. Consider the basic L-shape of the house and garage. Note how it lends itself to a large drive court. Observe the simplicity of the masses of brick and vertical character of the glass areas. Notice the inviting recessed double front doors. Around to the rear, the architectural interest is indeed extremely exciting. The glass areas are as dramatic as is the wood deck. The covered porch and the two covered terraces complete the facilities for gracious outdoor living fun.

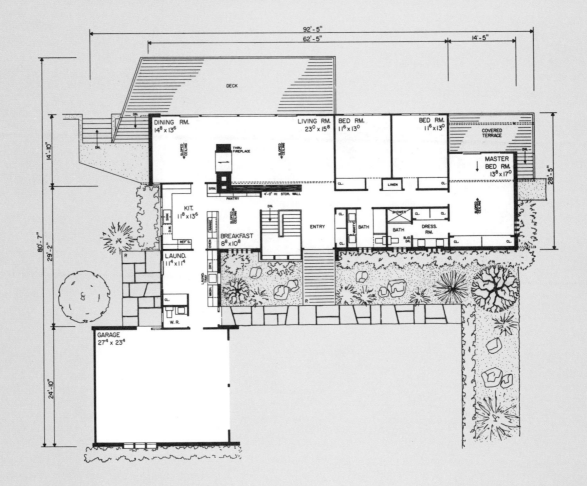

Design T71963 2,248 Sq. Ft. - Main Level; 1,948 Sq. Ft. - Lower Level; 42,422 Cu. Ft.

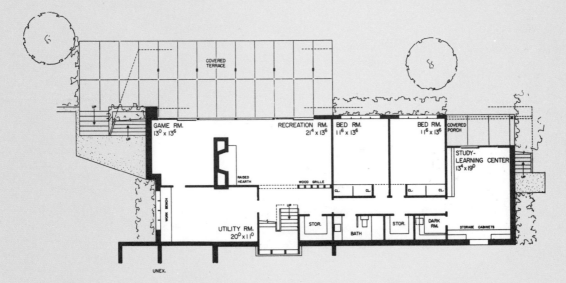

● Over four thousand square feet are available for use by the young, active family. And use them, they certainly will! There are five bedrooms to sleep a large active crew. The living areas are varied and numerous. In addition to the conventional formal living and dining rooms, there is a study/learning center. This is where all the mechanical paraphenalia like the tape recorder, film and slide projectors, phonograph, radio and television will be kept. A great way to keep all the equipment together. Note adjacent dark room. Then there is the recreation room with raised hearth fireplace. The game room will house the pool table, while the utility room will cater to the hobbyists. There are three full baths, plus an extra wash room and laundry adjacent to the kitchen.

Design T72719
2,363 Sq. Ft. - Main Level
1,523 Sq. Ft. - Lower Level; 47,915 Cu. Ft.

● If you have a flair for something different and useful at the same time, then expose the basement for hillside living. This design offers three large living areas: gathering room, family room and all-purpose activity room. Note the features in each of the three: balcony, sloping ceiling and thru-fireplace in the gathering room; deck and eating area in the family room; terrace and raised hearth fireplace in the activities room. The staircase to the lower level is delightfully open which adds to the spacious appeal of the entry hall. Cabinets and shelves are also a delightful feature of this area. Three bedrooms, the master bedroom suite on the main level with the other two on the lower level. An efficient U-shaped kitchen to easily serve the eating area of the family room and the formal dining room. The laundry is just a step away. The front projection of the two-car garage reduces the size of the lot required to build this exciting contemporary home.

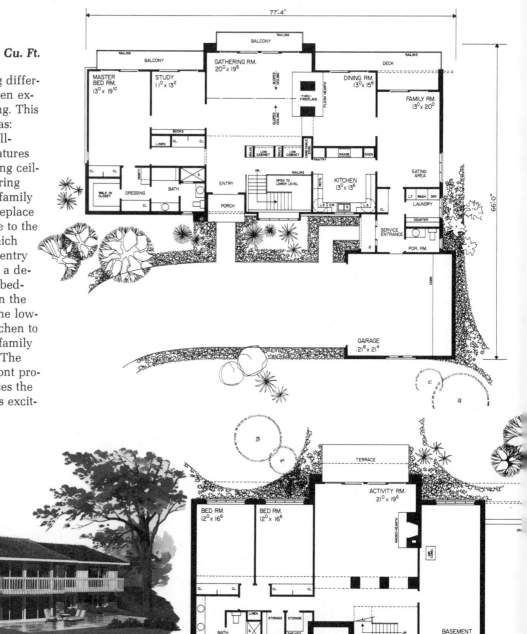

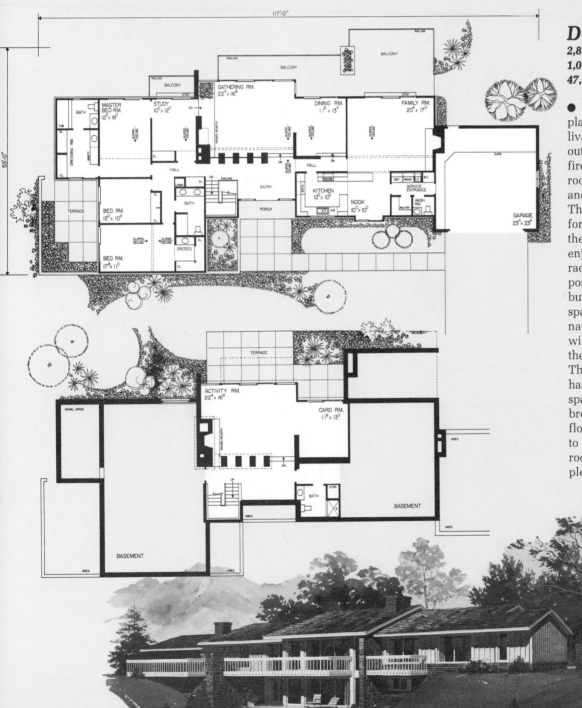

Design T72578
2,877 Sq. Ft. - Main Level
1,011 Sq. Ft. - Lower Level
47,525 Cu. Ft.

● How about three fireplaces in a delightfully livable floor plan! This outstanding home offers fireplaces in the gathering room, the family room and the activity room. That could make you look forward to winter. Also, the warm weather will be enjoyed on the rear terrace and balcony. The exposed lower level contributes an abundance of space which will enjoy natural light. Bulk items will be easily stored in the two basement areas. The country-size kitchen has an efficient work space and a separate breakfast nook. A first floor laundry is adjacent to the nook. Three bedrooms, including a complete master bedroom.

Design T72760

1,483 Sq. Ft. - Main Level
1,483 Sq. Ft. - Lower Level; 33,080 Cu. Ft.

● Here is contemporary design at its simple, yet dramatic, best. The modern adaptation of the mansard roof produces results that are interesting, indeed. The top of the roof itself is virtually flat and built-up with a gravel surface. The overhanging portion is made up of metal. While this is predominantly a frame house with vertical siding, there are brick masses which offer an attractive contrast. The rear view is unique with glass areas effectively shaded by overhanging roofs and balconies. Two of the terraces are covered, thus permitting inclement weather use. No rained-out cookouts here! A thru-fireplace separates the dining room from the sunken living room.

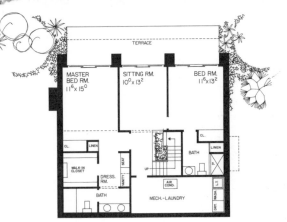

Floor Plan - Main Level

36'-0"

BALCONY

LIVING RM.
34⁸ x 13²

DINING AREA

STUDY-
BED RM.
14⁶ x 11¹⁰

NOOK
9⁰11¹⁴ x 8⁴

RAILING

DN.

UP

B.CL.

PANTRY

WALK IN
CLOSET

PDR. RM.

KITCHEN
14⁶ x 7⁸

REF'S.

D.W.

OVEN

STORAGE
12⁴ x 6⁸

CL.

ENTRY

PORCH

DN.

62'-0"

CURB

ENTRY
COURT

GARAGE
20⁸ x 20¹⁰

GATES

Floor Plan - Lower Level

TERRACE

MASTER
BED RM.
11⁶ x 15⁰

SITTING RM.
10⁰ x 13²

BED RM.
11⁶ x 13²

CL.

LINEN

CL.

LINEN

WALK IN
CLOSET

VANITY
SEAT

UP

BATH

S.

DRESS.
RM.

VANITY

AIR
COND.

W.

DRY

WASH

L.T.

BATH

MECH.-LAUNDRY

Design T72725 1,212 Sq. Ft. - Main Level
996 Sq. Ft. - Lower Level; 25,120 Cu. Ft.

● This contemporary mansard roof adaptation is ideal for a narrow hillside lot. The living/dining area is more than 34 foot wide. A great area to plan for individual needs. It has a raised hearth fireplace and three sets of sliding glass doors to the balcony. The staircase to the lower level is delightfully open with a dramatic view of the planting area below. Note the over-sized garage for extra storage.

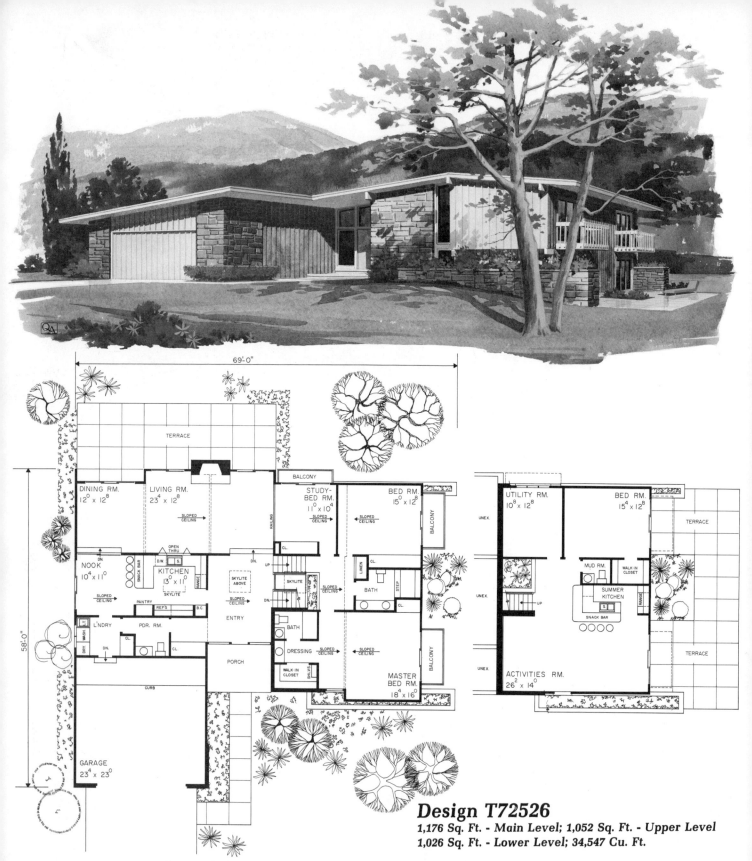

Design T72526

1,176 Sq. Ft. - Main Level; 1,052 Sq. Ft. - Upper Level
1,026 Sq. Ft. - Lower Level; 34,547 Cu. Ft.

● Here is an eye-catching multi-level which offers living patterns that will surely please the whole family. Flanking the front door, and above as well, are large glass panels which provide with the help of the skylite, plenty of natural light to the spacious entry. From this generous area traffic flows conveniently. To the left is the well-planned kitchen area. The breakfast nook, laundry, powder room and plenty of storage are nearby. Straight ahead is the sunken living room with the adjacent dining room. Having a sloping beamed ceiling and an abundance of glass, this will be another cheerful area. To the right, stairs lead to the upper level. Here two bedrooms, study and two baths are housed. Note the exceptional features including a planter, balcony and sunken tub. Also from the hall, there is access to the featured-packed lower level. How do you like that huge activities room?

TRI-LEVEL LIVING PATTERNS
. . . Multi-Level Homes for Contemporary Living
These designs feature homes with three levels of livability. Many employ sunken rooms, while others extend a full three stories. Such living patterns enjoy excellent zoning and traffic patterns.

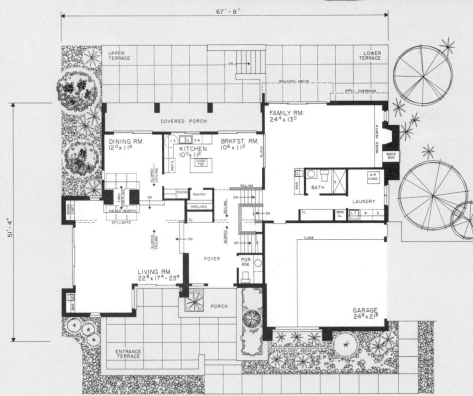

Design T72893
1,297 Sq. Ft. - Main Level;
1,256 Sq. Ft. - Upper Level
654 Sq. Ft. - Lower Level
49,198 Cu. Ft.

● Here is a contemporary split-level with a lot of appeal. To the right of the foyer and up a few steps you will find three bedrooms and a bath. Also, a master bedroom suite with an over-sized tub, shower, walk-in closet and sliding glass doors to a balcony. (One of the front bedrooms also has a balcony.) A sunken living room is on the main level. It has a wet bar and shares with the dining room a thru-fireplace, sloped ceiling and a skylight. A spacious kitchen and breakfast room are nearby. They offer easy access to the covered porch - ideal for summer meals. The lower level has a large family room with sliding glass doors to the lower terrace, another wet bar and a fireplace. The laundry, full bath, large closet and garage access are just steps away.

● This luxurious three-bedroom home offers comfort on many levels. Its modern design incorporates a rear garden room and conversation pit off a living room and dining room plus skylights in an adjacent family room with high sloped ceiling. Other features include an entrance court, activities room, modern kitchen, upper lounge, and master bedroom.

Design T72901
1,449 Sq. Ft. - Main Level
665 Sq. Ft. - Upper Level
448 Sq. Ft. - Master Bedroom Level
419 Sq. Ft. - Activities Room Level
45,720 Cu. Ft.

Design T72736
1,848 Sq. Ft. - Lower Level
212 Sq. Ft. - Main Level
1,263 Sq. Ft. - Upper Level
43,092 Cu. Ft.

● This Contemporary four-bedroom home is a charmer with wide overhangs, side balconies, and textured brick and wood exterior. Three bedrooms and a lounge are isolated on the upper level. An entrance landing leads down to a lower-level master bedroom, gathering room with thru fireplace, rear family room, modern L-shaped kitchen, and a combination dining/garden room off a rear terrace. Note the three-car garage with storage and covered porch.

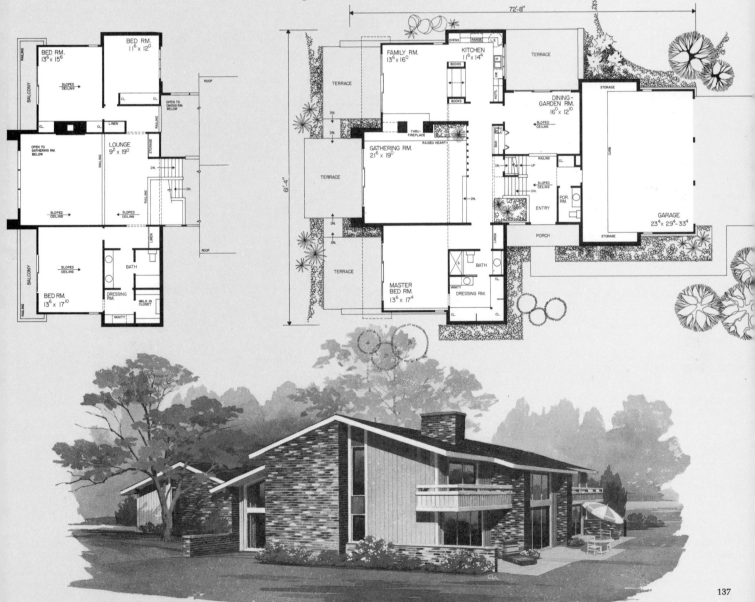

Design T72173

2,290 Sq. Ft. - Main Level; 1,621 Sq. Ft. - Upper Level
1,638 Sq. Ft. - Lower Level; 58,470 Cu. Ft.

68'-0"

● The rustic nature of this split-level design is captured by the rough-textured stone, natural-toned wood siding and wide, overhanging roof with exposed beams. Indoor-outdoor living relationships are outstanding. The foyer will be dramatic, indeed.

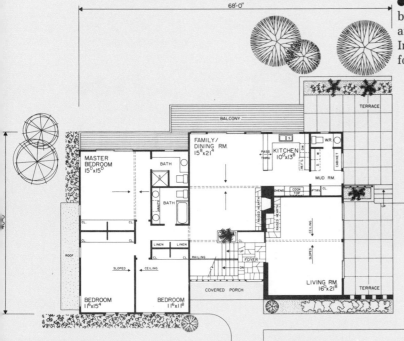

Design T72248
1,501 Sq. Ft. - Upper Level; 511 Sq. Ft. - Living Room Level
1,095 Sq. Ft. - Lower Level; 30,486 Cu. Ft.

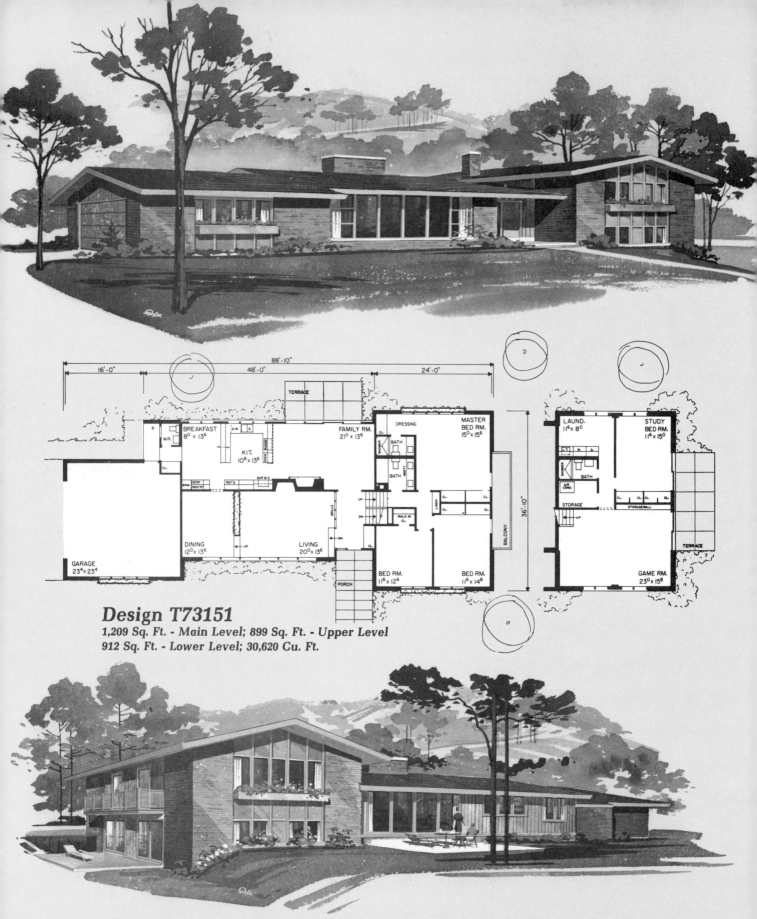

Design T73151
1,209 Sq. Ft. - Main Level; 899 Sq. Ft. - Upper Level
912 Sq. Ft. - Lower Level; 30,620 Cu. Ft.

● Split-level living can be great fun. And it certainly will be for the occupants of this impressive house. First and foremost, you and your family will appreciate the practical zoning. The upper level is the quiet sleeping level. List the features. They are many. The main level is zoned for both formal and informal living. Don't miss the sunken living room or the twin fireplaces. The lower level provides that extra measure of livability for all to enjoy.

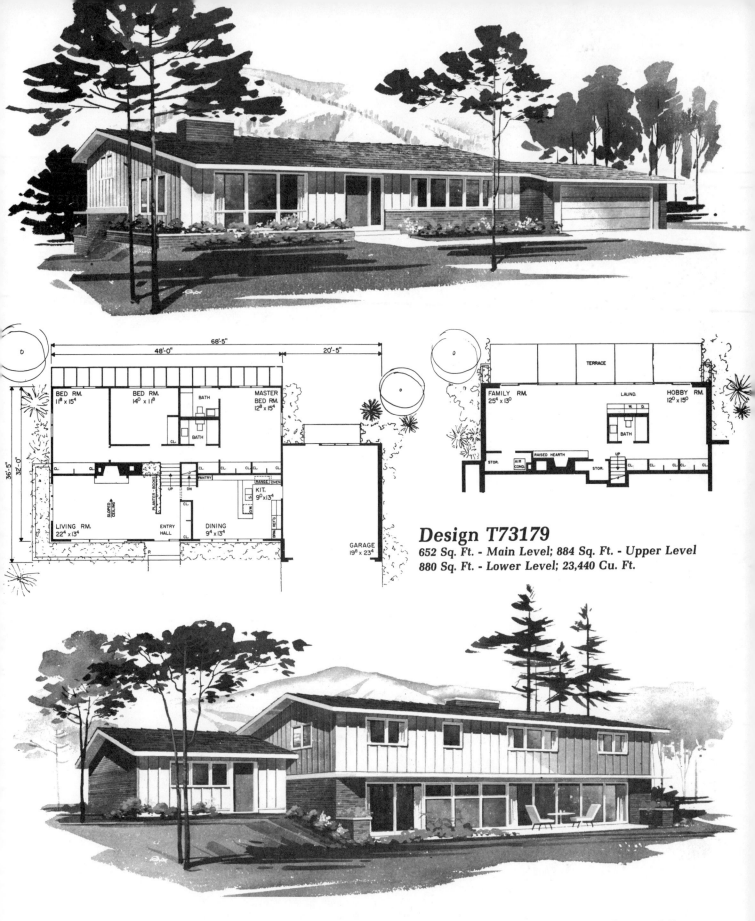

Design T73179
652 Sq. Ft. - Main Level; 884 Sq. Ft. - Upper Level
880 Sq. Ft. - Lower Level; 23,440 Cu. Ft.

● This tri-level home has four distinct areas, each performing its function to perfection. The sleeping area has two full baths, three big bedrooms and plenty of closets. The living area of the main level is spacious, has good light and is free of cross-room traffic. The dining-kitchen is efficient and lends itself to formal and informal dining. The lower level is bright, cheerful, has plenty of space and functions with the outdoors. Note extra full bath.

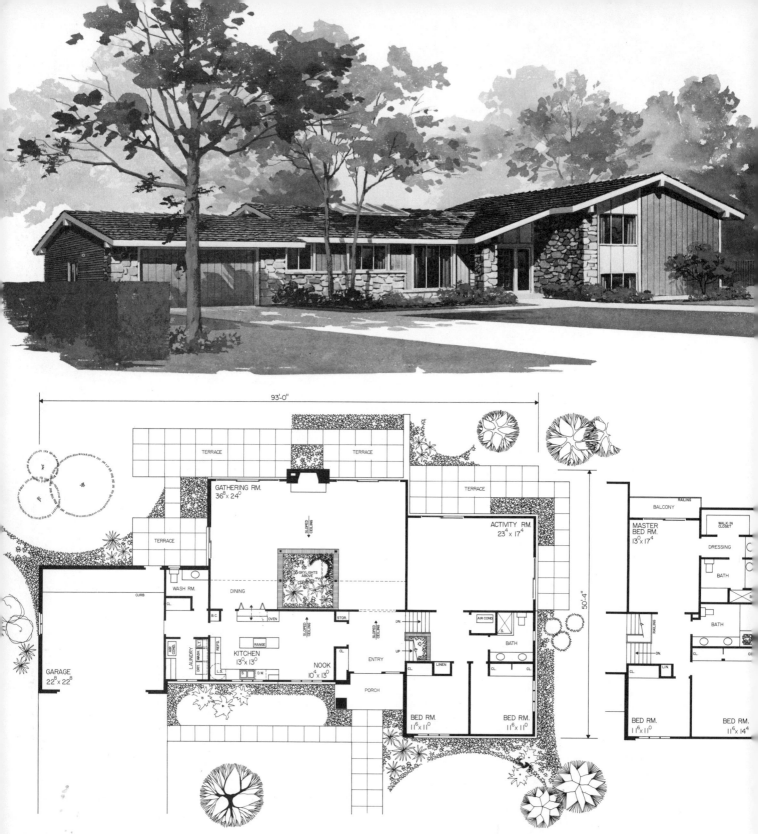

Design T72584 *1,604 Sq. Ft. - Main Level; 1,018 Sq. Ft. - Upper Level; 1,026 Sq. Ft. - Lower Level; 39,200 Cu. Ft.*

● Imagine an indoor garden with a skylight above in the huge gathering room plus a planter beside the lower level stairs. The gathering room also has a sloped ceiling, fireplace and two sets of sliding glass doors leading to the rear terrace and one set to the side terrace. That sure is luxury. But the appeal does not stop there. There are sloped ceilings in the foyer and breakfast nook. The kitchen has an island range, built-in oven and pass-thru to the dining room. Plus a large activities room. A great place for those informal activities. Five bedrooms in all to serve the large family. Including a master suite with a private balcony, dressing room, walk-in closet and bath.

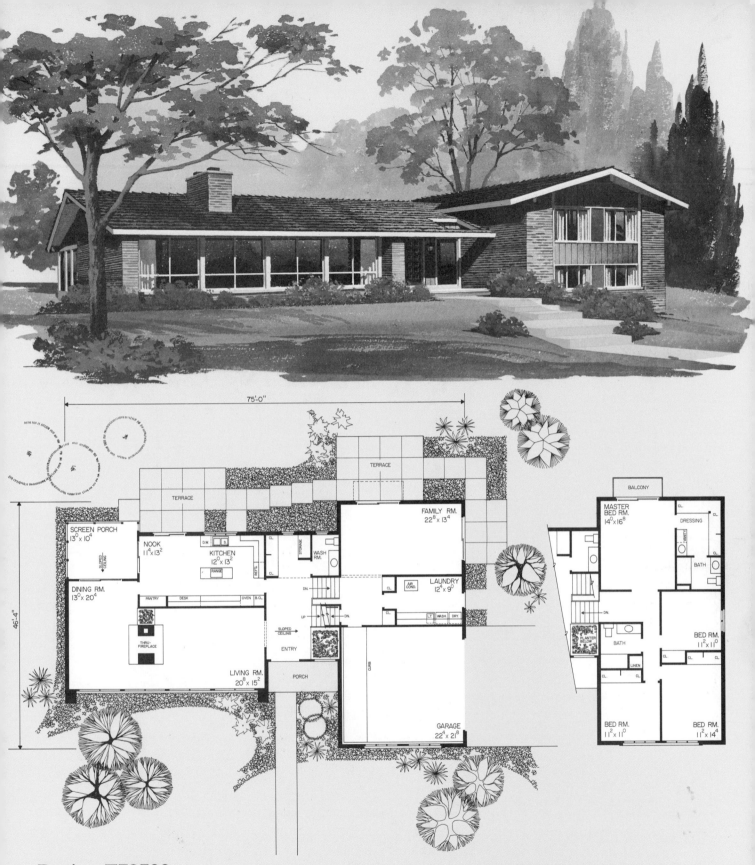

Design T72588 *1,354 Sq. Ft. - Main Level; 1,112 Sq. Ft. - Upper Level; 562 Sq. Ft. - Lower Level; 46,925 Cu. Ft.*

● A thru-fireplace with an accompanying planter for the formal dining room and living room. That's old-fashioned good cheer in a contemporary home. The dining room has an adjacent screened-in porch for outdoor dining in the summertime. There are companions for these two formal areas, an informal breakfast nook and a family room. Each having sliding glass doors to separate rear terraces. Built-in desk, pantry, ample work space and is-land range are features of the L-shaped kitchen. The large laundry on the lower level houses the heating and cooling equipment. Three family bedrooms, bath and master bedroom suite are on the upper level.

143

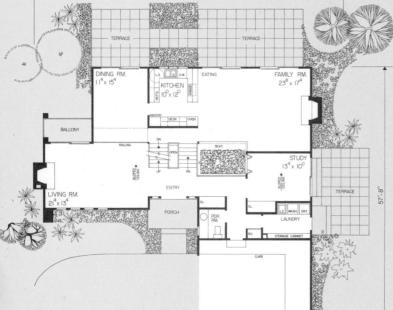

Design T72551

819 Sq. Ft. - Main Level; 818 Sq. Ft. - Upper Level
818 Sq. Ft. - Lower Level; 31,800 Cu. Ft.

● This multi-level design is perfect for a family that enjoys lots of livability. Sloped ceilings highlight a spacious living room and study. A few steps down is an efficient kitchen with an adjacent dining room. The large family room will be a great asset. The upper level has two bedrooms and a master bedroom. The master bedroom has doors that open for a view of the living room below. A unique feature is the skylight above the planting area of the lower level.

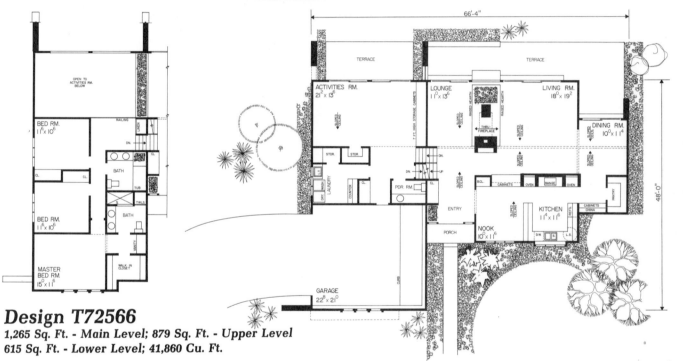

Design T72566

**1,265 Sq. Ft. - Main Level; 879 Sq. Ft. - Upper Level
615 Sq. Ft. - Lower Level; 41,860 Cu. Ft.**

● Spacious, this tri-level offers a lot of room and comfort. An efficient kitchen and an eating area is adjacent to the entry. A dining room is only a few steps away. The living room and lounge are divided by a fireplace. It is open, has raised hearth and an end planter. It will be the focal point of both rooms. Three bedrooms are on the upper level. The upper level hall is open for a view of the activities room below.

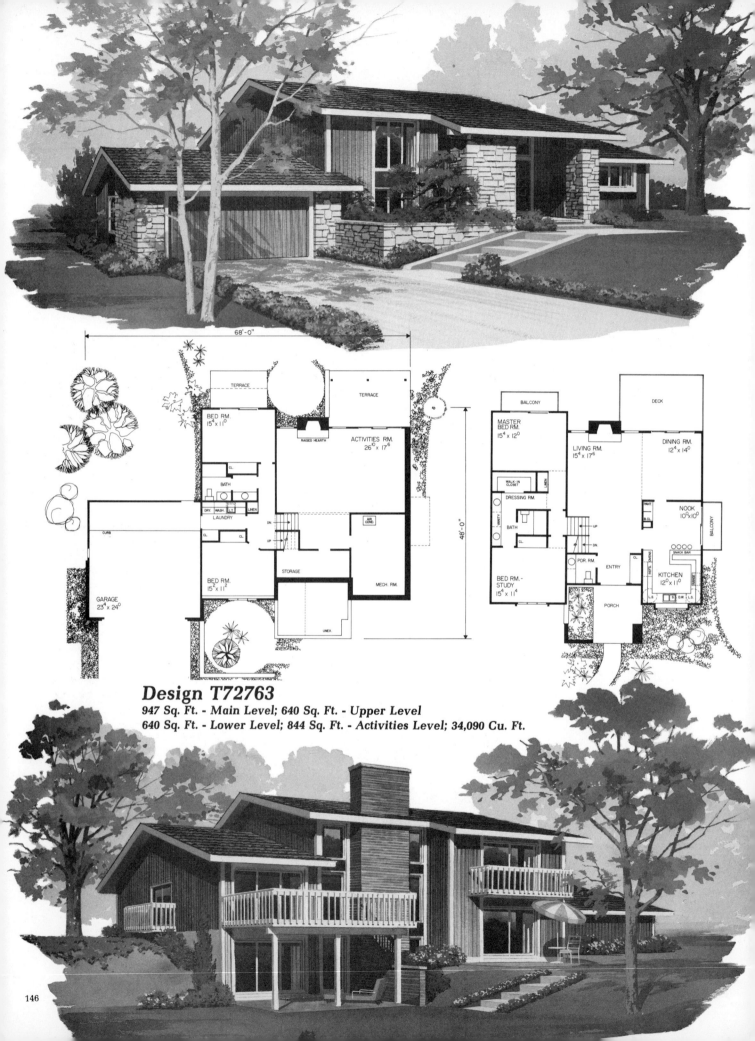

68'-0"

48'-0"

TERRACE

BED RM.
15⁴ x 11⁰

TERRACE

ACTIVITIES RM.
26¹⁰ x 17⁶

RAISED HEARTH

CL

BATH

DRY WASH L.T. LINEN
LAUNDRY

DN.

AIR COND.

CURB

UP

CL CL

BED RM.
15² x 11²

STORAGE

MECH. RM.

GARAGE
23⁴ x 24⁰

UNEX.

BALCONY

DECK

MASTER BED RM.
15⁴ x 12⁰

LIVING RM.
15⁴ x 17⁶

DINING RM.
12⁴ x 14⁰

WALK-IN CLOSET

LINEN

DRESSING RM.

VANITY

BATH

CL

UP

PANT.
BL.CL

NOOK
10⁰ x 10⁰

BALCONY

DN.

SNACK BAR

PDR. RM.

ENTRY

CL

REFR. OVENS

KITCHEN
12⁰ x 11⁰

BED RM.-
STUDY
15⁴ x 11⁴

PORCH

LS D.W. LS

Design T72763

947 Sq. Ft. - Main Level; 640 Sq. Ft. - Upper Level
640 Sq. Ft. - Lower Level; 844 Sq. Ft. - Activities Level; 34,090 Cu. Ft.

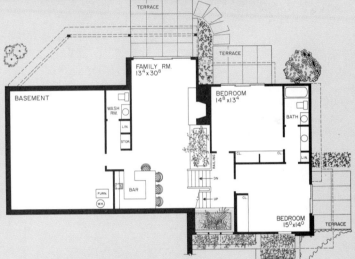

Design T72679 1,179 Sq. Ft. - Main Level
681 Sq. Ft. - Upper Level; 643 Sq. Ft. - Family Room Level
680 Sq. Ft. - Lower Level; 43,733 Cu. Ft.

● This spacious modern Contemporary home offers plenty of livability on many levels. Main level includes a breakfast room in addition to a dining room. Adjacent is a sloped-ceiling living room with raised hearth. The upper level features isolated master bedroom suite with adjoining study or sitting room and balcony. Family room level includes a long rectangular family room with adjoining terrace on one end and adjoining bar with washroom at the other end. A spacious basement is included. Two other bedrooms are positioned in the lower level with their own view of the terrace and quiet privacy. Note the rear deck.

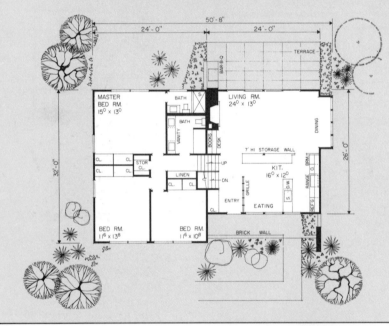

Design T71093
654 Sq. Ft. - Main Level; 768 Sq. Ft. - Upper Level
492 Sq. Ft. - Lower Level; 18,762 Cu. Ft.

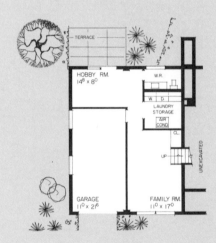

Design T72375
993 Sq. Ft. - Main Level; 1,064 Sq. Ft. - Upper Level
335 Sq. Ft. - Lower Level; 33,970 Cu. Ft.

● For those who like tri-level living, these three contemporary designs have much to offer. Their exteriors are most-distinctive. There are low-pitched, wide-overhanging roofs, effective use of contrasting exterior materials, raised planters and recessed front entrances. The interiors also are quite dramatic with sloped ceilings in Design 42375, right, and Design 42845, below, to enhance the spaciousness. Each of the designs has a fireplace and economically grouped plumbing facilities.

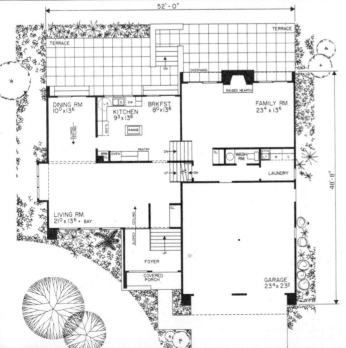

Design T72845
804 Sq. Ft. - Main Level; 1,089 Sq. Ft. - Upper Level
619 Sq. Ft. - Foyer and Lower Level; 36,030 Cu. Ft.

● This multi-level design will be ideal on a sloping site, both in the front and the rear of the house. The contemporary exterior is made up of vertical wood siding. The sloping roofline adds to the exterior appeal and creates a sloped ceiling in the formal living and dining rooms. An attractive bay window highlights the living room as will sliding glass doors in the dining room. The U-shaped kitchen and breakfast room also are located on this main level.

149

Design T72734 1,626 Sq. Ft. - Main Level; 1,033 Sq. Ft. - Upper Level; 1,273 Sq. Ft. - Lower Level; 47,095 Cu. Ft.

● If you have a desire for something delightfully different that offers unique, yet practical and enjoyable living patterns, then this house deserves careful study by all the members of your family. Having three bedrooms and a study on the upper level and a guest (or hobby) room on the lower level; it offers sleeping flexibility for the growing family. Notice how the living area looks down on the delightful planting area of the lower level. Also it shares a thru-fireplace with the study. Other features of the study include a 7 foot high book shelve, private balcony and separate stairs to the master bedroom. The outstanding U-shaped kitchen is flanked by the family and dining room. In addition to the living room, there is the huge, 32 foot activity room on the lower level. An abundance of storage space will be found in the three-car garage and the basement.

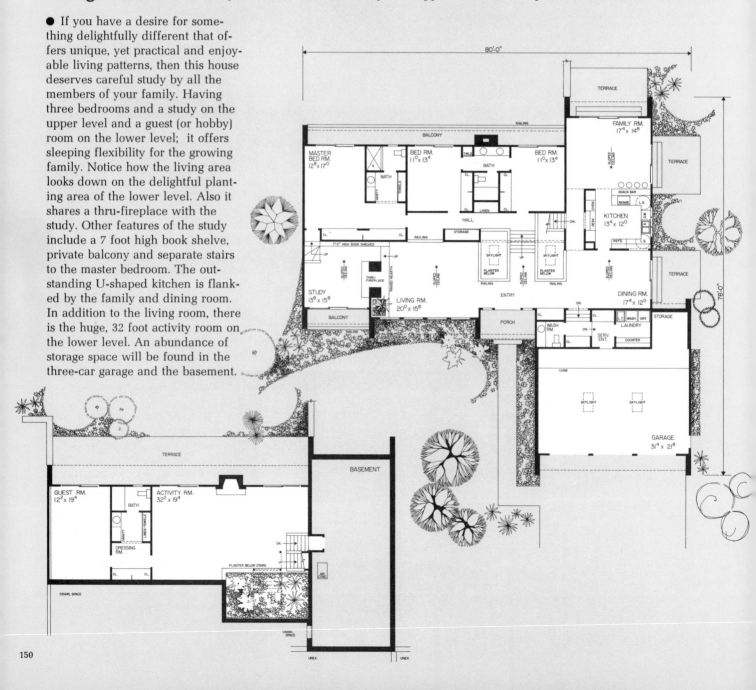

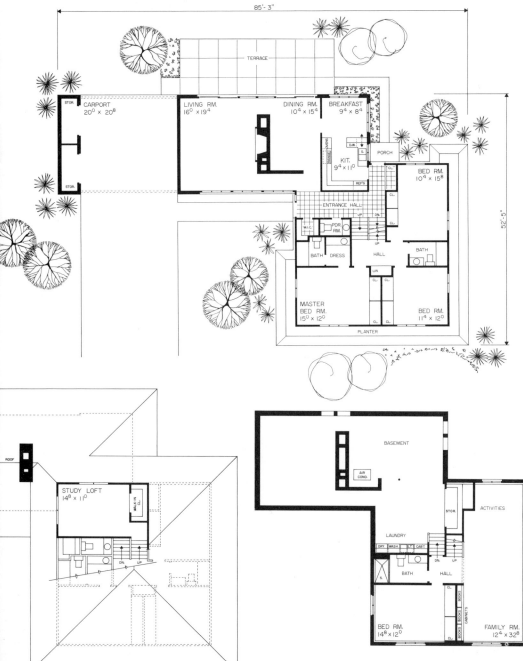

Design T72296

993 Sq. Ft. - Main Level
810 Sq. Ft. - Upper Level
842 Sq. Ft. - Lower Level
255 Sq. Ft. - Study Level
38,788 Cu. Ft.

● Here is real multi-level living with each level making a fine contribution to convenient living for the whole family. Including the basement, there are five distinct levels. The L-shaped plan gives birth to the distinctive contemporary exterior. The hip-roof has a wide, pleasing overhang. Just below is the unique, overhanging planter. If desired, this refreshing design could function wonderfully as a five bedroom home. The formal dining room and the breakfast room provide excellent eating facilities. The 32 foot lower level family room provides all the space necessary for multi-purpose activities. The basement offers an extra area for hobbies. Don't miss the laundry, three full baths and the powder room.

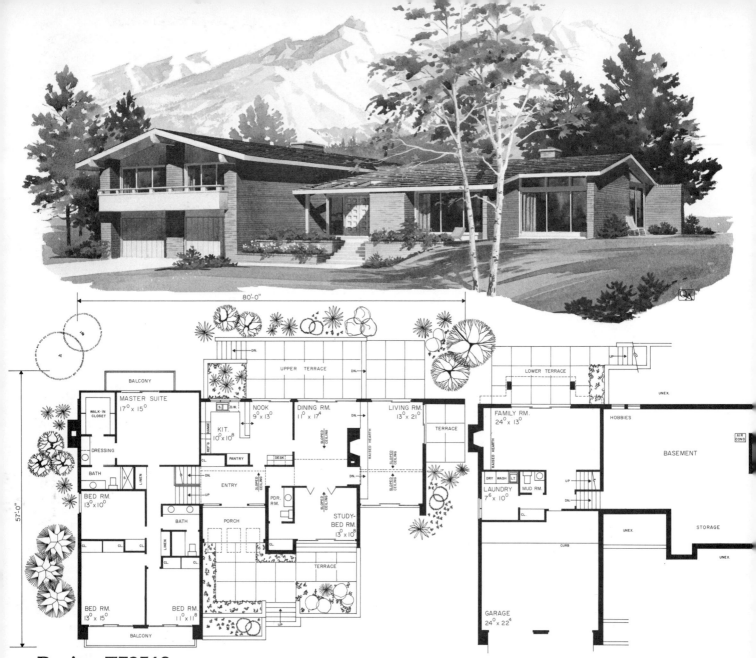

Design T72516 1,183 Sq. Ft. - Main Level; 1,248 Sq. Ft. - Upper Level; 607 Sq. Ft. - Lower Level; 41,775 Cu. Ft.

Floor plan labels (upper design):

80'-0"
57'-0"

BALCONY
MASTER SUITE 17⁰ x 15⁰
WALK-IN CLOSET
DRESSING
BATH
BED RM. 13⁰ x 10⁰
CL
BED RM. 13⁰ x 15⁰
CL CL
BED RM. 11⁰ x 11⁸
BALCONY
BATH
LINEN
DN
UP
ENTRY
PANTRY
DESK
KIT. 10⁰ x 10⁸
RANGE REF'G
NOOK 9⁰ x 13⁰
DW
UPPER TERRACE
DINING RM. 11⁰ x 17⁴
LIVING RM. 13⁰ x 21⁰
RAISED HEARTH
SLOPED CEILING
TERRACE
PDR. RM.
STUDY-BED RM. 13⁰ x 10⁰
PORCH
LINEN
TERRACE
UP
DN
LOWER TERRACE
UNEX.
FAMILY RM. 24⁰ x 13⁰
HOBBIES
BASEMENT
AIR COND.
RAISED HEARTH
LAUNDRY 7⁶ x 10⁰
DRY WASH LT
MUD RM.
CL
UP
DN
UNEX.
STORAGE
UNEX.
CURB
GARAGE 24⁰ x 22⁴

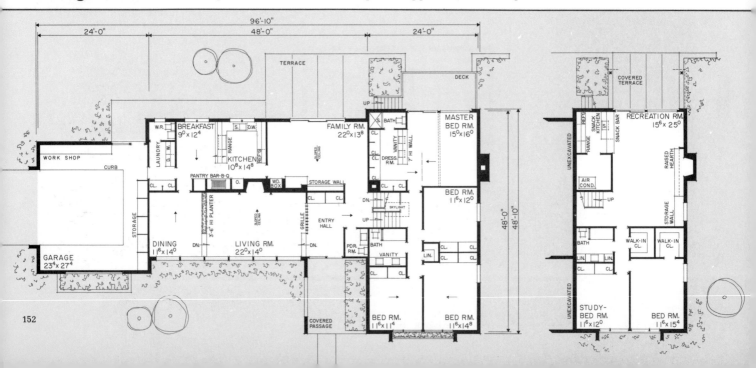

Floor plan labels (lower design):

96'-10"
24'-0" 48'-0" 24'-0"
48'-10"
48'-0"

TERRACE
DECK
UP
WORK SHOP
CURB
GARAGE 23⁴ x 27⁴
STORAGE
W.R.
BREAKFAST 9⁰ x 12⁴
LAUNDRY
W. D.
CL
RANGE REF'G
S. D.W.
KITCHEN 10⁸ x 14⁸
PANTRY BAR-B-Q
O.
WD. BOX
3'-6" HI PLANTER
SLOPED CEILING
DINING 11⁶ x 14⁰
LIVING RM. 22⁰ x 14⁰
DN
STORAGE WALL
GRILLE
ENTRY HALL
UP
DN
PDR. RM.
BATH
VANITY
FAMILY RM. 22⁰ x 13⁸
SLOPED CEILING
BATH
VANITY
DRESS. RM.
7' HI WALL
MASTER BED RM. 15⁰ x 16⁰
BED RM. 11⁶ x 12⁰
DN
SKYLIGHT
UP
LIN.
CL CL
BED RM. 11⁶ x 11⁴
BED RM. 11⁶ x 14⁸
COVERED PASSAGE
COVERED TERRACE
UNEXCAVATED
REF'G RANGE
SNACK KITCHEN
SNACK BAR
RECREATION RM. 15⁶ x 25⁰
AIR COND.
RAISED HEARTH
UP
STORAGE WALL
BATH
LIN. LIN.
WALK-IN CL.
WALK-IN CL.
STUDY-BED RM. 11⁶ x 12⁰
BED RM. 11⁶ x 15⁴
UNEXCAVATED

Design T72712
1,624 Sq. Ft. - Main Level; 1,100 Sq. Ft. - Upper Level
1,193 Sq. Ft. - Lower Level; 49,370 Cu. Ft.

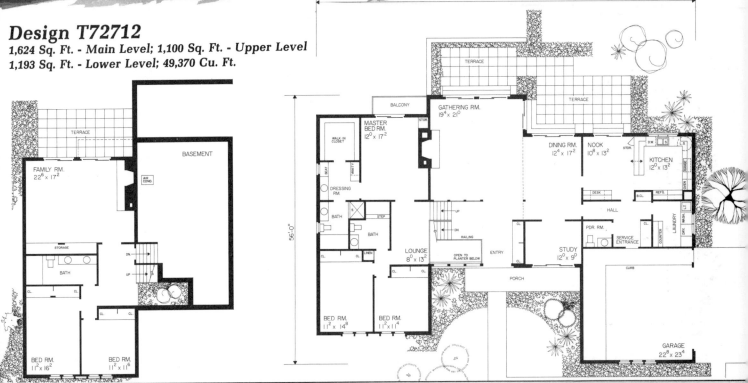

Design T71789 1,486 Sq. Ft. - Main Level; 1,200 Sq. Ft. - Upper Level; 1,200 Sq. Ft. - Lower Level; 39,516 Cu. Ft.

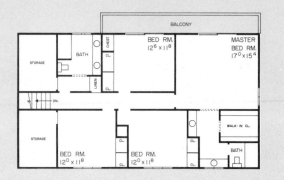

Design T72300

1,579 Sq. Ft. - Main Level
1,176 Sq. Ft. - Upper Level
321 Sq. Ft. - Lower Level
34,820 Cu. Ft.

● A T-shaped contemporary with just loads of livability. You may enter this house on the lower level through the garage, or by ascending the steps to the delightful terrace which leads to the main level front entry. Zoning of the interior is wonderful. Projecting to the front and functioning with the formal dining room is the living room. Projecting to the rear and functioning with the kitchen is the family room. Each of these two living areas features a fireplace, beamed ceiling and sliding glass doors to the outside. Also notice the nook, the laundry and the closet space. On the upper level there are four large bedrooms, two full baths, two storage rooms and an outdoor balcony. The lower level offers that fifth bedroom with a full bath nearby. Don't miss the storage facilities of the garage. Truly fine livability.

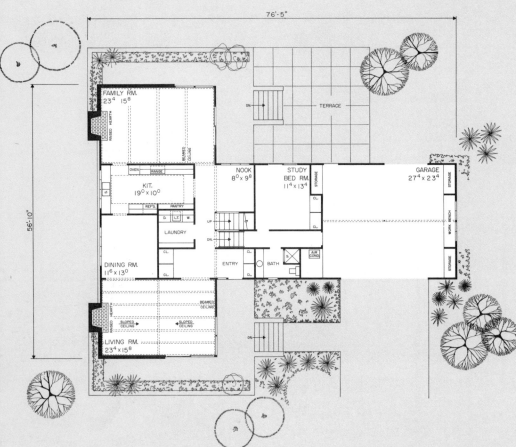

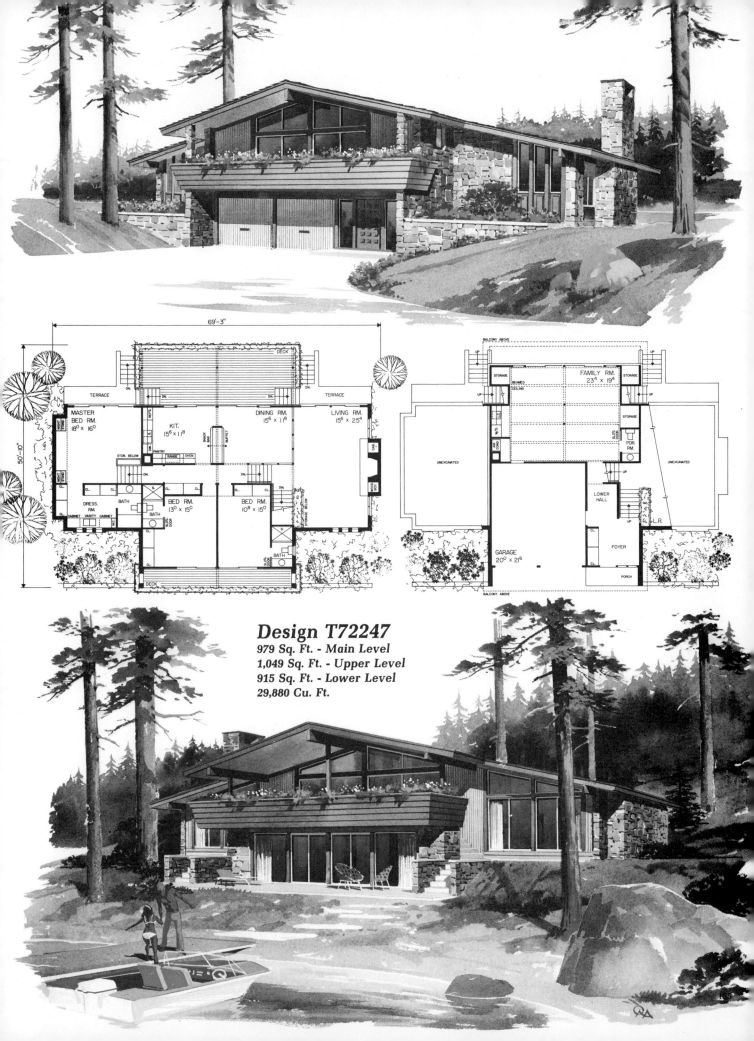

Design T72247

979 Sq. Ft. - Main Level
1,049 Sq. Ft. - Upper Level
915 Sq. Ft. - Lower Level
29,880 Cu. Ft.

69'-3"

50'-10"

TERRACE
TERRACE

DECK

MASTER
BED RM.
18⁰ x 16⁰

KIT.
15⁶ x 11⁸

DINING RM.
15⁶ x 11⁸

LIVING RM.
15⁶ x 25⁴

SNACK BAR

BUFFET

PANTRY

RANGE OVEN

STOR. BELOW

DRESS.
RM.

BATH

BATH

CL.

CL.

BED RM.
13⁰ x 15⁰

BED RM.
10⁸ x 15⁰

CL.

STORAGE BELOW

CABINET VANITY CABINET

BATH

DECK

BALCONY ABOVE

FAMILY RM.
23⁴ x 19⁴

STORAGE

BEAMED
CEILING

STORAGE

STORAGE

UNEXCAVATED

UNEXCAVATED

PDR.
RM.

LOWER
HALL

L.R.

GARAGE
20⁰ x 21⁶

FOYER

CL.

PORCH

BALCONY ABOVE

Design T72536 *1,077 Sq. Ft. - Main Level; 1,319 Sq. Ft. - Upper Level; 914 Sq. Ft. - Lower Level; 31,266 Cu. Ft.*

● Here are three levels of outstanding livability all packed in a delightfully contemporary exterior. The low pitched roof has a wide overhang with exposed rafter tails. The stone masses contrast effectively with the vertical siding and the glass areas. The extension of the sloping roof provides the recessed feature of the front entrance with the patterned double doors. The homemaker's favorite highlight will be the layout of the kitchen. No crossroom traffic here. Only a few steps from the formal and informal eating areas, it is the epitome of efficiency. A sloping beamed ceiling, sliding glass doors and a raised hearth fireplace enhance the appeal of the living room. The upper level offers the option of a fourth bedroom or a sitting room functioning with the master bedroom. Note the three balconies. On the lower level, the big family room, quiet study, laundry and extra washroom are present.

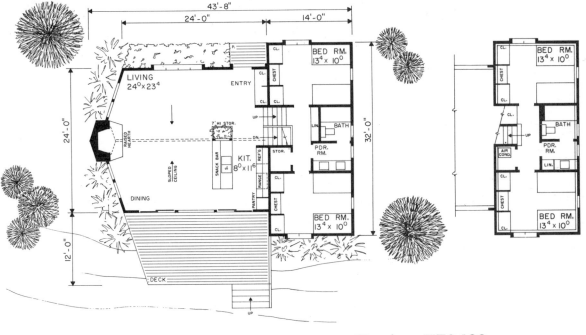

Design T72463
624 Sq. Ft. - Main Level; 448 Sq. Ft. - Upper Level
448 Sq. Ft. - Lower Level; 16,232 Cu. Ft.

● Here's a leisure home with multiple levels of livability and room for many sleepers. There are four bedrooms in all in this compact house. The main level of this plan houses the living areas. Open planning on this level has resulted in a spacious living, dining, and kitchen area. A raised-hearth fireplace is strategically located. Each of the two sleeping levels features two bedrooms, a compartmented bath, and excellent storage facilities. Use of double bunks will enable you to entertain a crowd on those glorious holiday weekends. Also note the built-in chests.

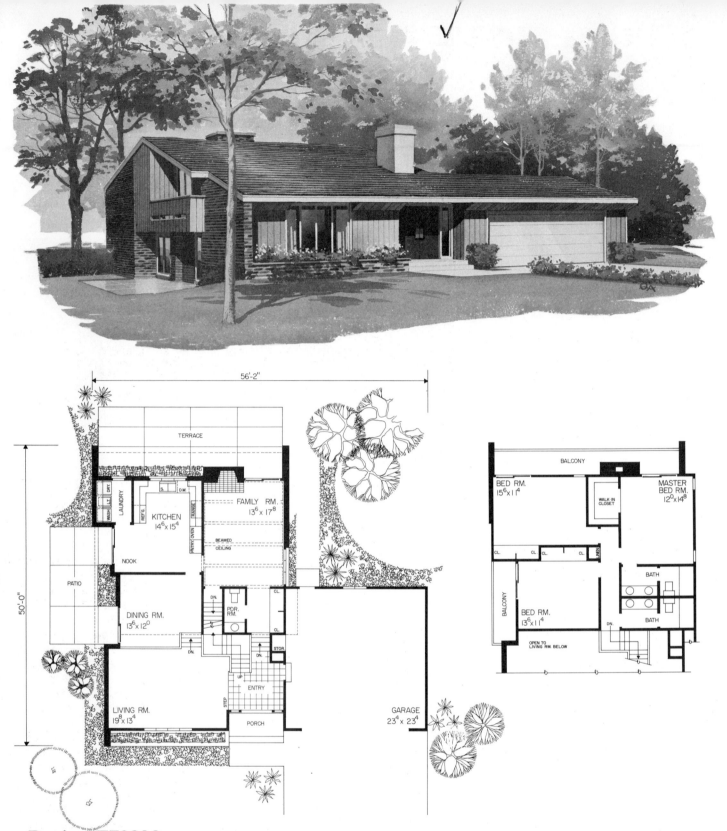

Design T72393 *392 Sq. Ft. - Entry Level; 841 Sq. Ft. - Upper Level; 848 Sq. Ft. - Lower Level; 24,980 Cu. Ft.*

● For those with a flair for something refreshingly contemporary both inside and out. This modest sized multi-level has a unique exterior and an equally interesting interior. The low-pitched, wide-overhanging roof protects the inviting double front doors and the large picture window. The raised planter and the side balcony add an extra measure of appeal. Inside, the living patterns will be delightful! The formal living room will look down into the dining room. Like the front entry, the living room has direct access to the lower level. The kitchen is efficient and spacious enough to accommodate an informal breakfast eating area. The laundry room is nearby. The all-purpose family room has beamed ceiling, fireplace and sliding glass doors to rear terrace. The angular, open stairwell to the upper level is dramatic, indeed. Notice how each bedroom has direct access to an outdoor balcony.

BI-LEVEL HOME DESIGNS

...Houses with Split Foyers
The bi-level home, sometimes called a raised ranch, usually involves a foyer near stairs. The short flight of stairs leads to another level. Hence the house "splits" at the foyer.

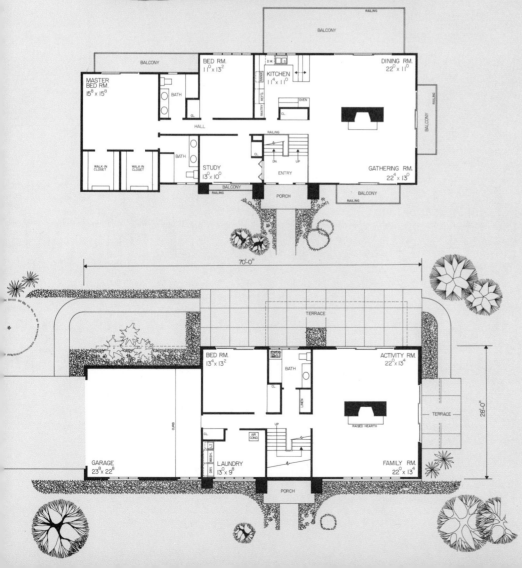

Design T72580
1,852 Sq. Ft. - Upper Level
1,297 Sq. Ft. - Lower Level
32,805 Cu. Ft.

● Indoor-outdoor living hardly could ask for more! And here's why. Imagine, five balconies and three terraces! These unique balconies add great beauty to the exterior while adding pleasure to those who utilize them from the interior. And there's more. This home has enough space for all to appreciate. Take note of the size of the gathering room, family room and activity room. There's also a large dining room. Four bedrooms too, for the large or growing family. Or three plus a study. Two fireplaces, one to service each of the two levels in this bi-level design. The rear terrace is accessible thru sliding glass doors from the lower level bedroom and activity room. The side terrace functions with the activity/family room area. The master suite has two walk-in closets and a private bath.

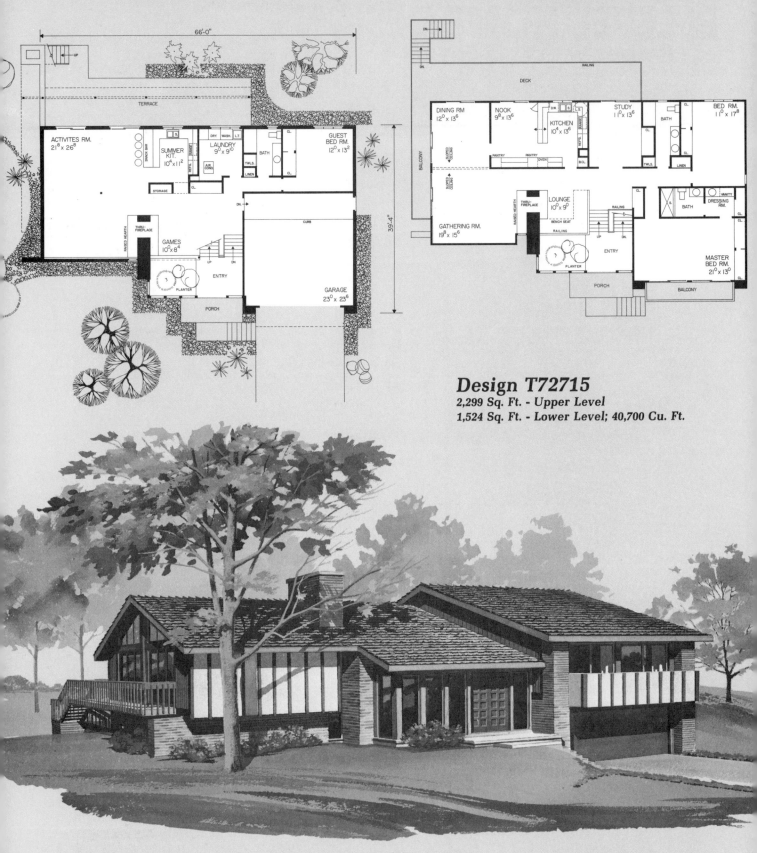

Design T72715
2,299 Sq. Ft. - Upper Level
1,524 Sq. Ft. - Lower Level; 40,700 Cu. Ft.

● A lounge with built-in seating and a thru-fireplace to the gathering room highlights this upper level. A delightful attraction to view upon entrance of this home. A formal dining room, study and U-shaped kitchen with breakfast nook are present, too. That is a lot of room. There's more! A huge activities room has a fireplace, snack bar and adjacent summer kitchen. This is the perfect set-up for teenage parties or family cook-outs on the terrace. The entire family certainly will enjoy the convenience of this area. All this, plus three bedrooms (optional four without the study), including a luxury master suite with its own outdoor balcony. The upper level, outdoor deck provides partial cover for the lower level terrace. This home offers outdoor living potential on both levels.

Design T72579

2,383 Sq. Ft. - Upper level
1,716 Sq. Ft. - Lower Level
43,842 Cu. Ft.

● A huge gathering room, almost 27' with a raised hearth fireplace in the center, sloped ceilings and separate areas for dining and games. Plus balconies on two sides and a deck on the third. A family room on the lower level of equal size to the gathering room with its own center fireplace and adjoining terrace. An activities room to enjoy more living space. A room both youngsters along with adults can utilize. There is an efficient kitchen and dining nook with a built-in desk. Four bedrooms, including a master suite with private bath, two walk-in closets and a private balcony. In fact, every room in the house opens onto a terrace, a deck or a balcony. Sometimes more than one! Indoor-outdoor living will be enjoyed to the maximum. With a total of over 4,000 square feet, there are truly years of gracious living ahead.

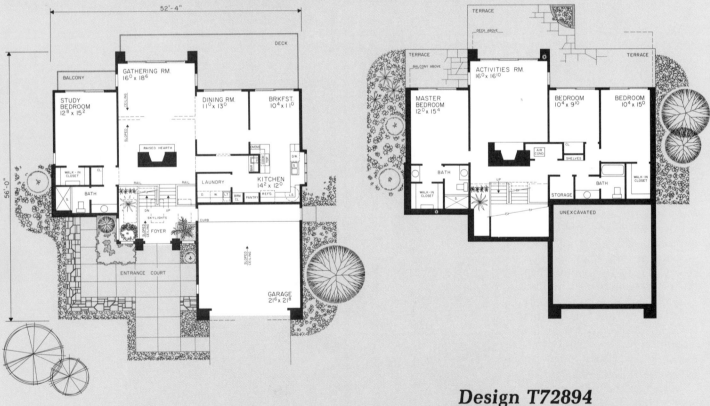

Design T72894
1,490 Sq. Ft. - Main Level
1,357 Sq. Ft. - Lower Level; 38,450 Cu. Ft.

● Contemporary, bi-level living will be enjoyed by all members of the family. Upon entering the foyer, complimented by skylights, stairs will lead you to the upper and lower levels. Up a few steps, you will find yourself in the large gathering room. The fire- place, sloped ceiling and the size of this room will make this a favorite spot. To the left is a study/bedroom with a full bath and walk-in closet. Notice the efficient kitchen and break- fast room with nearby wet bar. The lower level houses two bedrooms and a bath to one side; and a master bed- room suite to the other. Centered is a large activity room with raised-hearth fireplace. It will be enjoyed by all. Note - all of the rear rooms on both levels have easy access to the outdoors for excellent indoor-outdoor livability.

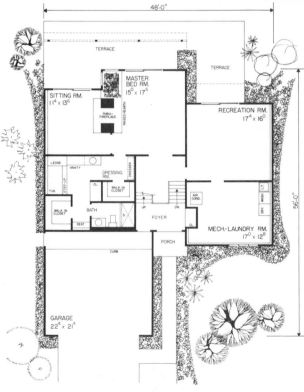

Design T72759

1,747 Sq. Ft. - Upper Level
1,513 Sq. Ft. - Lower Level; 34,540 Cu. Ft.

● A contemporary bi-level with a large bonus room on a third level over the garage. This studio will serve as a great room to be creative in or just to sit back in. The design also provides great indoor/outdoor living relationships with terraces and decks. The formal living/dining area has a sloped ceiling and built-in wet bar. The dramatic beauty of a raised hearth fireplace and built-in planter will be enjoyed by those in the living room. Both have sliding glass doors to the rear deck. The breakfast area will serve as a pleasant eating room with ample space for a table plus the built-in snack bar. The lower level houses the recreation room, laundry and an outstanding master suite. This master suite includes a thru-fireplace, sitting room, tub and shower and more.

Design T72669

826 Sq. Ft. - First Floor
1,535 Sq. Ft. - Second Floor
26,770 Cu. Ft.

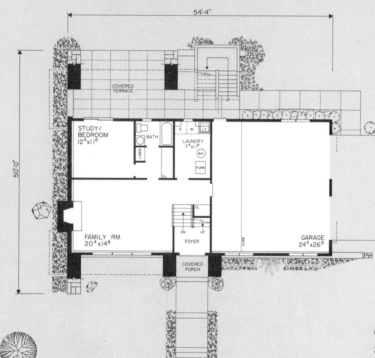

● This comfortable, efficient four-bedroom home offers good traffic flow and personal access to balconies from three upstairs bedrooms. There's a breakfast room adjacent to the kitchen upstairs, plus a dining room and living room also upstairs. An upper-level deck is also accessible from a rear entry. A bedroom/study downstairs opens into a covered terrace. Note the fireplace and first-floor family room, too!

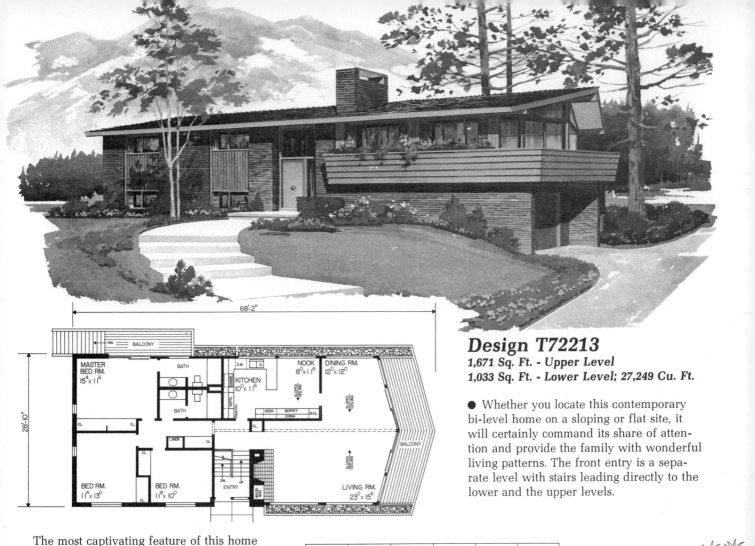

Design T72213

1,671 Sq. Ft. - Upper Level
1,033 Sq. Ft. - Lower Level; 27,249 Cu. Ft.

● Whether you locate this contemporary bi-level home on a sloping or flat site, it will certainly command its share of attention and provide the family with wonderful living patterns. The front entry is a separate level with stairs leading directly to the lower and the upper levels.

The most captivating feature of this home may very well be the spacious living and dining areas. An exposed beam is the apex of sloped ceilings. The projecting, glass-gabled end allows for a full measure of natural light. Two pairs of sliding glass doors open onto the balcony. The living balcony wraps around both front and rear to provide appealing planting areas. The kitchen is an efficient one in which to work, while the breakfast nook is but a step away. The sleeping zone has three bedrooms plus two full baths. Don't overlook the fireplace with its wood box.

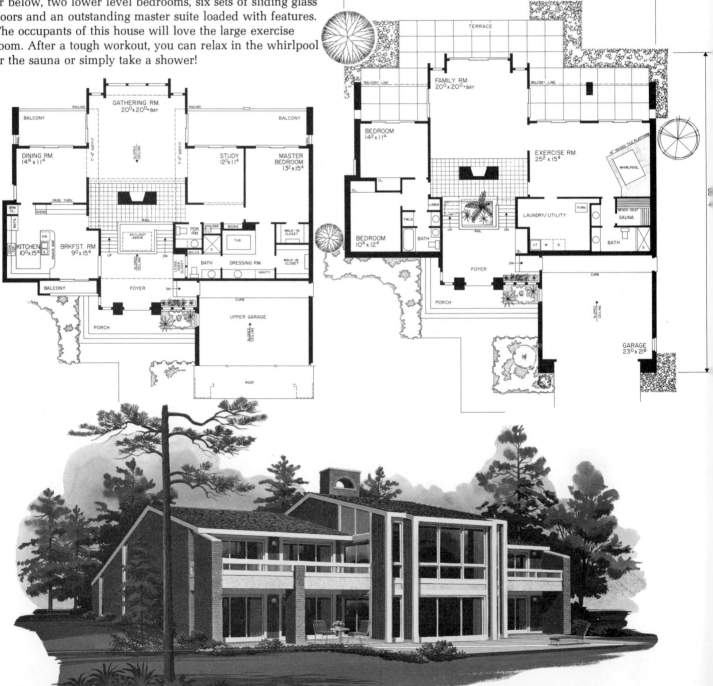

This attractive, contemporary bi-level will overwhelm you with its features: two balconies, an open staircase with planter below, two lower level bedrooms, six sets of sliding glass doors and an outstanding master suite loaded with features. The occupants of this house will love the large exercise room. After a tough workout, you can relax in the whirlpool or the sauna or simply take a shower!

Design T72856 1,801 Sq. Ft. - Upper Level
2,170 Sq. Ft. - Lower Level; 44,935 Cu. Ft.

Design T72868

1,203 Sq. Ft. - Upper Level
1,317 Sq. Ft. - Lower Level; 29,595 Cu. Ft.

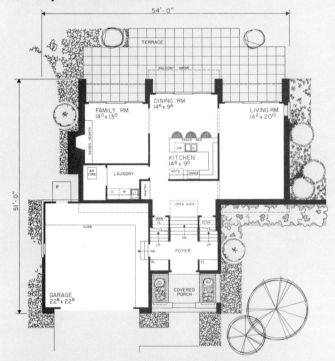

Common Living Areas – Sleeping Privacy

● Two couples sharing the expense of a house has got to be ideal and, of course, economical. The occupants of this house could do just that. The lower level, housing the kitchen, dining room, family and living rooms and the laundry facilities, is the common area to be shared by both couples. Centrally located, the kitchen and dining room act as a space divider to the living and family rooms so both couples can enjoy privacy.

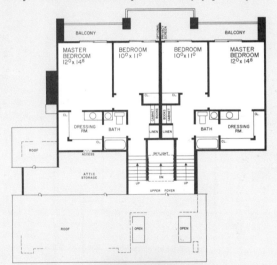

Separate stairways lead to the upper level from the skylit foyer. Each private area has two bedrooms, a dressing room and a full bath. Individual entrances can be locked for additional privacy. Sliding glass doors are in each of the rear rooms on both levels so the outdoors can be enjoyed to its fullest.

Design T72723
1,748 Sq. Ft. - Main Level
294 Sq. Ft. - Entry Level
743 Sq. Ft. - Upper Level
45,400 Cu. Ft.

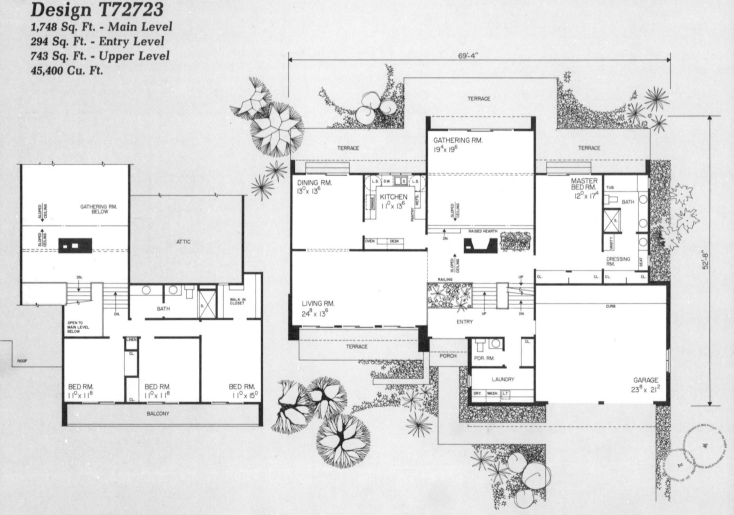

● Bi-level living that begins with a front entry level which houses a powder room and a laundry. The main level has a sunken gathering room! This area has a sloped ceiling, raised hearth fireplace, built-in planter and sliding glass doors to the rear terrace. Also a living room with an adjacent formal dining room. The U-shaped kitchen is a convenient work center with easy access to all areas. The master bedroom's occupants will enjoy their private bath, dressing room and sliding glass doors to another section of the rear terrace. The upper level is an entire sleeping zone. Three bedrooms and a bath will further serve the family. View the gathering room from the upper level.

Design T72735

1,545 Sq. Ft. – Upper Level
1,633 Sq. Ft. – Lower Level
33,295 Cu. Ft.

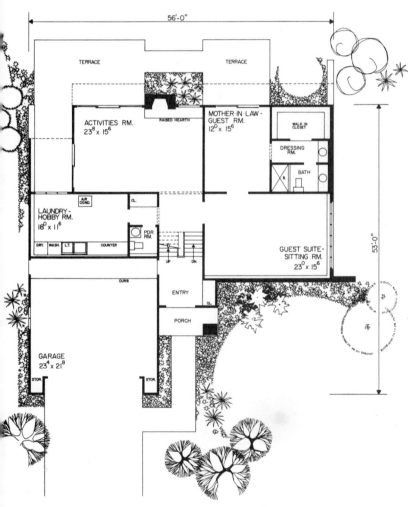

56'-0"

53'-0"

TERRACE   TERRACE

ACTIVITIES RM.
23⁸ x 15⁶

MOTHER·IN·LAW·
GUEST RM.
12⁰ x 15⁶

RAISED HEARTH

WALK-IN
CLOSET

DRESSING
RM.

BATH

AIR
COND.

LAUNDRY·
HOBBY RM.
18⁰ x 11⁶

CL.

PDR.
RM.

GUEST SUITE-
SITTING RM.
23⁰ x 15⁶

DRY. WASH. LT.   COUNTER

UP   DN.

CURB

ENTRY

CL.

PORCH

GARAGE
23⁴ x 21⁸

STOR.

STOR.

BALCONY   OPEN   OPEN   BALCONY

GATHERING RM.
23⁸ x 15⁶

MASTER
BED RM.
12⁰ x 15⁶

VANITY

DRESSING
RM.

BATH

DECK

SLOPED CEILING

DINING

WALK-IN
CLOSET

NOOK
11⁴ x 9⁶

LINEN

BATH

OVEN

KITCHEN
12⁰ x 11⁶

DN.

RAILING

CL.

B.CL.

DESK
BOOKS

PNTRY.

RANGE

D.W.

REFG.

DN.

SKYLIGHT

SLOPED CEILING

STUDY
9⁸ x 12⁰

CL.

BED RM.
11⁰ x 12⁰

CL.

ENTRY
BELOW

BALCONY

● Whether entering this house through the double front doors, or from the garage, access is gained to the lower level by descending seven stairs. Here, there is a bonus of livability. If desired, this level could be used to accommodate a live-in relative while still providing the family with a fine informal activities room and a separate laundry/hobby room and extra powder room. Up seven risers from the entry is the main living level. It has a large gathering room; a sizable nook which could be called upon to function as a separate dining room; an efficient kitchen with pass-thru to a formal dining area and a two bedroom, two bath and study sleeping zone. Don't miss the balconies and deck.

169

Design T72319 1,343 Sq. Ft. - Upper Level
980 Sq. Ft. - Lower Level; 23,290 Cu. Ft.

● This rectangular, bi-level home will be economical to build. The wide overhanging, low-pitched roof enhances the appeal of the exterior. Inside, there are four bedrooms, two on each level, a family activities area, plus a more formal, living room with an adjacent dining room and an efficient kitchen opening into the breakfast room.

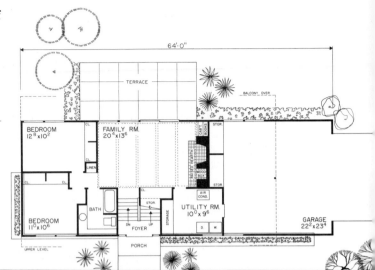

Design T72567 1,773 Sq. Ft. - Upper Level; 1,356 Sq. Ft. - Lower Level; 35,750 Cu. Ft.

Design T71220 1,456 Sq. Ft. - Upper Level
862 Sq. Ft. - Lower Level; 22,563 Cu. Ft.

● This fresh, contemporary exterior sets the stage for exceptional livability. Measuring only 52 across the front, this bi-level home offers the large family outstanding features. Whether called upon to function as a four or five bedroom home, there is plenty of space in which to move around.

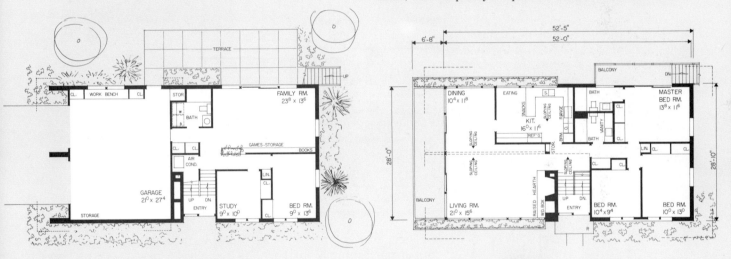

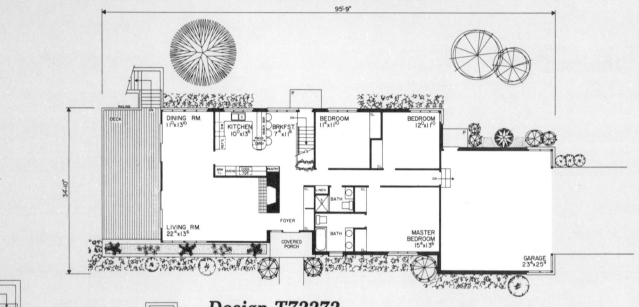

Design T72272

1,731 Sq. Ft. - Main Level
672 Sq. Ft. - Lower Level; 27,802 Cu. Ft.

● Certainly not a huge house. But one, nevertheless, that is long on livability and one that surely will be fun to live in. With its wide-overhanging hip roof, this unadorned facade is the picture of simplicity. As such, it has a quiet appeal all its own. The living-dining area is one of the focal points of the plan. It is wonderfully spacious. The large glass areas and the accessibility, through sliding glass doors, of the outdoor balcony are fine features. For recreation, there is the lower level area which opens onto a large terrace covered by the balcony above.

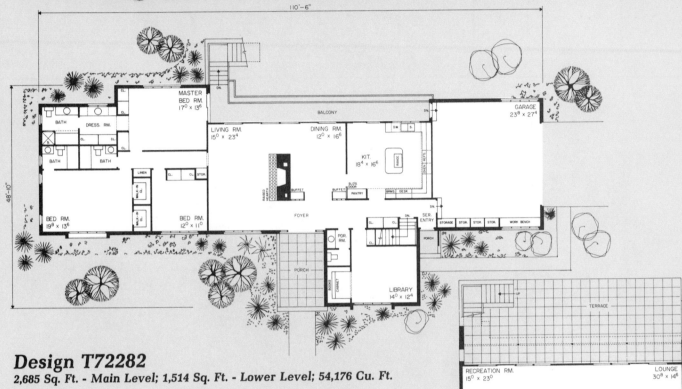

Design T72282
2,685 Sq. Ft. - Main Level; 1,514 Sq. Ft. - Lower Level; 54,176 Cu. Ft.

● If your building site does not have a natural contour to the rear, you may want to consider creating a change in topography yourself. Here is a very satisfying result of exposing a partial basement. In this case, an additional 1,514 square feet of livability has been created. Notice how this lower level now becomes the informal living area of the house.

Design T71310 1,040 Sq. Ft. - Upper Level
694 Sq. Ft. - Lower Level; 17,755 Cu. Ft.

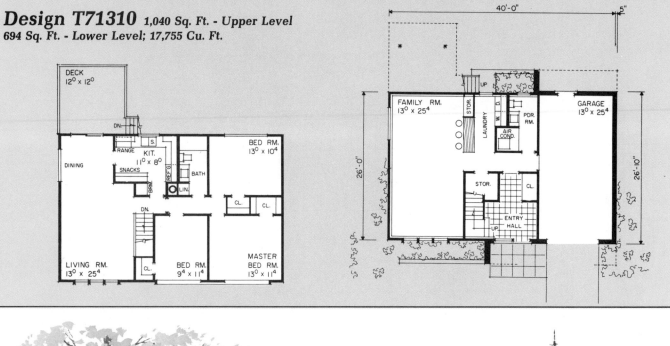

DECK
12⁰ x 12⁰

DN.

DINING

RANGE
S.
KIT.
11⁰ x 8⁰
SNACKS
BRM.
REF'G
BATH
LIN.
CL.

BED RM.
13⁰ x 10⁴

DN.
CL.
CL.
CL.

LIVING RM.
13⁰ x 25⁴

BED RM.
9⁴ x 11⁴

MASTER
BED RM.
13⁰ x 11⁴

40'-0"
5"

FAMILY RM.
13⁰ x 25⁴
STOR.
UP
LAUNDRY
W. D.
PDR. RM.
AIR COND.
GARAGE
13⁰ x 25⁴

26'-0"
26'-10"

STOR.
CL.

ENTRY HALL
UP

● The gathering room is separated from the dining room by a stone wall and a short flight of stairs. Dining and breakfast rooms both have sliding glass doors leading to a rear terrace and are within convenient reach of the U-shaped kitchen. Two bedrooms and two baths are in a separate wing. The master suite opens to the terrace.

BASEMENT

STOR.

AIR COND.

CRAWL SPACE

LAUNDRY
BATH
LIN
STORAGE

UP
CL.

LOW STORAGE

GUEST BEDROOM
11⁰ x 10¹⁰

GARAGE
20⁰ x 22⁴

UNEX.

62'-0"

TERRACE

DINING RM.
12⁸ x 13⁰

BRKFST RM.
10⁰ x 11⁰

DW
S
KITCHEN
11⁰ x 13⁴

BATH
S

MASTER BEDROOM
12¹⁰ x 14¹⁰

LINEN

UP
OVEN
PN'TRY
BRM
CL.
CL.

CL.
STONE WALL

CL.
CL.
LIN
CL.

RAILING

FOYER

34'-0"

GATHERING RM.
17⁰ x 16⁸

COVERED PORCH

STUDY BEDROOM
11¹⁰ x 11²

BATH

BEDROOM
11⁶ x 13⁶

11'-0"

ENTRANCE COURT

DN.

UNEX.

Design T71842 1,747 Sq. Ft. - Upper Level; 937 Sq. Ft. - Lower Level; 27,212 Cu. Ft.

Design T72885 1,922 Sq. Ft. Upper Level
492 Sq. Ft. - Lower Level; 34,640 Cu. Ft.

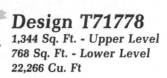

Design T71778
**1,344 Sq. Ft. - Upper Level
768 Sq. Ft. - Lower Level
22,266 Cu. Ft**

● Interesting? You bet it is. The low-pitched, wide overhanging roof, the vertical siding and the dramatic glass areas give the facade of this contemporary bi-level house an appearance all its own.

Design T71704
**1,498 Sq. Ft. - Upper Level
870 Sq. Ft. - Lower Level
23,882 Cu. Ft.**

● The bi-level concept of living has become popular. This is understandable, for it represents a fine way in which to gain a maximum amount of extra livable area beneath the basic floor plan.

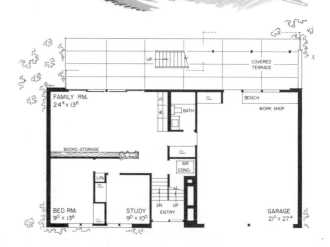

MORE TWO-STORY HOMES

... for Contemporary Living

The popular two-story design represents a most economical use of construction dollars by stacking. Two levels of livability facilitates traffic patterns in larger homes and allows zoning for private areas such as sleeping quarters and other rooms.

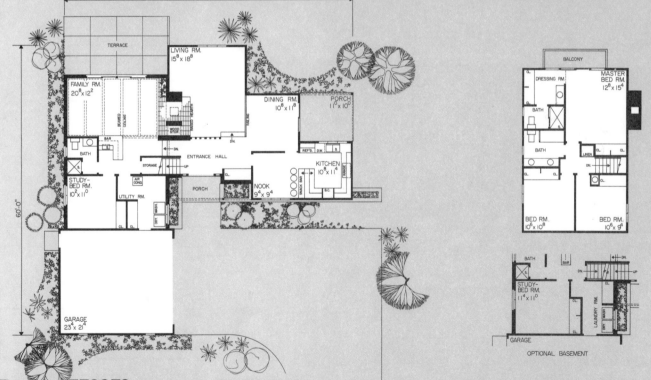

Design T72379   1,525 Sq. Ft. - First Floor; 748 Sq. Ft. - Second Floor; 26,000 Cu. Ft.

● A house that has "everything" may very well look just like this design. Its exterior is well-proportioned and impressive. Inside the inviting double front doors, there are features galore. The living room and family room level are sunken. Separating these two rooms is a dramatic thru fireplace. A built-in bar, planter and beamed ceiling highlight the family room. Nearby is a full bath and a study which could be utilized as a fourth bedroom. The fine functioning kitchen has a pass-thru to the snack bar in the breakfast nook. The adjacent dining room overlooks the living room and has sliding doors to the covered porch. Upstairs three bedrooms, two baths and an outdoor balcony will serve the family with ease. Blueprints for this design include optional basement details.

Design T72711 975 Sq. Ft. - First Floor
1,024 Sq. Ft. - Second Floor; 31,380 Cu. Ft.

● Special features! A complete master suite with a private balcony plus two more bedrooms and a bath upstairs. The first floor has a study with a storage closet. A convenient snack bar between kitchen and dining room. The kitchen offers many built-in appliances. Plus a gathering room and dining room that measures 31 feet wide. Note the curb area in the garage and fireplace in gathering room.

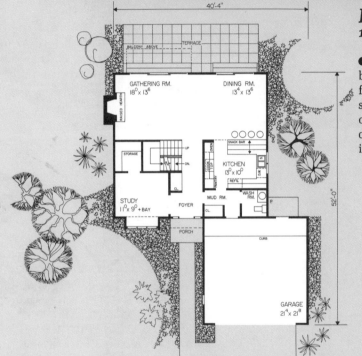

Design T72748
1,232 Sq. Ft. - First Floor
720 Sq. Ft. - Second Floor
27,550 Cu. Ft.

● This four bedroom contemporary will definitely have appeal for the entire family. The U-shaped kitchen-nook area with its built-in desk, adjacent laundry/washroom and service entrance will be very efficient for the busy kitchen activities. The living and family rooms are both sunken one step.

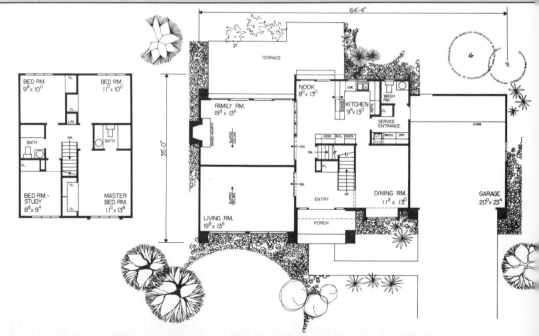

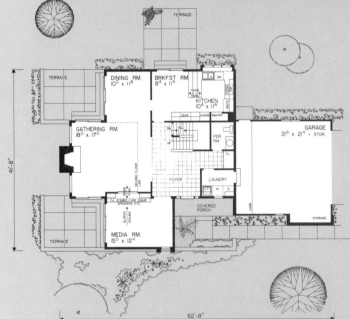

Design T72910 1,221 Sq. Ft. - First Floor
767 Sq. Ft. - Second Floor; 33,370 Cu. Ft.

● This two-story home offers excellent zoning by room functions and modern amenities for comfort. Bedrooms are located upstairs for privacy. There's also an upper gathering room, in addition to a downstairs gathering room. Notice also the media room for stereos/VCRs, plush master bedroom with whirlpool, modern kitchen, and balcony.

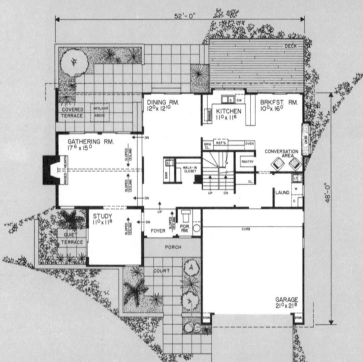

Design T72823
1,370 Sq. Ft. - First Floor
927 Sq. Ft. - Second Floor
34,860 Cu. Ft.

● The street view of this contemporary design features a small courtyard entrance as well as a private terrace off the study. Inside the livability will be outstanding. This design features spacious first floor activity areas that flow smoothly into each other. In the gathering room a raised hearth fireplace creates a dramatic focal point. An adjacent covered terrace, featuring a skylight, is ideal for outdoor dining and could be screened in later for an additional room.

Design T72828 First Floor: 817 Sq. Ft. - Living Area; 261 Sq. Ft. - Foyer & Laundry
Second Floor: 852 Sq. Ft. - Living Area; 214 Sq. Ft. - Foyer & Storage; 34,690 Cu. Ft.

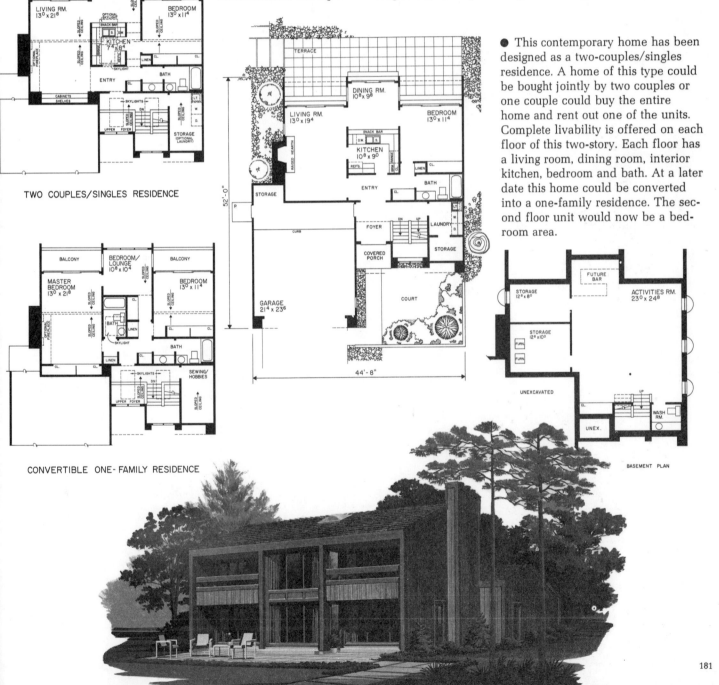

Two couples/singles residence plan labels:
- BALCONY
- DINING RM. 10⁸ x 10⁴
- BALCONY
- LIVING RM. 13⁰ x 21⁸
- BEDROOM 13⁰ x 11⁴
- OPTIONAL SKYLIGHT
- SNACK BAR
- KITCHEN 7⁴ x 8⁴
- SLOPED CEILING
- OPTIONAL FIREPLACE
- LINEN
- BATH
- ENTRY
- CABINETS SHELVES
- SKYLIGHTS
- UPPER FOYER
- STORAGE (OPTIONAL LAUNDRY)
- W. D.

TWO COUPLES/SINGLES RESIDENCE

Convertible one-family residence plan labels:
- BALCONY
- BEDROOM/LOUNGE 10⁸ x 10⁴
- BALCONY
- MASTER BEDROOM 13⁰ x 21⁸
- BEDROOM 13⁰ x 11⁴
- OPTIONAL FIREPLACE
- BATH
- LINEN
- SKYLIGHT
- SEWING/HOBBIES
- SKYLIGHTS
- UPPER FOYER

CONVERTIBLE ONE-FAMILY RESIDENCE

First floor plan labels:
- TERRACE
- DINING RM. 10⁸ x 9⁸
- LIVING RM. 13⁰ x 19⁴
- BEDROOM 13⁰ x 11⁴
- RAISED HEARTH
- SNACK BAR
- KITCHEN 10⁸ x 9⁰
- REF'D.
- LINEN
- CL.
- BATH
- ENTRY
- STORAGE
- CURB
- FOYER
- LAUNDRY
- DN UP
- COVERED PORCH
- STORAGE
- GARAGE 21⁴ x 23⁶
- COURT
- 52'-0"
- 44'-8"

Basement plan labels:
- STORAGE 12⁸ x 8⁰
- FUTURE BAR
- ACTIVITIES RM. 23⁰ x 24⁸
- STORAGE 12⁸ x 10⁰
- FURN.
- FURN.
- UNEXCAVATED
- UNEX.
- CL.
- UP
- WASH RM.

BASEMENT PLAN

● This contemporary home has been designed as a two-couples/singles residence. A home of this type could be bought jointly by two couples or one couple could buy the entire home and rent out one of the units. Complete livability is offered on each floor of this two-story. Each floor has a living room, dining room, interior kitchen, bedroom and bath. At a later date this home could be converted into a one-family residence. The second floor unit would now be a bedroom area.

Design T71879
1,008 Sq. Ft. - First Floor
1,008 Sq. Ft. - Second Floor
27,518 Cu. Ft.

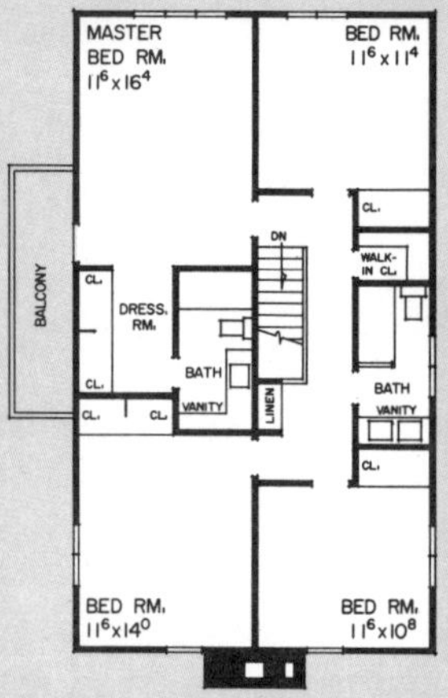

First Floor plan labels:
TERRACE
48'-0"
24'-0" 24'-0"
STOR.
BREAKFAST 9⁶ x 7⁴
FAMILY RM. 11⁶ x 15⁰
GARAGE 23⁸ x 21⁴
CURB
STOR.
SINK
KIT. 11⁶ x 9⁰
RANGE OVEN
REF'G
DN
22'-0"
42'-0"
DINING RM. 11⁶ x 12⁰
W.R.
CL.
UP
ENTRY
R
20'-0"
LIVING RM. 23⁴ x 12⁰

Second Floor plan labels:
MASTER BED RM. 11⁶ x 16⁴
BED RM. 11⁶ x 11⁴
BALCONY
DRESS. RM.
DN
CL.
WALK-IN CL.
CL.
BATH
VANITY
LINEN
BATH
VANITY
CL.
BED RM. 11⁶ x 14⁰
BED RM. 11⁶ x 10⁸

● This contemporary two-story will be most economical to build. Thus, the return on your construction dollar will be weighted in your favor. Consider: four bedrooms - three for the kids and one for the parents; one main bath and one private bath with dressing room for Mr. and Mrs.; two distinct eating areas - the informal breakfast room and the formal dining room; a family room only a step removed from the rear terrace and a quiet living room off by itself.

● Here is another contemporary, two-story design which offers fine contemporary living patterns. There are four bedrooms, 2½ baths and formal and informal living and dining areas. The fireplace with its raised hearth in the family room is flanked with bookshelves. Blueprints for this design include details for an optional non-basement.

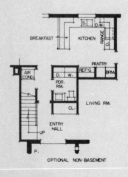

Design T71908
1,122 Sq. Ft. - First Floor
896 Sq. Ft. - Second Floor; 27,064 Cu. Ft.

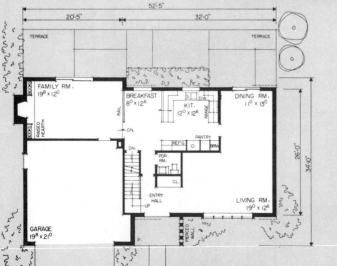

First Floor plan labels:
52'-5"
20'-5" 32'-0"
TERRACE
TERRACE
BOOKS
FAMILY RM. 19⁸ x 12⁰
RAISED HEARTH
BOOKS
RAIL
BREAKFAST 8⁰ x 12⁶
KIT. 12⁰ x 12⁶
S.
D.W.
RANGE
DINING RM. 11⁰ x 13⁰
DN.
DN.
REF'G
O.
PANTRY
BRM.
PDR. RM.
CL.
ENTRY HALL
UP
LIVING RM. 19⁰ x 12⁶
26'-0"
34'-0"
VAULT
GARAGE 19⁸ x 21⁰
PIERCED WALL
P.

Second Floor plan labels:
BED RM. 12⁰ x 11⁰
BATH
MASTER BED RM. 11⁴ x 16⁸
CL.
DN.
CL.
BATH
LIN.
CL.
WALK-IN CL.
BED RM. 10⁸ x 10⁴
CL.
BED RM. 14⁸ x 10⁴

Optional non-basement plan labels:
BREAKFAST
KITCHEN
S.
D.W.
RANGE
O.
AIR COND.
D.
W.
PANTRY
REF'G
BRM.
PDR. RM.
CL.
LIVING RM.
ENTRY HALL
UP
P.
OPTIONAL NON-BASEMENT

● This two-story contemporary offers a variety of living patterns for your family. To the right of the spacious entrance hall, you will find a large living room with a fireplace. A few steps away is a nice-sized dining room with adjacent kitchen and breakfast area. Note, the bar and pantry. A spacious family room with beamed ceiling and fireplace is ideal for entertaining guests. Also featured on this floor is a laundry room and adjacent washroom. Three bedrooms are upstairs, along with a full bath and the master bedroom with full bath and dressing room. Notice the luxury of the private balcony.

Design T71878 1,384 Sq. Ft. - First Floor
1,320 Sq. Ft. - Second Floor; 37,384 Cu. Ft.

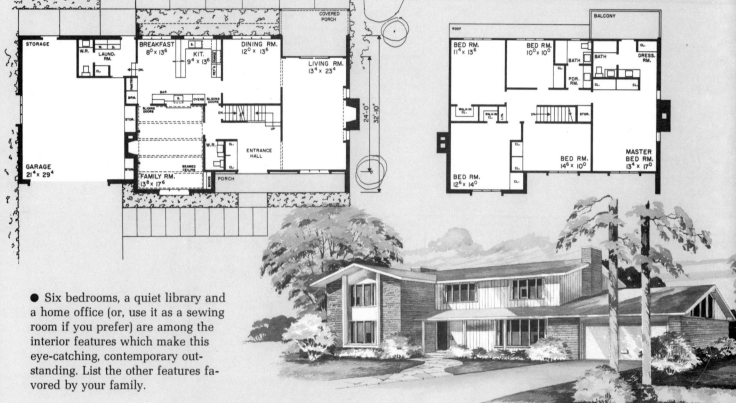

● Six bedrooms, a quiet library and a home office (or, use it as a sewing room if you prefer) are among the interior features which make this eye-catching, contemporary outstanding. List the other features favored by your family.

Design T71899 1,790 Sq. Ft. - First Floor
1,514 Sq. Ft. - Second Floor; 47,058 Cu. Ft.

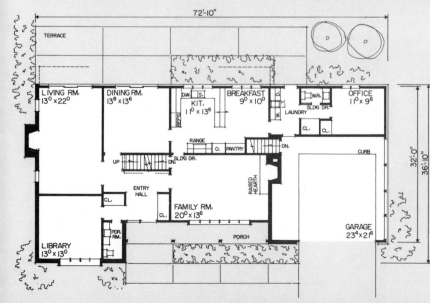

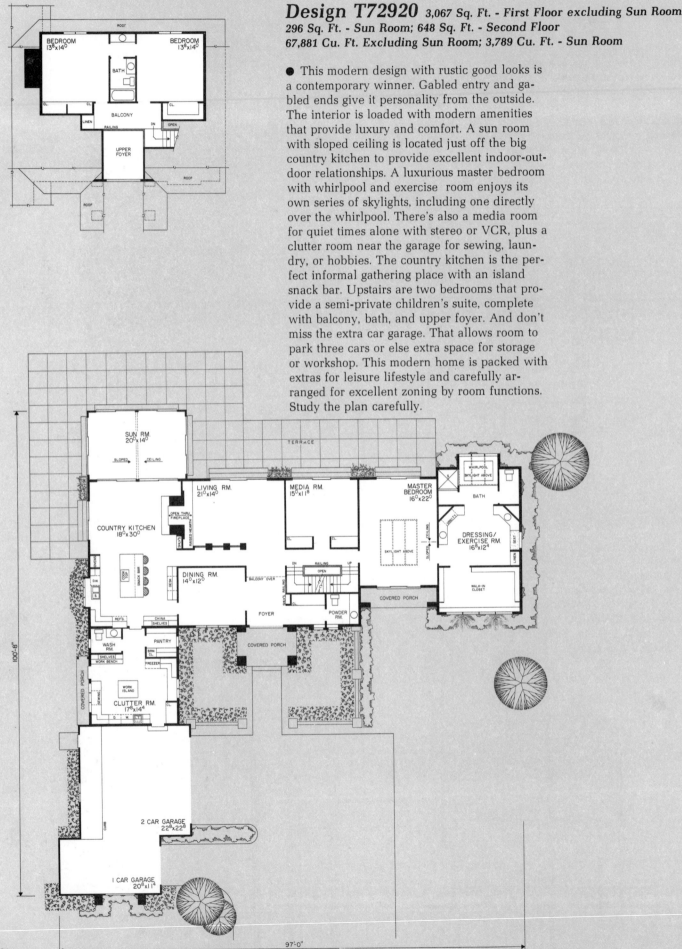

Design T72920 3,067 Sq. Ft. - First Floor excluding Sun Room
296 Sq. Ft. - Sun Room; 648 Sq. Ft. - Second Floor
67,881 Cu. Ft. Excluding Sun Room; 3,789 Cu. Ft. - Sun Room

● This modern design with rustic good looks is a contemporary winner. Gabled entry and gabled ends give it personality from the outside. The interior is loaded with modern amenities that provide luxury and comfort. A sun room with sloped ceiling is located just off the big country kitchen to provide excellent indoor-outdoor relationships. A luxurious master bedroom with whirlpool and exercise room enjoys its own series of skylights, including one directly over the whirlpool. There's also a media room for quiet times alone with stereo or VCR, plus a clutter room near the garage for sewing, laundry, or hobbies. The country kitchen is the perfect informal gathering place with an island snack bar. Upstairs are two bedrooms that provide a semi-private children's suite, complete with balcony, bath, and upper foyer. And don't miss the extra car garage. That allows room to park three cars or else extra space for storage or workshop. This modern home is packed with extras for leisure lifestyle and carefully arranged for excellent zoning by room functions. Study the plan carefully.

Excellent zoning and luxurious comforts for modern lifestyle . . .

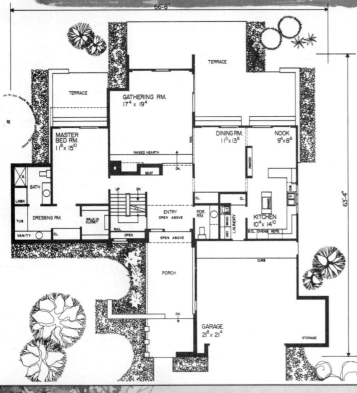

Design T72729 1,590 Sq. Ft. - First Floor
756 Sq. Ft. - Second Floor; 39,310 Cu. Ft.

● Entering this home will be a pleasure through the sheltered walk-way to the double front doors. And the pleasure and beauty does not stop there. The entry hall and sunken gathering room are open to the upstairs for added dimension. There is fine indoor-outdoor living relationships in this design. Note the private terrace, a living terrace plus the balcony.

Design T72178 1,441 Sq. Ft. - First Floor; 1,415 Sq. Ft. - Second Floor; 40,206 Cu. Ft.

● The spacious, front entry routes traffic most effectively to all of the areas of this wonderfully livable home. The front living room is separated from the sunken, rear family room by the four foot high built-in storage wall. The result is a tremendously spacious living zone. The kitchen is big and efficient. Upstairs there are four large bedrooms and three full baths.

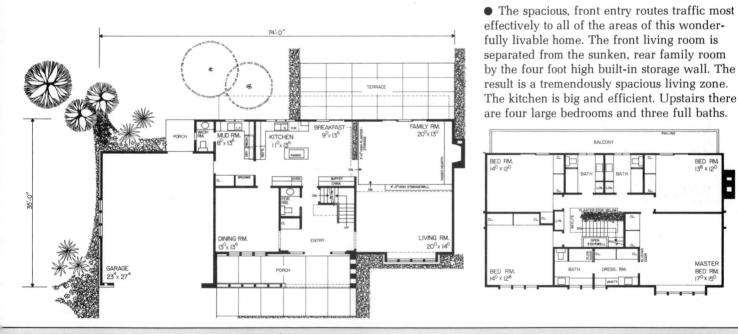

Design T72602 1,154 Sq. Ft. - First Floor
1,120 Sq. Ft. - Second Floor; 30,370 Cu. Ft.

● Varying roof planes, wide overhangs, interestingly shaped blank wall areas and patterned, double front doors provide the distinguishing characteristics of this contemporary design. The extension of the front wall results in a private, outdoor patio area accessible from the living room. There is a fine feeling of spaciousness inside this plan. The living area features open planning. Upstairs, four good-sized bedrooms and two baths.

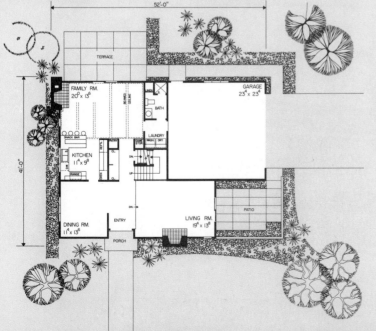

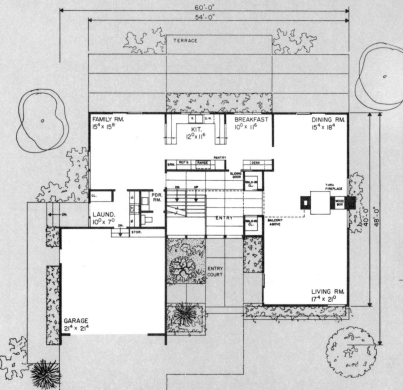

TERRACE

FAMILY RM.
15⁴ x 15⁸

KIT.
12⁰ x 11⁶

BREAKFAST
10⁰ x 11⁶

DINING RM.
15⁴ x 18⁴

BRK. REF'G RANGE PANTRY DESK

SLIDING DOOR

WALK-IN CL.

PDR. RM.

LAUND.
10⁰ x 7⁰

STOR.

CL.

ENTRY

BALCONY ABOVE

WALK-IN CL.

ENTRY COURT

THRU FIREPLACE

WOOD BOX

LIVING RM.
17⁴ x 21⁰

GARAGE
21⁴ x 21⁴

60'-0"
54'-0"
48'-0"
40'-0"

Design T72123

1,624 Sq. Ft. - First Floor
1,335 Sq. Ft. - Second Floor
42,728 Cu. Ft.

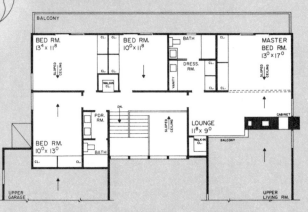

BALCONY

BED RM.
13⁴ x 11⁸

SLOPED CEILING

WALK-IN CL.

BED RM.
10⁰ x 11⁸

BATH

DRESS. RM.

VANITY

MASTER BED RM.
13⁰ x 17⁰

SLOPED CEILING

BED RM.
10⁰ x 13⁰

PDR. RM.

BATH

CL.

DN.

SLOPED CEILING

LOUNGE
11⁸ x 9⁰

WALK-IN

BALCONY

CABINET

UPPER GARAGE

UPPER LIVING RM.

● Inside there is close to 3,000 square feet of uniquely planned floor area. The spacious, well-lighted entry has, of course, a high sloping ceiling. The second floor ceiling also slopes and, consequently, adds to the feeling of spaciousness.

Design T72130 1,608 Sq. Ft. - First Floor; 924 Sq. Ft. - Second Floor; 34,949 Cu. Ft.

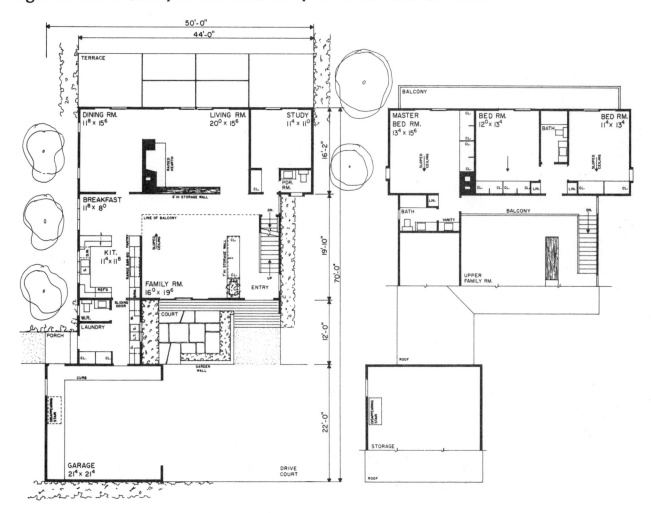

● Ring in the new. Here is a fresh forward-looking design which exemplifies some of the up-to-date imagery of today's architecture. This contemporary is a good study in the interest developed by the introduction of angles. These angles, plus the varying roof planes, blank wall masses, simple glass areas and the overall shape resulting from the orientation of the living components, make this an outstanding design. Inside, the floor planning will offer a lifetime of enjoyable living patterns. Study the various room relationships. Notice the practical zoning which results in a separation of functions to guarantee convenient living. Observe the homemaker's kitchen/laundry area. Also, formal dining, living rooms.

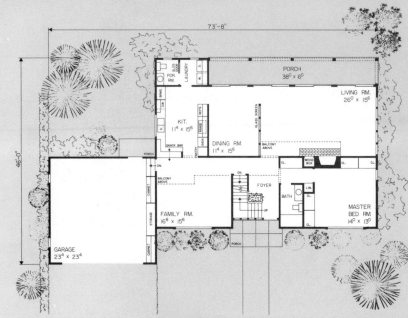

Design T72246 1,651 Sq. Ft. - First Floor
1,161 Sq. Ft. - Second Floor; 52,382 Cu. Ft.

● This contemporary design has a trace of chalet in its ancestry. Sloping ceilings, open planning and plenty of glass assure an atmosphere of spaciousness throughout the interior.

Design T72772
1,579 Sq. Ft. - First Floor
1,240 Sq. Ft. - Second Floor; 39,460 Cu. Ft.

● This four-bedroom two-story contemporary design is sure to suit your growing family needs. The rear U-shaped kitchen, flanked by the family and dining rooms, will be very efficient to the busy homemaker. Parents will enjoy all the convenience of the master bedroom suite.

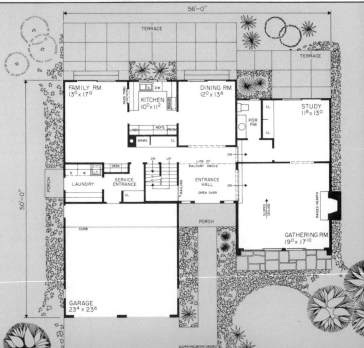

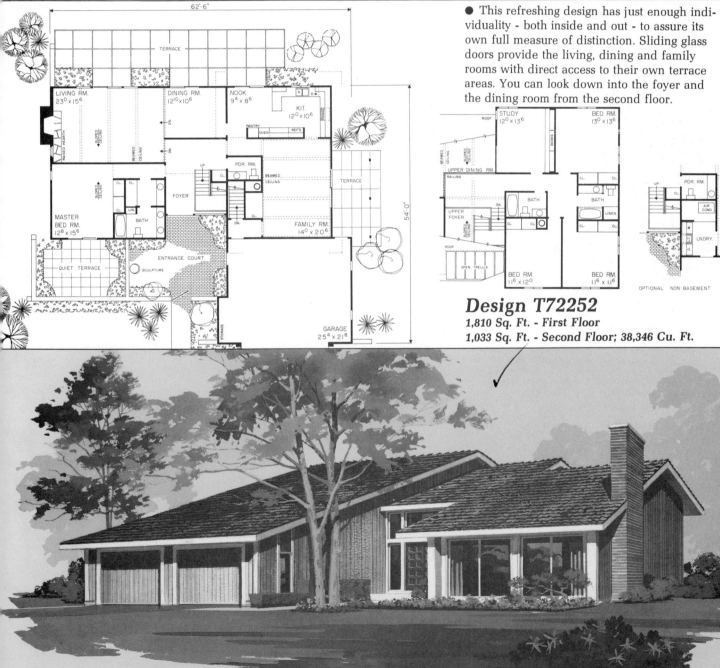

The floor plan includes the following labeled areas:

- TERRACE
- LIVING RM. 23⁰ x 15⁶
- DINING RM. 12¹⁰ x 10⁶
- NOOK 9⁴ x 8⁶
- KIT. 12⁰ x 10⁶
- PANTRY / OVEN / REF'S
- RAISED HEARTH
- SLOPED CEILING
- BEAMED CEILING
- PDR. RM.
- BEAMED CEILING
- MASTER BED RM. 12⁸ x 15⁶
- CL. / CL. / LIN.
- BATH
- FOYER
- UP
- DN.
- TERRACE
- FAMILY RM. 14⁰ x 20⁶
- QUIET TERRACE
- ENTRANCE COURT
- SCULPTURE
- STORAGE
- GARAGE 25⁴ x 21⁸

Dimensions: 62'-6" / 54'-0"

● This refreshing design has just enough individuality - both inside and out - to assure its own full measure of distinction. Sliding glass doors provide the living, dining and family rooms with direct access to their own terrace areas. You can look down into the foyer and the dining room from the second floor.

Second floor plan labels:

- ROOF
- STUDY 12⁰ x 13⁶
- BED RM. 13⁰ x 13⁶
- BOOKS
- BEAMED CEILING / SLOPED CEILING
- UPPER DINING RM.
- RAILING
- UPPER FOYER
- BATH
- BATH
- CL. / CL. / CL. / CL. / LINEN
- DN.
- ROOF
- OPEN TRELLIS
- BED RM. 11⁶ x 12⁰
- BED RM. 11⁶ x 11⁶
- UP
- PDR. RM.
- AIR COND.
- LNDRY.
- OPTIONAL NON-BASEMENT

Design T72252
1,810 Sq. Ft. - First Floor
1,033 Sq. Ft. - Second Floor; 38,346 Cu. Ft.

Design T72377 1,170 Sq. Ft. - First Floor
815 Sq. Ft. - Second Floor; 22,477 Cu. Ft.

● What an impressive, up-to-date home. Its refreshing configuration will command a full measure of attention. Note that all of the back rooms on the first floor are a couple steps lower than the entry and living room area. Separating the living room and the slightly lower level is a thru-fireplace, which has a raised hearth in the family room. Four bedrooms, serviced by two full baths, comprise the second floor which looks down into the living room.

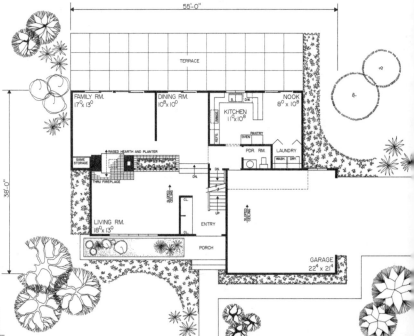

Design T72390 1,368 Sq. Ft. - First Floor
1,428 Sq. Ft. - Second Floor; 37,734 Cu. Ft.

● If yours is a large family and you like the architecture of the Far West, don't look further. Particularly if you envision building on a modest sized lot. Projecting the garage to the front contributes to the drama of this two-story. Its stucco exterior is beautifully enhanced by the clay tiles of the varying roof surfaces. The focal point, of course, is the five bedroom, three bath second floor. Four bedrooms have access to the outdoor balcony.

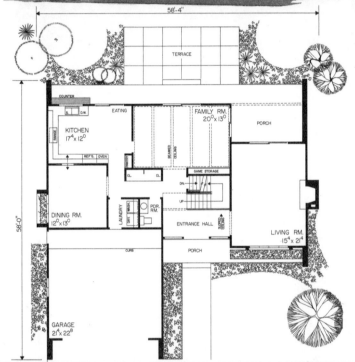

Design T72309
1,719 Sq. Ft. - First Floor
456 Sq. Ft. - Second Floor; 22,200 Cu. Ft.

● Study this floor plan carefully. The efficiency of the kitchen could hardly be improved upon. It is strategically located to serve the formal dining room, the family room and even the rear terrace. The sleeping facilities are arranged in a most interesting manner. The master bedroom with its attached bath and dressing room will enjoy a full measure of privacy on the first floor. A second bedroom is also on this floor and has a full bath nearby. Upstairs, there are two more bedrooms and a bath.

193

Design T72582

1,195 Sq. Ft. - First Floor
731 Sq. Ft. - Second Floor
32,500 Cu. Ft.

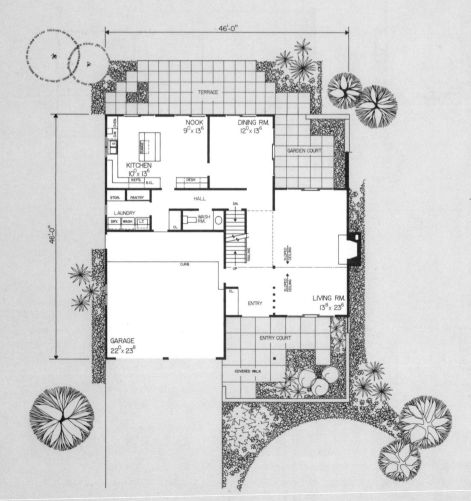

● This distinctive two-story will command attention wherever built. One of its significant features is that it doesn't require a huge piece of property. In slightly less than 2,000 square feet it offers tremendous livability. As a bonus, the basement can function as the family recreation and hobby areas. Of particular interest is the first floor laundry room. Don't miss the fine kitchen layout, the formal and informal dining facilities and the sloping ceiling of the living room. Notice the outstanding outdoor living facilities. Upstairs, three bedrooms and two baths will be found.

Design T71978 1,280 Sq. Ft. - First Floor
960 Sq. Ft. - Second Floor; 24,031 Cu. Ft.

● Why not make your next two-story home one with a contemporary facade? Surely, it can be agreed that such an exterior can be as attractive, well-proportioned and distinctive as its traditional counterpart. Study each floor carefully. This design has much to offer in the way of total comfort for the family. Particularly noteworthy are the sleeping and bath accommodations on the second floor. Study the entire plan.

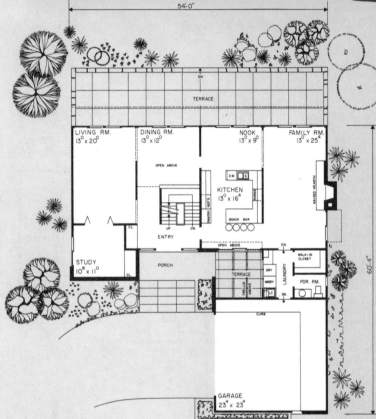

54'-0"

TERRACE

LIVING RM.
13⁰ x 20⁰

DINING RM.
13⁰ x 12⁰

NOOK
13⁰ x 9⁰

FAMILY RM.
13⁰ x 25⁴

OPEN ABOVE

KITCHEN
13⁰ x 16⁰

SNACK BAR

ENTRY

STUDY
10⁸ x 11⁰

PORCH

OPEN ABOVE

WALK-IN CLOSET

TERRACE

LAUNDRY

POR. RM.

CURB

GARAGE
23⁴ x 23⁴

60'-4"

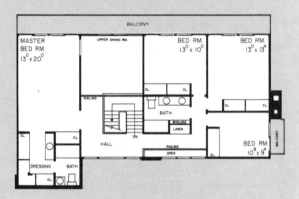

BALCONY

MASTER BED RM.
13⁰ x 20⁰

UPPER DINING RM.

BED RM.
13⁰ x 10⁰

BED RM.
13⁰ x 13⁴

RAILING

BATH

SHELVES

LINEN

HALL

DRESSING

BATH

RAILING

OPEN

BED RM.
10⁸ x 9⁴

BALCONY

Design T72509
1,634 Sq. Ft. - First Floor
1,304 Sq. Ft. - Second Floor
44,732 Cu. Ft.

● A two-story with more livability will be hard to find. Notice how the various rooms are oriented with the terrace and balcony. The dining room has a high ceiling so its activities can be viewed from the upstairs hall.

Design T72709

2,471 Sq. Ft. - First Floor
2,038 Sq. Ft. - Second Floor
73,125 Cu. Ft.

● A lower-level conversation pit! Above, a skylight. And on the first and second floors, open balconies. . .offering a view of both the conversation pit and skylight. That's just the beginning. Develop the basement area around the conversation pit and add 1,435 square feet to your informal living area. The gathering room features a balcony overlooking an indoor garden . . . part of the scenery in the family room. Fireplace in both those rooms. An enormous kitchen with a walk-in pantry, island range, built-in desk. Four large bedrooms, including a luxury master suite. Observe the storage potential.

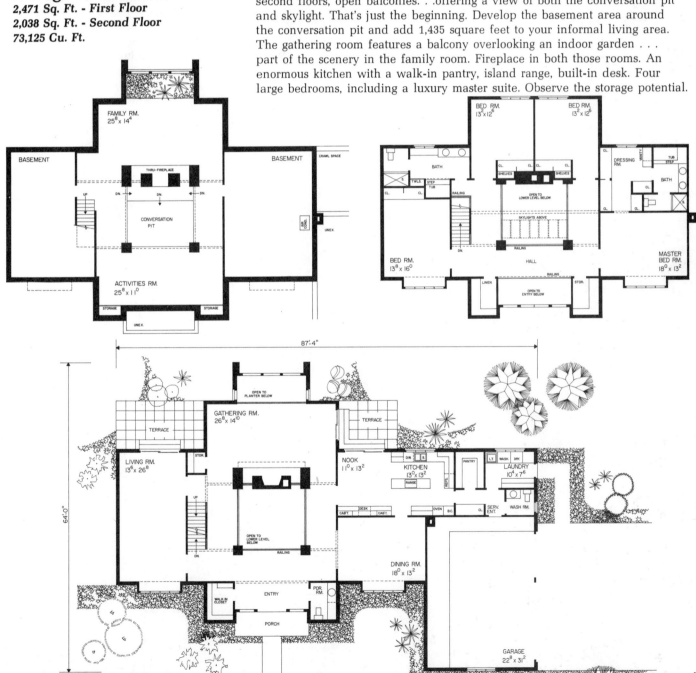

Design T71877

1,162 Sq. Ft. - First Floor
883 Sq. Ft. - Second Floor
27,617 Cu. Ft.

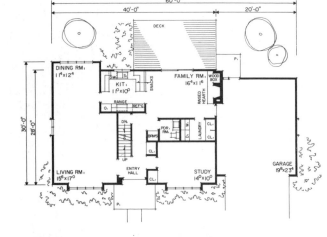

● This simple, straightforward plan has much to offer in the way of livability and economical construction costs. Worthy of particular note are the excellent traffic patterns and the outstanding use of space. Notice the cozy family room with its raised hearth fireplace, wood box and sliding glass doors to the sweeping outdoor deck. The efficient kitchen is flanked by the informal snack bar and the formal dining area. Open planning between the living and dining areas promotes a fine feeling of spaciousness. The study is a great feature. It may function as just that or become, the sewing or TV room, the guest room or even the fourth bedroom.

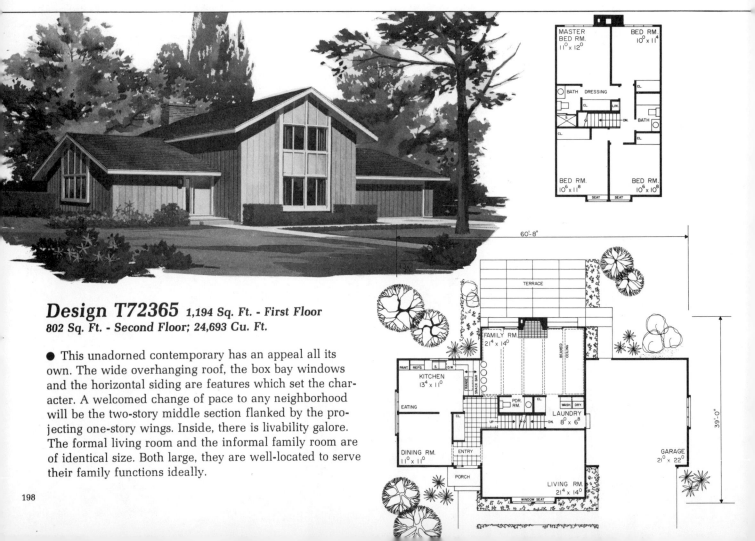

Design T72365 1,194 Sq. Ft. - First Floor

802 Sq. Ft. - Second Floor; 24,693 Cu. Ft.

● This unadorned contemporary has an appeal all its own. The wide overhanging roof, the box bay windows and the horizontal siding are features which set the character. A welcomed change of pace to any neighborhood will be the two-story middle section flanked by the projecting one-story wings. Inside, there is livability galore. The formal living room and the informal family room are of identical size. Both large, they are well-located to serve their family functions ideally.

MORE ONE-STORY HOMES
. . . Under 2,000 Sq. Ft. Contemporary designs often come in compact sizes, packed with comfort plus practical living features for modern lifestyles.

Design T72818 1,566 Sq. Ft.; 20,030 Cu. Ft.

● This is most certainly an outstanding contemporary design. Study the exterior carefully before your journey to inspect the floor plan. The vertical lines are carried from the siding to the paned windows to the garage door. The front entry is recessed so the overhanging roof creates a covered porch.

Note the planter court with privacy wall. The floor plan is just as outstanding. The rear gathering room has a sloped ceiling, raised hearth fireplace, sliding glass doors to the terrace and a snack bar with pass-thru to the kitchen. In addition to the gathering room, there is the living room/study. This

room could be utilized in a variety of ways depending on your family's choice. The formal dining room is convenient to the U-shaped kitchen. Three bedrooms and two closely located baths are in the sleeping wing. This plan includes details for the construction of an optional basement.

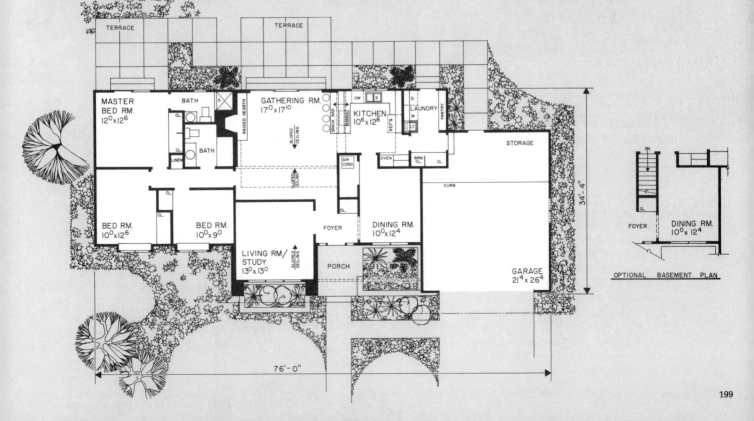

Design T72703
1,445 Sq. Ft.; 30,300 Cu. Ft.

● This modified, hip-roofed contemporary design will be the answer for those who want something both practical, yet different, inside and out. The covered front walk sets the stage for entering a modest sized home with tremendous livability. The focal point will be the pleasant conversation lounge. It is sunken, partically open to the other living areas and shares the enjoyment of the thru-fireplace with the living room. There are two bedrooms, two full baths and a study. The kitchen is outstanding.

Design T72753
1,539 Sq. Ft.; 31,910 Cu. Ft.

● In this day and age of expensive building sites, projecting the attached garage from the front line of the house makes a lot of economic sense. It also lends itself to interesting roof lines and plan configurations. Here, a pleasing covered walkway to the front door results. A privacy wall adds an extra measure of design appeal and provides a sheltered terrace for the study/bedroom. You'll seldom find more livability in 1,539 square feet. Imagine, three bedrooms, two baths, a spacious living/dining area and a family room.

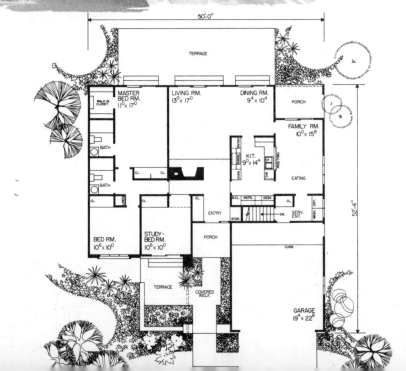

Design T72744
1,381 Sq. Ft.; 17,530 Cu. Ft.

● Here is a practical and an attractive contemporary home for that narrow building site. It is designed for efficiency with the small family or retired couple in mind. Sloping ceilings foster an extra measure of spaciousness. In addition to the master bedroom, there is the study that can also serve as the second bedroom or as an occasional guest room. The single bath is compartmented and its dual access allows it to serve living and sleeping areas more than adequately. Note raised hearth fireplace, snack bar, U-shaped kitchen, laundry, two terraces, etc.

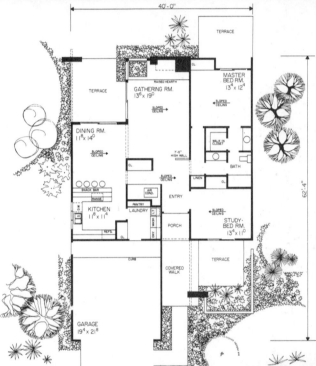

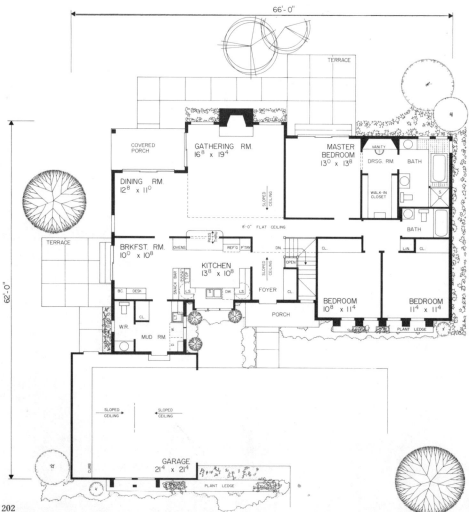

Design T72912
1,864 Sq. Ft.; 45,343 Cu. Ft.

● This modern design with smart Spanish styling incorporates careful zoning by room functions with lifestyle comfort. All three bedrooms, including a master bedroom suite, are isolated at one end of the one-story home for privacy and out of traffic patterns. Entry to a breakfast room and kitchen is possible through a mud room off the garage. That's good news for people carrying groceries from car to kitchen or people with muddy shoes during inclement weather. The modern kitchen includes a snack bar and cook top with multiple access to breakfast room, side foyer, and pass-thru to hallway. There's also a nearby formal dining room. A large rear gathering room features sloped ceiling and its own fireplace. Note the two-car garage and built-in plant ledge in front. Gabled end window treatment plus varied roof lines further enhance the striking appearance of this efficient design.

Design T72913 1,835 Sq. Ft.; 42,998 Cu. Ft.

● This smart design features multi-gabled ends, varied roof lines, and vertical windows. It also offers efficient zoning by room functions and plenty of modern comforts for Contemporary family lifestyle. A covered porch leads through a foyer to a large central gathering room with fireplace, sloped ceiling, and its own special view of a rear terrace. A modern kitchen with snack bar has a pass-thru to a breakfast room with view of the terrace. There's also an adjacent dining room. A media room isolated along with bedrooms from rest of the house offers a quiet private area for listening to stereos or VCRs. A master bedroom suite includes its own whirlpool. A large two-car garage includes extra storage.

Design T72330
1,854 Sq. Ft.; 30,001 Cu. Ft.

● Your family will never tire of the living patterns offered by this appealing home with its low-pitched, wide over-hanging roof. The masonry masses of the exterior are pleasing. While the blueprints call for the use of stone, you may wish to substitute brick veneer. Sloping ceiling and plenty of glass will assure the living area of a fine feeling of spaciousness. The covered porches enhance the enjoy-ment of outdoor living. Two baths serve the three bedroom sleeping area.

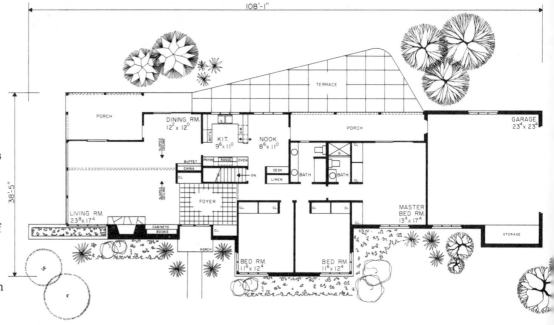

Design T73165
1,940 Sq. Ft.; 20,424 Cu. Ft.

● A practical plan with a contemporary facade. The center entrance encourages fine traffic circulation. To the right of the entry hall is the formal living area with its sunken living room and sepa-rate dining room separated by an attractive built-in planter. To the left of the entry hall is the three bedroom, two full bath sleeping zone. At the end of the entrance hall is the in-formal living area featuring the family room, efficient kitchen and laundry room.

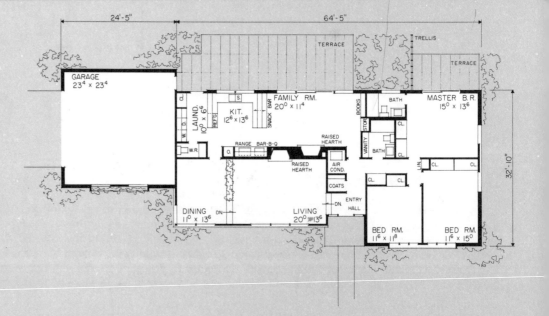

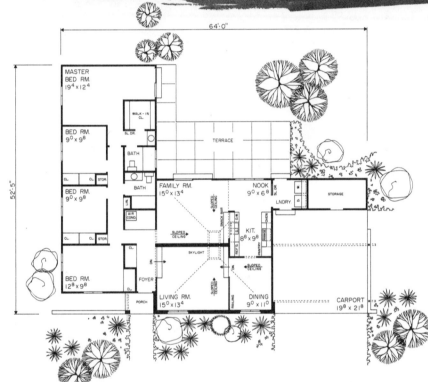

MASTER BED RM. 19⁴ x 12⁴

WALK-IN CL.

BED RM. 9⁰ x 9⁸

BATH

BATH

BED RM. 9⁰ x 9⁸

AIR COND.

BED RM. 12⁸ x 9⁸

FOYER

PORCH

TERRACE

FAMILY RM. 15⁰ x 13⁴

SLOPED CEILING

SLOPED CEILING

SKYLIGHT

SLOPED CEILING

LIVING RM. 15⁰ x 13⁴

NOOK 9⁰ x 6⁸

LNDRY.

KIT. 8⁸ x 9⁸

SLOPED CEILING

DINING 9⁰ x 11⁰

STORAGE

CARPORT 19⁸ x 21⁸

64'-0"

52'-5"

Design T72312
1,703 Sq. Ft.; 18,801 Cu. Ft.

● If you like contemporary living patterns to go with your refreshingly distinctive exterior, this four bedroom design may be the perfect choice for you and your family. Essentially of frame construction with vertical siding, brick veneer is used prudently to foster an appealing contrast in exterior materials. The covered front entrance leads to the centered foyer which effectively routes traffic to the well-zoned interior. The living and dining rooms function together for formal entertaining. The family room, nook and kitchen also function well together. This informal living zone is readily accessible to the rear terrace.

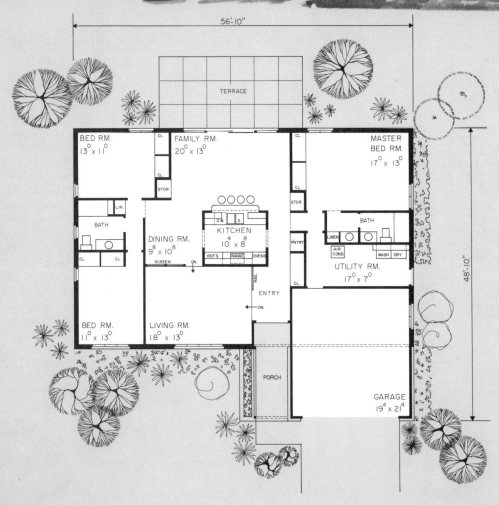

TERRACE

BED RM.
13⁰ x 11

FAMILY RM.
20⁰ x 13⁰

MASTER
BED RM.
17⁰ x 13⁰

CL.

CL.

STOR.

CL.

CL.

STOR.

LIN.

BATH

KITCHEN
4⁸
10 x 8

D.W. S.

BATH

LINEN

DINING RM.
9⁸ x 10⁸

AIR
COND.

WASH DRY

UTILITY RM.
17⁰ x 7⁰

REF'G RANGE OVENS

PNTRY

SCREEN

DN.

CL.

RAIL

ENTRY

DN.

BED RM.
11⁰ x 13⁰

LIVING RM.
18⁰ x 13⁰

PORCH

GARAGE
19⁴ x 21⁴

56'-10"

48'-10"

Design T72351 1,862 Sq. Ft.; 22,200 Cu. Ft.

● The extension of the wide over-hanging roof of this distinctive home provides shelter for the walkway to the front door. A raised brick planter adds appeal to the outstanding exterior design. The living patterns offered by this plan are delightfully different, yet ex-tremely practical. Notice the separation of the master bedroom from the other two bedrooms. While assuring an extra measure of quiet privacy for the parents, this master bedroom location may be ideal for a live-in-relative. Locating the kitchen in the middle of the plan frees up valuable outside wall space and leads to interesting planning. The front living room is sunken for dramatic appeal and need not have any cross-room traffic. The utility room houses the laundry and the heating and cooling equipment.

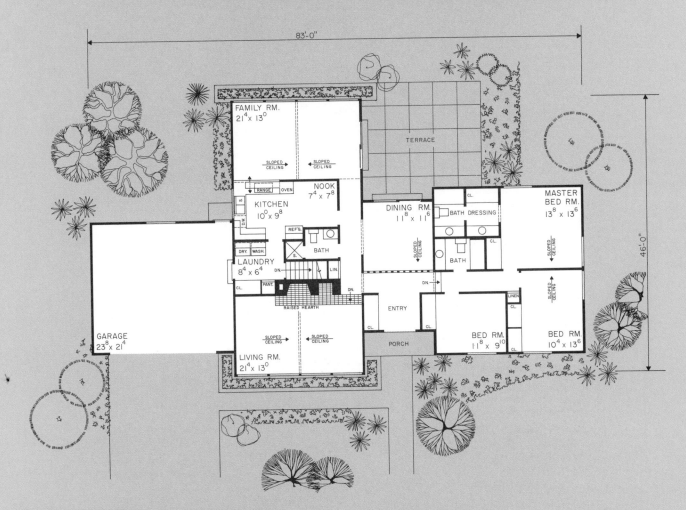

FAMILY RM. 21⁴ x 13⁰

TERRACE

SLOPED CEILING   SLOPED CEILING

NOOK 7⁴ x 7⁸

RANGE   OVEN

KITCHEN 10⁰ x 9⁸

REF'G.

DINING RM. 11⁸ x 11⁶

BATH   DRESSING

CL.

MASTER BED RM. 13⁸ x 13⁶

SLOPED CEILING

DRY.   WASH.

BATH

LAUNDRY 8⁴ x 6⁴

DN.   LIN.

SLOPED CEILING

CL.

BATH

CL.

PANT.

DN.

GARAGE 23⁸ x 21⁴

RAISED HEARTH

ENTRY

CL.   CL.

LINEN

CL.

SLOPED CEILING

SLOPED CEILING   SLOPED CEILING

PORCH

BED RM. 11⁸ x 9¹⁰

CL.

BED RM. 10⁴ x 13⁶

LIVING RM. 21⁴ x 13⁰

83'-0"

46'-0"

Design T72363 *1,978 Sq. Ft.; 27,150 Cu. Ft.*

● You will have a lot of fun deciding what you like best about this home with its eye-catching glass-gabled living room and wrap-around raised planter. A covered porch shelters the double front doors. Projecting to the rear is a family room identical in size with the formal living room. Between these two rooms there are features galore. There is the efficient kitchen with pass-thru and informal eating space. Then, there is the laundry with a closet, pantry and the basement stairs nearby. Also, a full bath featuring a stall shower. The dining room has a sloped ceiling and an appealing, open vertical divider which acts as screening from the entry. The three bedroom, two bath sleeping zone is sunken. The raised hearth fireplace in the living room has an adjacent wood box.

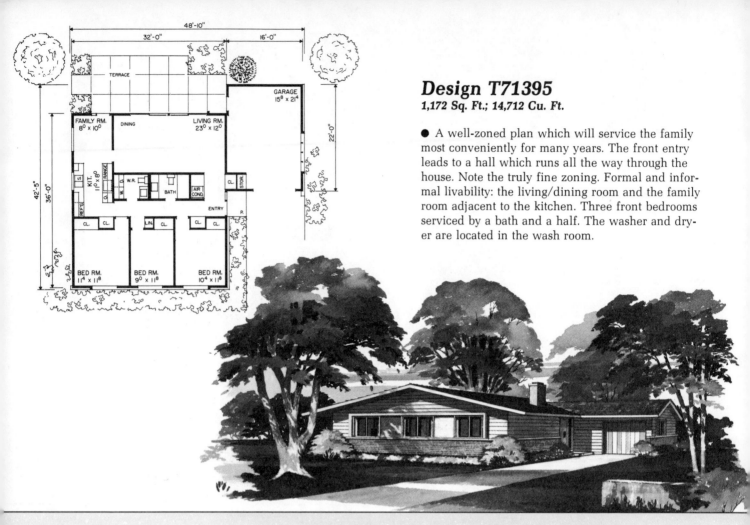

Design T71395
1,172 Sq. Ft.; 14,712 Cu. Ft.

● A well-zoned plan which will service the family most conveniently for many years. The front entry leads to a hall which runs all the way through the house. Note the truly fine zoning. Formal and informal livability: the living/dining room and the family room adjacent to the kitchen. Three front bedrooms serviced by a bath and a half. The washer and dryer are located in the wash room.

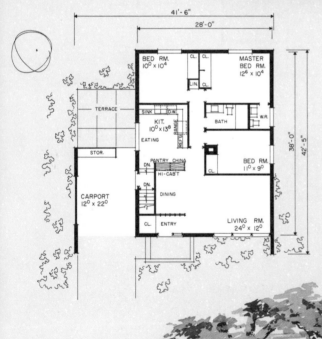

Design T71808
1,118 Sq. Ft.; 19,952 Cu. Ft.

● Contemporary design takes many forms. It is noted for its straight-forward simplicity and its effective use of materials. This appealing design reflects a pleasing use of brick masses and large glass areas. The low-pitched roof has a wide overhang which helps maintain that desired ground-hugging appearance. Cleverly planned, each square foot makes its contribution to complete livability. A full basement adds extra space for hobbies and recreation. The attached carport shields the service entrance and functions with the outdoor terrace.

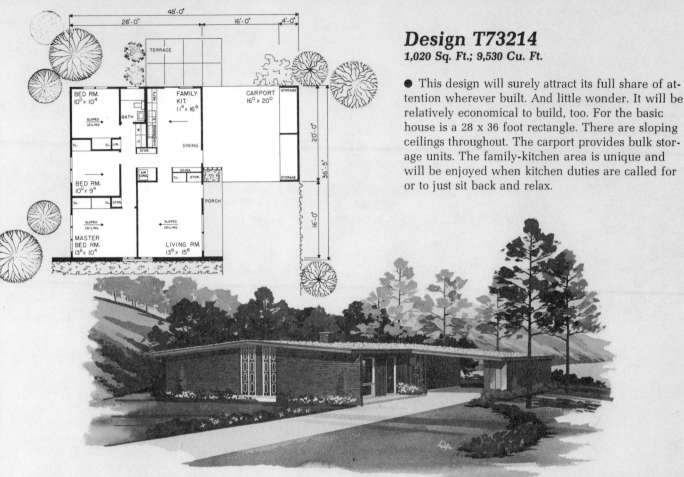

Design T73214
1,020 Sq. Ft.; 9,530 Cu. Ft.

● This design will surely attract its full share of attention wherever built. And little wonder. It will be relatively economical to build, too. For the basic house is a 28 x 36 foot rectangle. There are sloping ceilings throughout. The carport provides bulk storage units. The family-kitchen area is unique and will be enjoyed when kitchen duties are called for or to just sit back and relax.

Design T71379
864 Sq. Ft.; 8,778 Cu. Ft.

● This low-cost, efficiently-planned, house is custom-designed for a retired person or couple. The compact arrangement of rooms all on one level makes it easy to move from one area to another, inside or out, quickly and without exertion. A large hobby and storage room is ideal for pursuing favorite projects, such as woodworking or gardening. Sliding glass doors across the back of living-dining area make terrace easily accessible from kitchen for outdoor meals and entertaining. Each of the two bedrooms has a built-in chest adjacent to closet.

Design T72591 1,428 Sq. Ft.; 21,725 Cu. Ft.

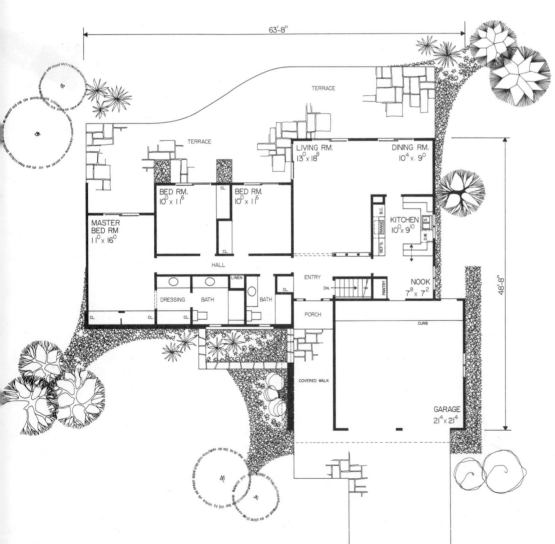

● A flowing terrace! The point of unity between interior and exterior in this distinctive home. This unusual terrace is accessible from every room except the kitchen . . . but designed to provide privacy as well. Inside, the spacious living and dining rooms feature two sets of sliding glass doors onto the terrace . . . allowing parties to spill outside during warm weather. And offering a scenic view all year round. Three bedrooms, all with sliding doors onto the terrace. Including a master suite with a dressing room and private bath. Plus its own secluded section of the terrace . . . perfect for solitary sunbathing or romantic nightcaps. Good times and easy work! There's an efficient kitchen with lots of work space and a large storage pantry. Plus a separate breakfast nook to make casual meals convenient and pleasant. This home creates its own peaceful enviroment! It's especially pleasing to people who love the outdoors.

Design T72702
1,636 Sq. Ft.; 38,700 Cu. Ft.

● A rear living room with a sloping ceiling, built-in bookcases, a raised hearth fireplace and sliding glass doors to the rear living terrace highlight this design. If desired, bi-fold doors permit this room to function with the adjacent study. An open railing next to the stairs to the basement recreation area fosters additional spaciousness. The kitchen has plenty of cabinet and cupboard space. It features informal eating space and is but a step or two from the separate dining room. Note side dining terrace. Each of the three rooms in the sleeping wing has direct access to outdoor living. The master bedroom highlights a huge walk-in wardrobe closet, dressing room with built-in vanity and private bath with large towel storage closet. Projecting the two-car garage with its twin doors to the front not only contributes to an interesting exterior, but reduces the size of the building site required for this home.

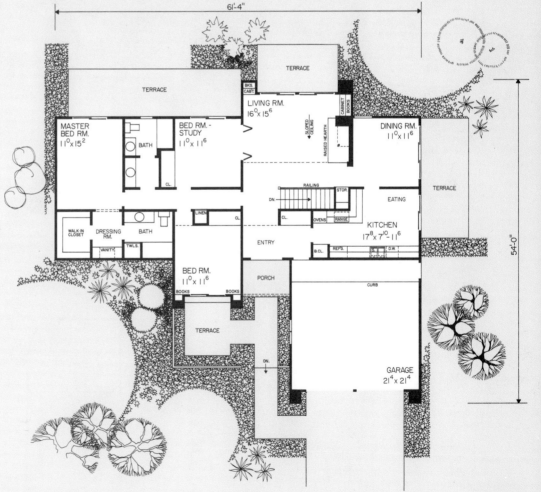

● A well-planned, medium sized contemporary home with plenty of big-house features. The brick line of the projected bedroom wing extends toward the projected two-car garage to form an attractive front court. The large glass panels below the overhanging roof are a dramatic feature. In addition to the two full baths, there is an extra wash room easily accessible from the kitchen/family room area as well as the outdoors. The laundry equipment is strategically located.

Design T71342
1,560 Sq. Ft.; 13,256 Cu. Ft.

● Here is a relatively low-cost home with a majority of the features found in today's high priced homes. The three-bedroom sleeping area highlights two full baths. The living area is a huge room of approximately 25 feet in depth zoned for both formal living and dining activities. The kitchen is extremely well-planned and includes a built-in desk and pantry. The family room has a snack bar and sliding glass doors to the terrace. Blueprints include optional basement details.

Design T71357
1,258 Sq. Ft.; 13,606 Cu. Ft.

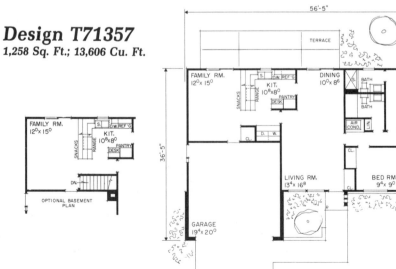

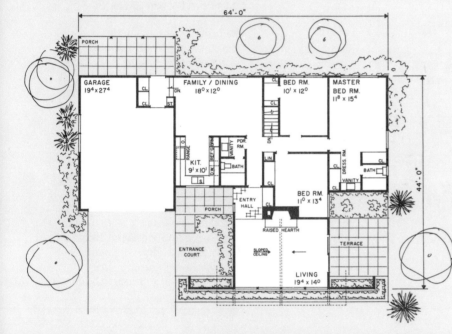

Design T71065
1,492 Sq. Ft.; 24,407 Cu. Ft.

● Here is a refreshing design that reflects all that is so appealing in good up-to-date exterior detailing and practical, efficient floor planning. The low pitched, wide overhanging roof, the glass gabled end with exposed rafters, the raised planter and the extended wing walls are all delightful exterior features. Of particular interest, is the formation of the front entrance court and side terrace resulting from the extension of the front living room wall. Inside, there is much to excite the new occupants. The quietly, formal living room will have plenty of light. The strategically located kitchen is ideal to view approaching callers. Master bedroom with bath, vanity and dressing room housing two closets will be welcomed by the parents.

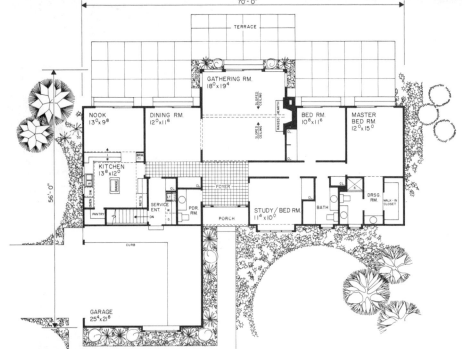

Design T72792
1,944 Sq. Ft.; 37,505 Cu. Ft.

● Indoor-outdoor living hardly could be improved upon in this contemporary design. All of the rear rooms have sliding glass doors to the large terrace. Divide the terrace in three parts and the nook and dining room have access to a dining terrace, the gathering room to a living terrace and two bedrooms to a lounging terrace. A delightful way to bring the outdoors view inside. Other fine features include the efficient kitchen which has plenty of storage space and an island range, a first floor laundry with stairs to the basement and a powder room adjacent to the front door.

Design T72797
1,791 Sq. Ft.; 37,805 Cu. Ft.

● The exterior appeal of this delightful one-story is sure to catch the attention of all who pass by. The overhanging roof adds an extra measure of shading along with the privacy wall which shelters the front court and entry. The floor plan also will be outstanding to include both leisure and formal activities. The gathering room has a sloped ceiling, sliding glass door to rear terrace and a thru-fireplace to the family room. This room also has access to the terrace and it includes the informal eating area. A pass-thru from the U-shaped kitchen to the eating area makes serving a breeze. Formal dining can be done in the front dining room. The laundry area is adjacent to the kitchen and garage and houses a washroom. Peace and quiet can be achieved in the study. The sleeping zone consists of three bedrooms and two full back-to-back baths. Additional space will be found in the basement.

Design T72875
1,913 Sq. Ft.; 36,271 Cu. Ft.

● This elegant Spanish design incorporates excellent indoor-outdoor living relationships for modern families who enjoy the sun and comforts of a well planned new home. Note the overhead openings for rain and sun to fall upon a front garden, while a twin arched entry leads to the front porch and foyer. Inside the floor plan features a modern kitchen with pass-thru to a large gathering room with fireplace. Other features include a dining room, laundry room, a study off the foyer, plus three bedrooms including master bedroom with its own whirlpool.

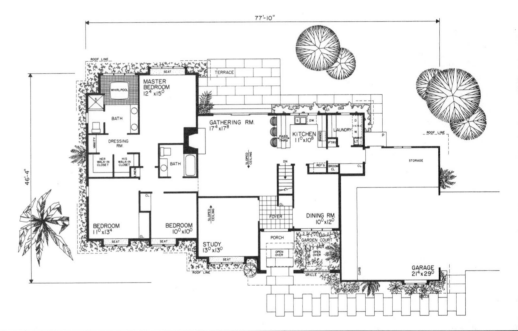

58'-0"

28'-0"

60'-0"

TERRACE

MASTER BED RM. 14⁴ x 11⁴

PDR. RM. VANITY

BATH

WALK-IN CL.

BATH

AIR COND.

LIVING RM. 18⁰ x 13⁸

FAMILY RM. 13⁴ x 17⁰

HEARTH RAISED

SLOPED CEILING

3'-6" HI STORAGE

GLASS GABLE

SLOPED CEILING

CL. CL. LIN.

BED RM. 11⁰ x 13⁶

BED RM. 11⁸ x 10⁰

LIN. CL.

ENTRY

GLASS GRILLE

SLOPED CEILING

DINING RM. 11⁸ x 13⁶

KIT. 13⁴ x 10⁴

RANGE BAR-B-Q

SINK

REF'G

D.W.

LAUND. TRAY

PANTRY

W.R.

MUD RM. 10⁰ x 10⁰

CL.

CURB

GARAGE 21⁴ x 21⁴

Design T71947 1,764 Sq. Ft.; 18,381 Cu. Ft.

● When it comes to housing your family, if you are among the contemporary-minded, you'll want to give this L-shaped design a second, then even a third, or fourth, look. It is available as either a three or four bedroom home. If you desire the three bedroom, 58 foot wide design order blueprints for T71947; for the four bedroom, 62 foot wide design, order T71948. Inside, you will note a continuation of the contemporary theme with sloping ceilings, exposed beams and a practical 42 inch high storage divider between the living and dining rooms. Don't miss the mud rooms.

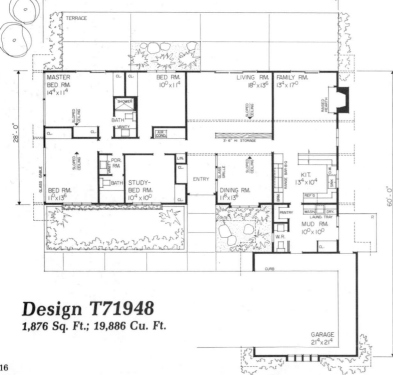

62'-0"

28'-0"

60'-0"

TERRACE

MASTER BED RM. 14⁴ x 11⁴

CL. CL.

BED RM. 10⁰ x 11⁴

SHOWER

BATH

VANITY

AIR COND.

LIVING RM. 18⁰ x 13⁶

FAMILY RM. 13⁴ x 17⁰

RAISED HEARTH

SLOPED CEILING

3'-6" HI STORAGE

GLASS GABLE

SLOPED CEILING

CL.

BED RM. 11⁰ x 13⁶

PDR. RM.

BATH

STUDY-BED RM. 10⁴ x 10⁰

LIN. CL.

ENTRY

GLASS GRILLE

SLOPED CEILING

DINING RM. 11⁸ x 13⁶

KIT. 13⁴ x 10⁴

RANGE BAR-B-Q

SINK

REF'G

D.W.

WASH. DRY.

PANTRY

W.R.

MUD RM. 10⁰ x 10⁰

CURB

Design T71948
1,876 Sq. Ft.; 19,886 Cu. Ft.

GARAGE 21⁴ x 21⁴

Design T72234 1,857 Sq. Ft.; 22,748 Cu. Ft.

● The clean lines of this flat-roof design with privacy wall, side vertical glass, and skylights make it a Contemporary winner. Comforts include a rear family room with fireplace plus built-in desk and bookshelves. A front living room enjoys a fireplace, too, plus view of a side terrace. A modern L-shaped kitchen is situated just adjacent to a laundry room for convenience and also enjoys a view of a rear terrace. All three bedrooms, including a master suite, are isolated for privacy at one end of the house. A large two-car garage includes built-in workbench and storage. Notice the wide front foyer.

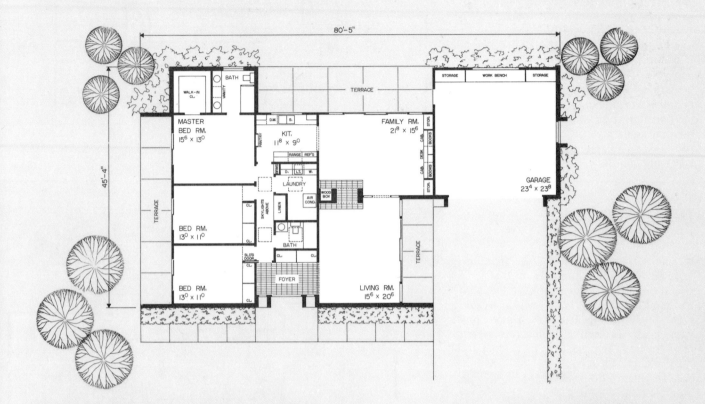

Design T71917
1,728 Sq. Ft.; 32,486 Cu. Ft.

● Imagine your family living in this appealing one-story home. Think of how your living habits will adjust to the delightful patterns offered here. Flexibility is the byword; for there are two living areas — the front, formal living room and the rear, informal family room. There are two dining areas — the dining room overlooking the front yard and the breakfast room looking out upon the rear yard. There are outstanding bath facilities — a full bath for the master bedroom and one that will be handy to the living areas as a powder room. Then there is the extra wash room just where you need it — handy to the kitchen, the basement and the outdoors.

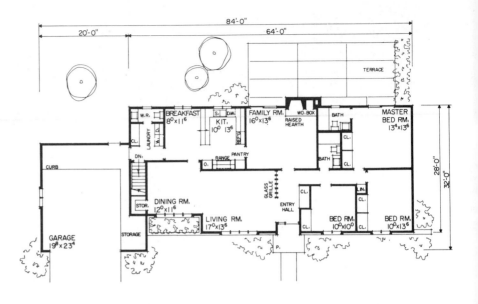

Design T71891
1,986 Sq. Ft.; 23,022 Cu. Ft.

● There is much more to a house than just its exterior. And while the appeal of this home would be difficult to beat, it is the living potential of the interior that gives this design such a high ranking. The sunken living room with its adjacent dining room is highlighted by the attractive fireplace, the raised planter and the distinctive glass panels.
A raised hearth fireplace, snack bar and sliding glass doors which open to the outdoor deck are features of the family room. The work center area is efficient. It has plenty of storage space and a laundry area.

Design T71396
1,664 Sq. Ft.; 30,229 Cu. Ft.

● Three bedrooms, 2½ baths, a formal dining area, a fine family room and an attached two-car garage are among the highlights of this frame home. The living-dining area is delightfully spacious with the fireplace wall, having book shelves at each end, functioning as a practical area divider. The many storage units found in this home will be a topic of conversion. The cabinets above the strategically located washer and dryer, the family room storage wall and walk-in closet and the garage facilities are particularly noteworthy. Blueprints show how to build this house with and without a basement.

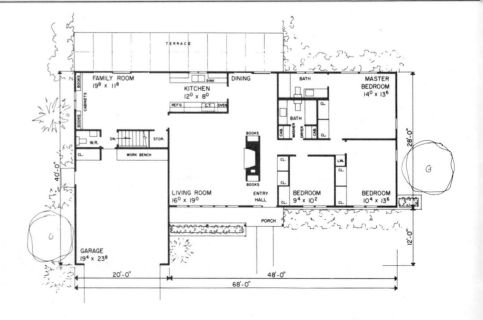

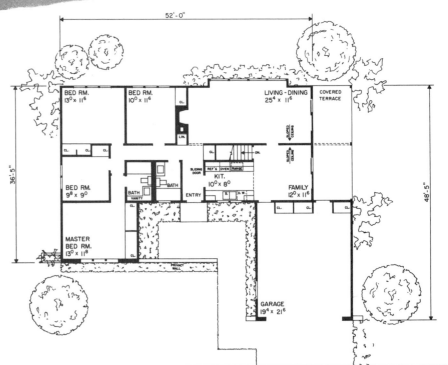

Design T73207
1,460 Sq. Ft.; 25,068 Cu. Ft.

● Four bedrooms to satisfy the sleeping requirements of the large or growing family. In addition, there are two full baths nearby. They have a common plumbing wall to enable the installation of these two baths to represent a worthwhile savings. The bath for the master bedroom is also handy to the other three bedrooms. It has a built-in vanity. The main bath is strategically located only a few steps from the kitchen as well as the living area. The kitchen is conveniently located near the front door with the kitchen window overseeing the front yard. The living/dining room will enjoy the fireplace wall. Along with the living/dining room, the family room has sloped ceiling and access to the covered terrace.

Design T71943 1,565 Sq. Ft.; 17,985 Cu. Ft.

● This home will be a great investment. It starts right out representing economy because it will not require a wide expensive building site. The projecting two-car garage in no way affects the modest, overall, 50 foot width of the house. The favorable economics go even further. In less than 1,600 square feet there is a long list of convenient living features. They begin, of course, with the four sizable bedrooms. Two full baths with back-to-back plumbing will adequately serve the large family. A spacious living room overlooks the rear terrace and has a glass grille room divider. It also features fine wall space for flexible furniture placement. The informal, all-purpose family room functions with the kitchen and terrace.

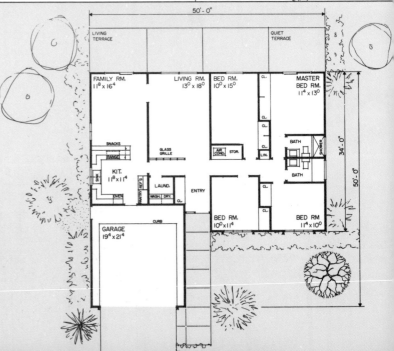

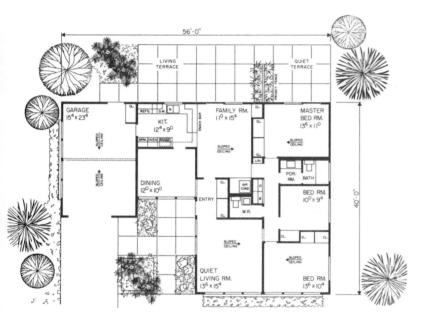

Design T71057
1,320 Sq. Ft.; 13,741 Cu. Ft.

● Here is a relatively small contemporary with 1,320 square feet that is just loaded with livability. Its overall dimension of 56 feet means that it won't require a big, expensive piece of property either. The flexibility of the floor planning is great, too. Notice the room locations. The three bedrooms and compartmented bath occupy the far end of the house. The living room is by itself and will have privacy. The dining room is next to the kitchen and enjoys a view of the front court area. The family room functions ideally with the kitchen and the rear terrace. Other features include the wash room, the sloped ceilings, the snack bar, the attached garage, sliding glass doors and an abundance of closets.

221

Design T71281
1,190 Sq. Ft.; 21,920 Cu. Ft.

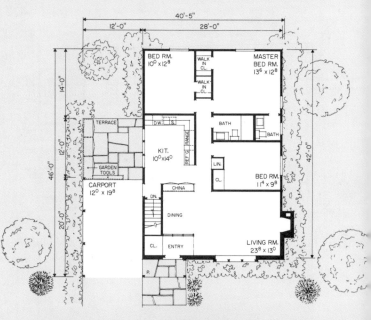

● Whatever you call it, contemporary or traditional, or even transitional, the prudent incorporation of newer with old design features results in a pleasant facade. The window and door detailing is obviously from an early era; while the low-pitched roof and the carport are features of relatively more recent vintage. Inside, there is an efficient plan which lends itself to the activities of the small family. As a home for a retired couple, or a young newlywed couple, this will be a fine investment. Certainly it will not require a big, expensive piece of property. The plan offers two full baths, three bedrooms, an excellent L-shaped kitchen, 23-foot living and dining area and a basement. Note side terrace.

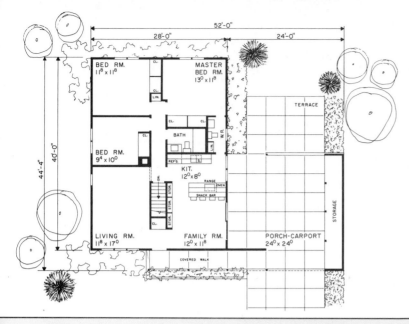

Design T73195
1,120 Sq. Ft.; 20,440 Cu. Ft.

● This 28 x 40 foot rectangle is a fine example of how delightful and refreshing contemporary design can become. Though simple in basic construction and floor planning, this home has an abundance of exterior appeal and interior livability. Observe the low-pitched, wide overhanging roof, the attached 24 foot square covered porch/carport, the effective glass area and vertical siding, plus the raised planter. The center entrance is flanked by the formal living room and the informal, all-purpose family room. A snack bar is accessible from the kitchen. Sliding glass doors lead to the outdoor living area. In addition to the main bath there is an extra wash room handy to both the master bedroom and the kitchen.

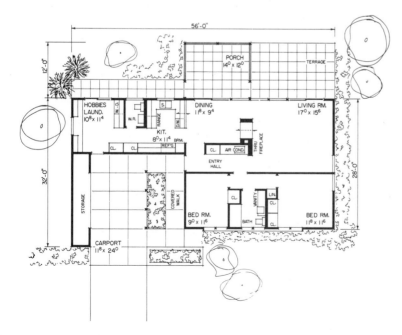

Design T71216
1,184 Sq. Ft,; 10,656 Cu. Ft.

● Whether called upon to function as a home for a retired couple or for a small family, this frame, non-basement design will provide wonderful livability. The covered walk with its adjacent planting areas makes for a pleasing approach to the front door. The thru-fireplace may be enjoyed from both formal areas—the living room and the separate dining room. Glass sliding doors lead to the cheerful enclosed porch. A pass-thru from the kitchen facilitates the serving of meals in the dining area. A wash room is conveniently located between the kitchen and hobbies/laundry room and is handy from the outdoors. The general area has an abundance of counter, cupboard and closet space.

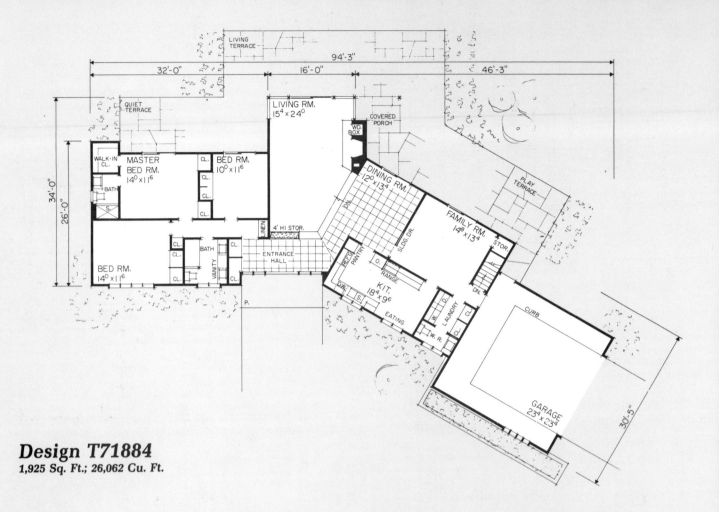

Design T71884
1,925 Sq. Ft.; 26,062 Cu. Ft.

● If you are searching for something with an air of distinction both inside and out then search no more. You could hardly improve upon what this home has to offer. You will forever be proud of the impressive hip-roof, angular facade. Its interest will give it an identity all its own. As for the interior, your everyday living patterns will be a delight, indeed. And little wonder, clever zoning and a fine feeling of spaciousness set the stage. As you stand in the entrance hall, you look across the tip of a four foot high planter into the sunken living room. Having an expanse of floor space, the wall of windows and the raised hearth fireplace, the view will be dramatic. Notice covered porch, play terrace and quiet terrace which will provide great outdoor enjoyment.

Design T72106
1,520 Sq. Ft.; 30,658 Cu. Ft.

● Take a serious look at this highly integrated plan. It has a simple, straightforward, up-to-date exterior which will be pleasing on any site, whether out in the country or on a city block. The interior design will be just as pleasing and serve the family admirably for many years. Three bedrooms, one-and-a-half baths, formal and informal living areas plus a basement for additional space are just a portion of the delightful qualities that this home has to offer.

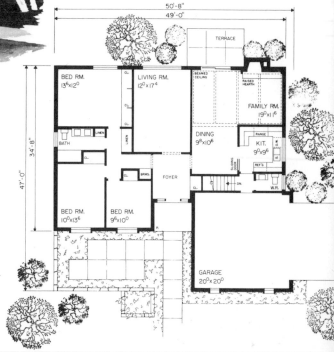

Design T71254
1,588 Sq. Ft.; 24,181 Cu. Ft.

● This is a great home for a relatively narrow building site. Measuring only 48 feet in width, this home could be located on almost any lot. The L-shaped configuration conveniently provides an area for a pool or an exceptionally large terrace or garden. In either case it will be a great place to enjoy the outdoors. The indoors will be enjoyed in the many conveniently located rooms including both formal and informal areas.

225

Design T73203
1,291 Sq. Ft.; 23,625 Cu. Ft.

● The degree to which your family's living patterns will be efficient will depend upon the soundness of the basic floor plan. Here is an exceptionally practical arrangment for a medium sized home. Traffic patterns will be most flexible. The work area is strategically located close to the front door and it will function ideally with both the indoor and outdoor informal living areas. The master bath will serve the living room and the sleeping area. The second bath will serve the work area, the family room and third bedroom. Note stall shower.

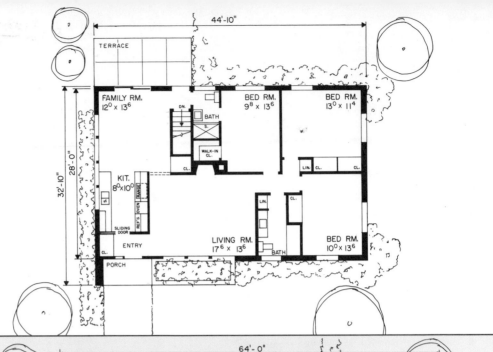

Design T73212
1,493 Sq. Ft.; 16,074 Cu. Ft.

● Imagine ushering your first visitors through the front door of your new home. After you have placed their coats in the big closet in the front entry, you will show them your three sizable bedrooms and the two full baths. Next, you will take them through the separate dining area, the efficient kitchen and into the large family room with its wall of built-in storage units. Your visitors will comment about the sliding glass doors which open onto the terrace from the family room.

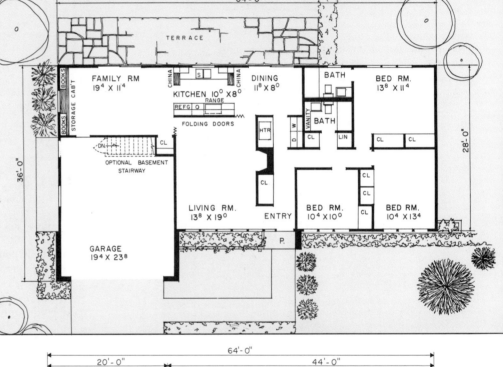

Design T71072
1,232 Sq. Ft.; 22,484 Cu. Ft.

● Low-pitched overhanging roof, vertical siding and patterned masonry screen wall create a charming exterior for this house. A fireplace divides the living room from the entry hall. Seven-foot high cabinets separate the kitchen from the living/dining area. The dining area opens through sliding glass doors to a private covered porch and the rear terrace. The informal area is enhanced by a wall of windows overlooking the terrace and a three-foot high built-in planter. For recreation and bulk storage there is a full basement.

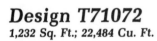
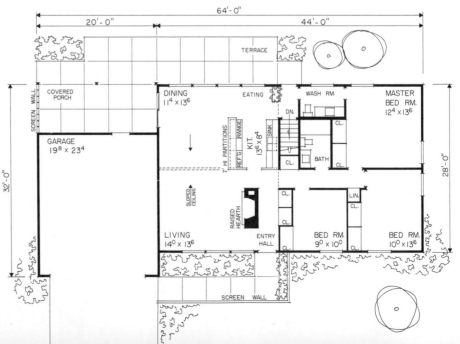

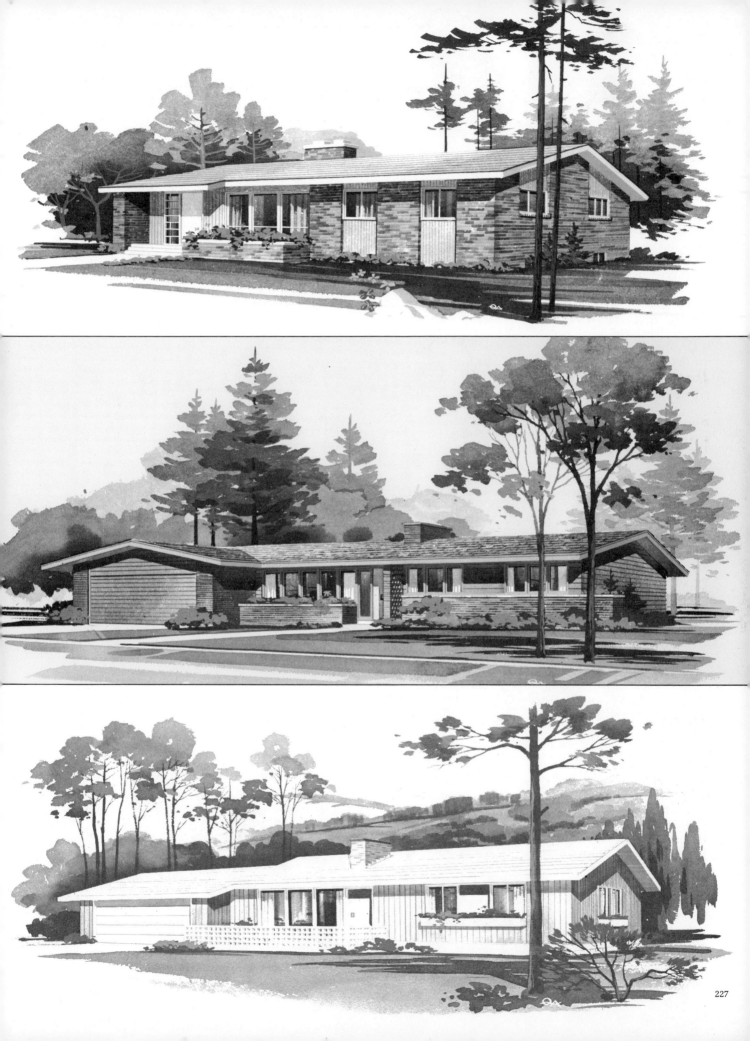

Design T72824
1,550 Sq. Ft.; 34,560 Cu. Ft.

● Low-maintenance and economy in building are the outstanding exterior features of this sharp, one-story design. It is sheathed in long-lasting cedar siding and trimmed with stone for an eye-appealing facade. Entrance to this home takes you through a charming garden courtyard. Then through a covered walk to the front porch. The garage, extending from the front of the house, serves two purposes; to reduce lot size and to buffer the interior of the house from street noise. Sliding glass doors are featured in each of the main rooms for easy access to the outdoors. A sun porch is tucked between the study and gathering rooms. Optional non-basement details are included with the purchase of this design.

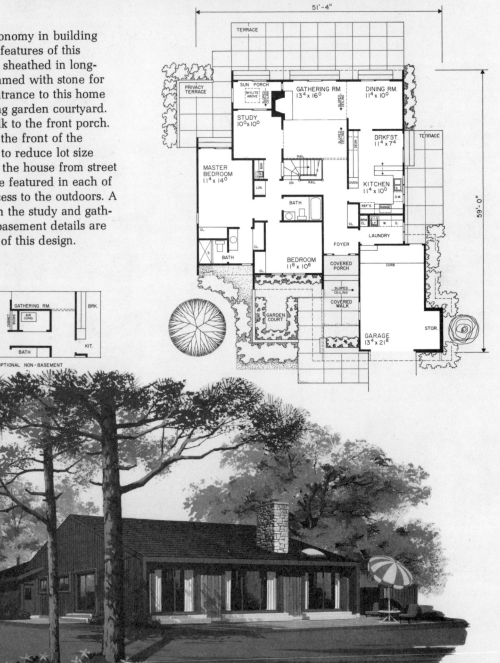

Design T72706 1,746 Sq. Ft.; 36,800 Cu. Ft.

● Here's a Contemporary design with a choice of exteriors. You can select the above Contemporary exterior, T72706, the French facade in T72705, or the Traditional exterior in T72704. All come with the same Contemporary floor plan with careful attention to modern living patterns. Note the large gathering room with raised-hearth fireplace and sliding glass doors that lead to a rear terrace. The adjacent master bedroom and dining room also are accessible to terrace by sliding glass doors. A modern kitchen includes a handy dining nook. There's a formal dining room, too. All three bedrooms are isolated for privacy at one end of the house. The 19-foot entry off the covered porch is impressive and offers double entry to the gathering room.

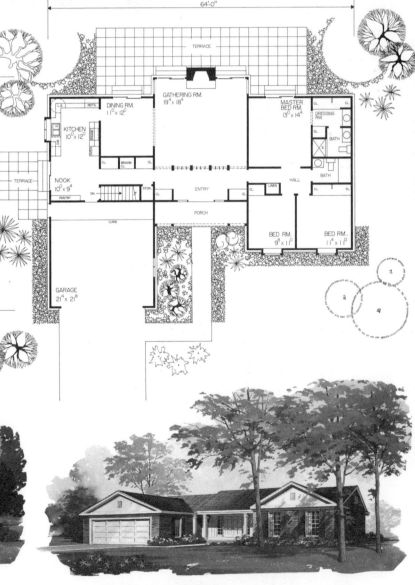

Design T72705 1,746 Sq. Ft.; 37,000 Cu. Ft.

Design T72704 1,746 Sq. ft.; 38,000 Cu. Ft.

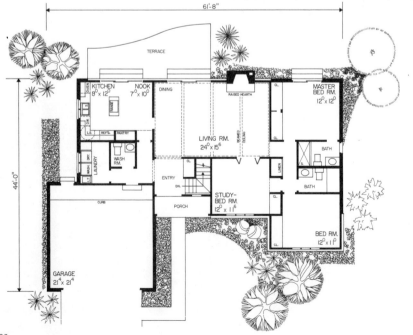

Design T72565
1,540 Sq. Ft.; 33,300 Cu. Ft.

● This modest sized floor plan has much to offer in the way of livability. It may function as either a two or three bedroom home. The living room is huge and features a fine, raised hearth fireplace. The open stairway to the basement is handy and will lead to what may be developed as the recreation area. In addition to the two full baths, there is an extra washroom. Adjacent is the laundry room and the service entrance from the garage. The blueprints you order for this design will show details for each of the three delightful elevations above. Which is your favorite? The Tudor, the Colonial or the Contemporary?

Design T72505
1,366 Sq. Ft.; 29,329 Cu. Ft.

● This design offers you a choice of three distinctively different exteriors. Which is your favorite? Blueprints show details for all three optional elevations. A study of the floor plan reveals a fine measure of livability. In less than 1,400 square feet there are features galore. An excellent return on your construction dollar. In addition to the two eating areas and the open planning of the gathering room, the indoor-outdoor relationships are of great interest. The basement may be developed for recreational activities. Be sure to note the storage potential, particularly the linen closet, the pantry, the china cabinet and the broom closet.

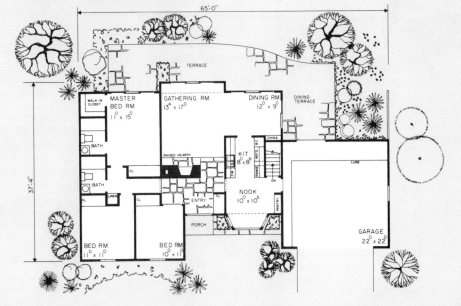

Design T71387
1,488 Sq. Ft.; 16,175 Cu. Ft.

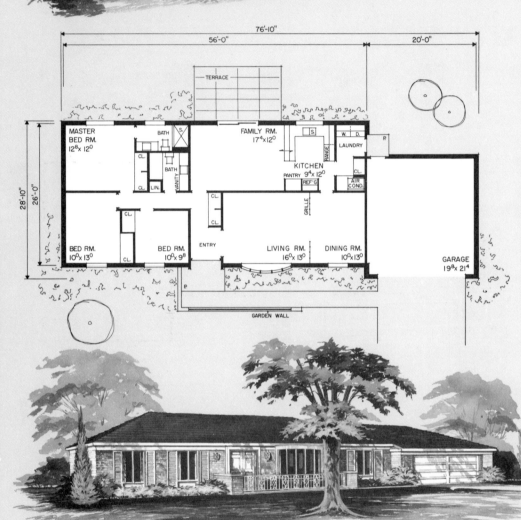

● Your choice of exterior goes with this Contemporary floor plan. If your tastes include a liking for Contemporary facades, then Design T71387 above will provide a lifetime of satisfaction. On the other hand, should you prefer French Provincial, then Design T71389 below may be your choice. Those who enjoy the warmth and charm of Colonial adaptations will probably select Design T71388 at bottom. Contrast the varying window treatments on the three different exteriors, plus the contrasting treatments of double front doors, garage doors, and roof lines. Regardless of your choice of exteriors, this three-bedroom floor plan offers efficent zoning, good traffic patterns, and comfort to suit modern lifestyles.

Design T71389
1,488 Sq. Ft.; 18,600 Cu. Ft.

Design T71388
1,488 Sq. Ft.; 18,600 Cu. Ft.

Design T71865
1,589 Sq. Ft.; 25,626 Cu. Ft.

● Here's a compact three-bed-room floor plan with a choice of contrasting exteriors. If you prefer the sleek, straightforward look of Contemporary styling, then Design T71865 likely will be your choice. But perhaps you prefer the more distinctive colonial appearance of Design T71864 below. Maybe you will select the formal hip-roof exterior of French styling in Design T71866 at bottom. Regardless of your choice of facades, you're certain to appreciate the delightful proportions of this floor plan, designed for modern family lifestyles. The floor plan features two and a half baths, formal living and dining rooms, a snack bar, and mud room. In the Contemporary design, the master bedroom has a window located in the left side of the elevation wall. Each exterior highlights an effective use of wood siding and stone (or brick in the case of French Design T71886).

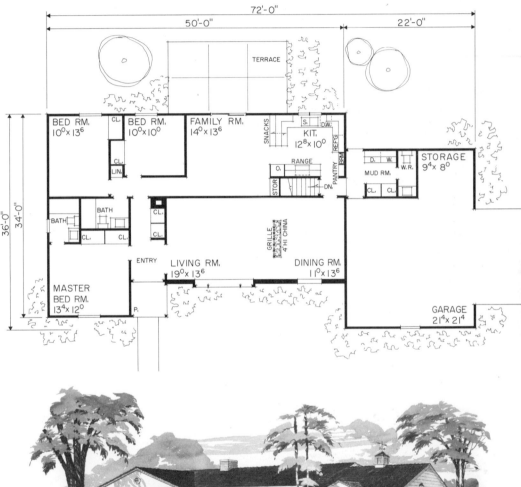

Design T71864
1,598 Sq. Ft.; 27,611 Cu. Ft.

Design T71866
1,598 Sq. Ft.; 27,248 Cu. Ft.

Design T71383
1,382 Sq. Ft.; 15,448 Cu. Ft.

● This efficient modern floor plan with choice of exterior styles includes three bedrooms, two full baths, separate dining room, formal living room, modern kitchen, plus an informal family room in less than 1,400 square feet. This represents a bargain in home planning. The plan also includes an attached two-car garage plus optional basement. Each of the exteriors you may select is predominantly brick. The Contemporary styling facade is Design T71383 above. Traditional Design T71305 below features both stone and vertical boards and battens with brick on the other three sides. Note the double front doors of French Design T71382 at bottom. Notice the difference in window treatments. Observe the location of stairs when this plan is built with a basement.

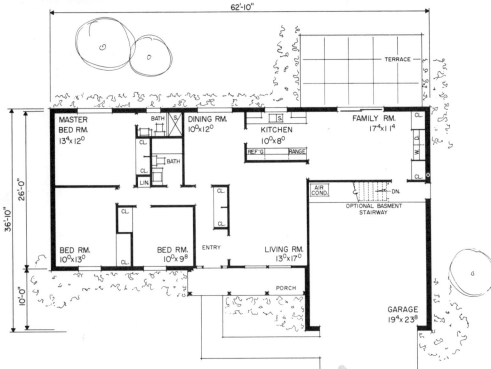

Floor plan annotations:

62'-10"

MASTER BED RM. 13⁴x12⁰

BATH

DINING RM. 10⁰x12⁰

KITCHEN 10⁰x8⁰

FAMILY RM. 17⁴x11⁴

TERRACE

CL.

BATH

CL.

LIN.

REF'G RANGE

W. D.

CL.

36'-10"   26'-0"   10'-0"

BED RM. 10⁰x13⁰

CL.

CL.

BED RM. 10⁰x9⁸

CL.

CL.

ENTRY

AIR COND.

OPTIONAL BASMENT STAIRWAY

DN.

LIVING RM. 13⁰x17⁰

PORCH

GARAGE 19⁴x23⁸

Design T71305
1,382 Sq. Ft.; 16,584 Cu. Ft.

Design T71382
1,382 Sq. Ft.; 17,164 Cu. Ft.

Design T71307 1,357 Sq. Ft.; 14,476 Cu. Ft.

● These three stylish exteriors have the same practical, L-shaped floor plan. Design T71307 (above) features a low-pitched, wide-overhanging roof, a pleasing use of horizontal siding and brick and an enclosed front flower court. Design T71380 (below) has its charm characterized by the pediment gables, the effective window treatment and the masses of brick. Design T71381 (bottom) is captivating because of its hip-roof, its dentils, panelled shutters and lamppost. Each of these three designs has a covered front porch. Inside, there is an abundance of livability. The formal living and dining area is spacious, and the U-shaped kitchen is efficient. There is informal eating space, a separate laundry and a fine family room. Note the sliding glass doors to the terrace. The blueprints include details for building either with or without a basement. Observe the pantry of the non-basement plan.

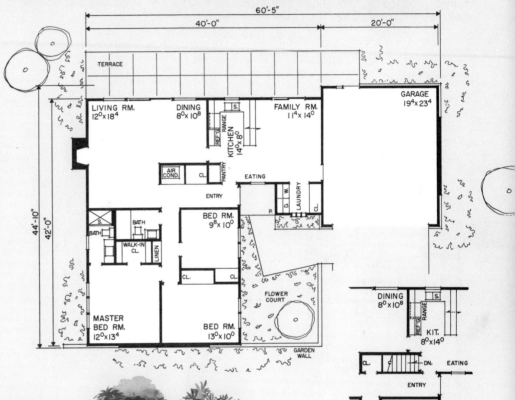

Design T71380
1,399 Sq. Ft.; 17,937 Cu. Ft.

Design T71381
1,399 Sq. Ft.; 17,937 Cu. Ft.

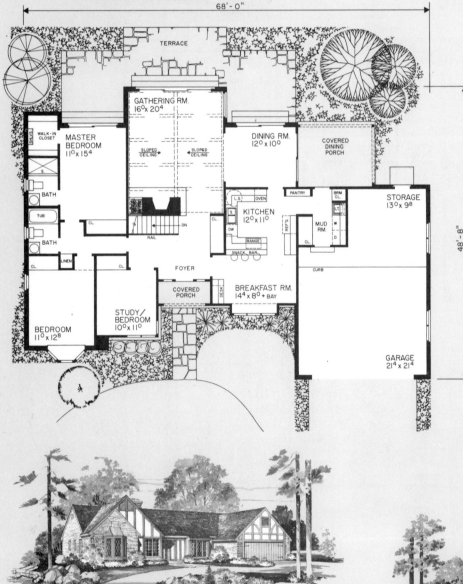

68'-0"

TERRACE

GATHERING RM.
16⁰ x 20⁴

SLOPED CEILING   SLOPED CEILING

MASTER BEDROOM
11⁰ x 15⁴

WALK-IN CLOSET

BATH

TUB

BATH

DINING RM.
12⁰ x 10⁰

COVERED DINING PORCH

PANTRY

OVEN

L.S.

KITCHEN
12⁰ x 11⁰

DW

RANGE

SNACK BAR

RAIL   DN

STORAGE
13⁰ x 9⁸

MUD RM.

BRM. CL.

W

D

48'-8"

FOYER

COVERED PORCH

DESK

BREAKFAST RM.
14⁴ x 8⁰ + BAY

CURB

BEDROOM
11⁰ x 12⁸

STUDY/BEDROOM
10⁰ x 11⁰

LINEN

CL.

CL.

GARAGE
21⁴ x 21⁴

Design T72803
1,679 Sq. Ft.; 36,755 Cu. Ft.

● This modern one-story house with optional non-basement plan comes in your choice of three exterior styles. Contemporary Design T72803 above mixes fieldstone and vertical wood siding on its facade. Tudor Design T72802 below combines half-timbered stucco and brick for its English facade. (Note the authentic bay window in the front bedroom.) Spanish-inspired Design T72804 at bottom employs stuccoed arches, multi-paned windows, and a gracefully sloped roof for its facade. All three exciting exteriors share one modern and efficient floor plan with three bedrooms (or two bedrooms with optional study).

M.B.R.   GATHERING RM.   D.R.

CL.

AIR COND.

CL.   K.

FOYER

STUDY   PORCH   B.R.

OPTIONAL NON - BASEMENT

Design T72802
1,729 Sq. Ft.; 42,640 Cu. Ft.

Design T72804
1,674 Sq. Ft.; 35,465 Cu. Ft.

Design T72807
1,576 Sq. Ft.; 35,355 Cu. Ft.

● This modern three-bedroom plan comes in three different exterior styles, each giving the house an entirely new personality. Contemporary Design T72807 above features sleek, clean lines. Traditional Design T72805 below becomes a romantic stone-and-shingle cottage. English Tudor Design T72806 at bottom is a brick and half-timbered stucco facade. All share floor plans designed for modern living patterns. A breakfast room off the kitchen/snack bar commands its own jutting view of the backyard. Adjacent are a dining room and large sloped-ceiling living room with fireplace. The living room commands a view of the side yard and rear.

58'-0"

50'-4"

COVERED PORCH

SKYLIGHT   SKYLIGHT   SKYLIGHT

BRKFST. RM.
13⁴ x 11¹⁰

LIVING RM.
13⁴ x 17²

DINING RM.
8⁰ x 9¹⁰

SNACK BAR

MUD RM.

STORAGE

KITCHEN
13⁴ x 9⁶

OVEN   REF'G.

FOYER

BATH

TV/STUDY BEDROOM
10⁰ x 10⁴

COVERED PORCH

GARAGE
19⁸ x 19⁰ + STOR.

WALK-IN CLOSET

MASTER BEDROOM
13⁶ x 12⁰

BEDROOM
13⁶ x 10⁸ + BAY

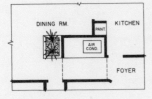

DINING RM.   KITCHEN

PANT.   AIR COND.

FOYER

OPTIONAL NON-BASEMENT

Design T72806
1,584 Sq. Ft.; 41,880 Cu. Ft.

Design T72805
1,547 Sq. Ft.; 40,880 Cu. Ft.

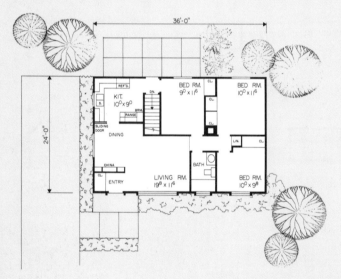

Design T72167
864 Sq. Ft.; 16,554 Cu. Ft.

● This 36' x 24' contemporary rectangle will be economical to build whether you construct the basement design at left, T72167, or the non-basement version below, T72168.

Design T72168
864 Sq. Ft.; 9,244 Cu. Ft.

● This non-basement design features a storage room and a laundry area with cupboards above the washer and dryer. Notice the kitchen eating space.

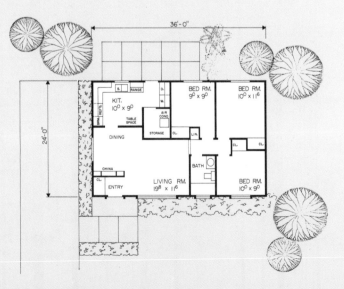

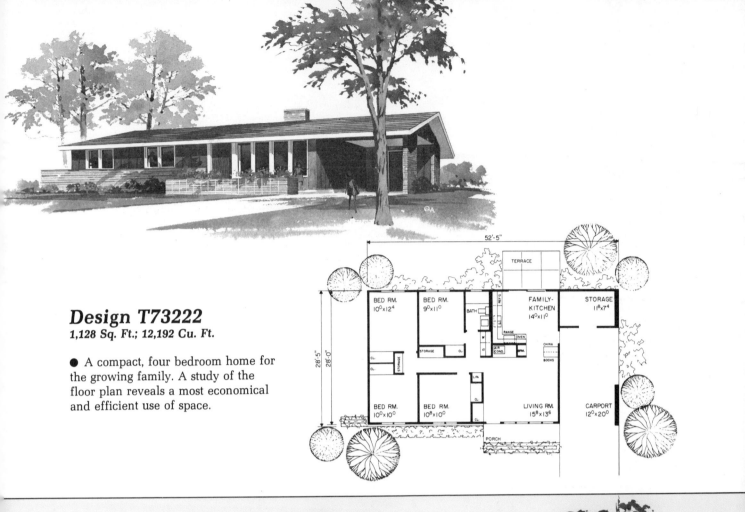

Design T73222
1,128 Sq. Ft.; 12,192 Cu. Ft.

● A compact, four bedroom home for the growing family. A study of the floor plan reveals a most economical and efficient use of space.

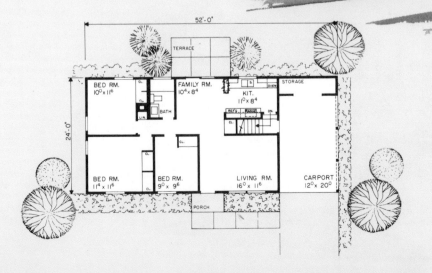

Design T73224
960 Sq. Ft.; 17,453 Cu. Ft.

● This three bedroom frame home has a wide overhanging hip-roof and an attached carport with a storage unit. Family room-kitchen area is spacious.

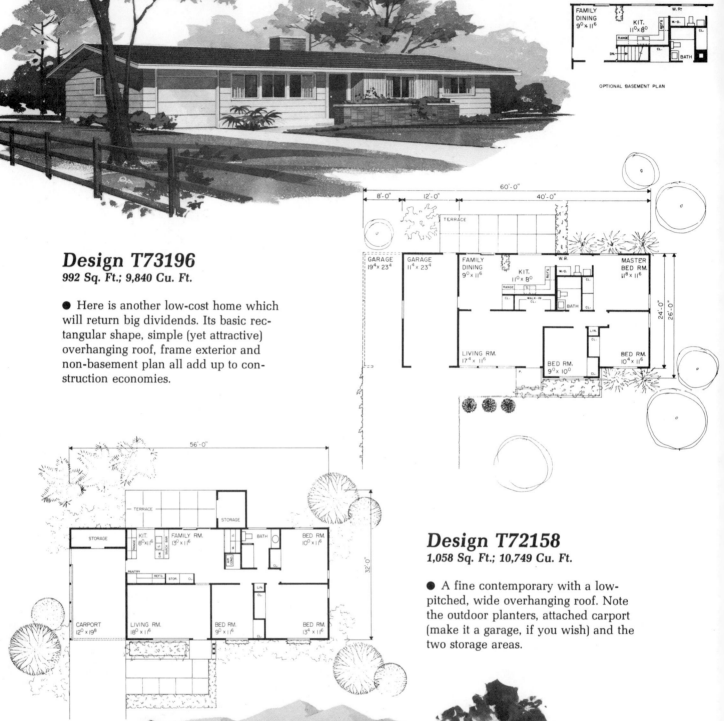

FAMILY DINING 9⁰ x 11⁶
KIT. 11⁰ x 8⁰
W. R.
BATH

OPTIONAL BASEMENT PLAN

Design T73196
992 Sq. Ft.; 9,840 Cu. Ft.

● Here is another low-cost home which will return big dividends. Its basic rectangular shape, simple (yet attractive) overhanging roof, frame exterior and non-basement plan all add up to construction economies.

TERRACE
60'-0"
8'-0" 12'-0" 40'-0"

GARAGE 19⁴ x 23⁴
GARAGE 11⁴ x 23⁴
FAMILY DINING 9⁰ x 11⁶
KIT. 11⁰ x 8⁰
W. R.
MASTER BED RM. 11⁸ x 11⁶
BATH
WALK-IN CL.
24'-0"
26'-0"
LIVING RM. 17⁴ x 11⁶
BED RM. 9⁰ x 10⁰
LIN
BED RM. 10⁴ x 11⁶

56'-0"

TERRACE
STORAGE
STORAGE
KIT. 8⁰ x 11⁶
FAMILY RM. 13⁰ x 11⁶
BATH
BED RM. 10⁰ x 11⁶
32'-0"
PANTRY
CARPORT 12⁰ x 19⁸
LIVING RM. 18⁰ x 11⁶
BED RM. 9⁰ x 11⁶
BED RM. 13⁴ x 11⁶
LIN

Design T72158
1,058 Sq. Ft.; 10,749 Cu. Ft.

● A fine contemporary with a low-pitched, wide overhanging roof. Note the outdoor planters, attached carport (make it a garage, if you wish) and the two storage areas.

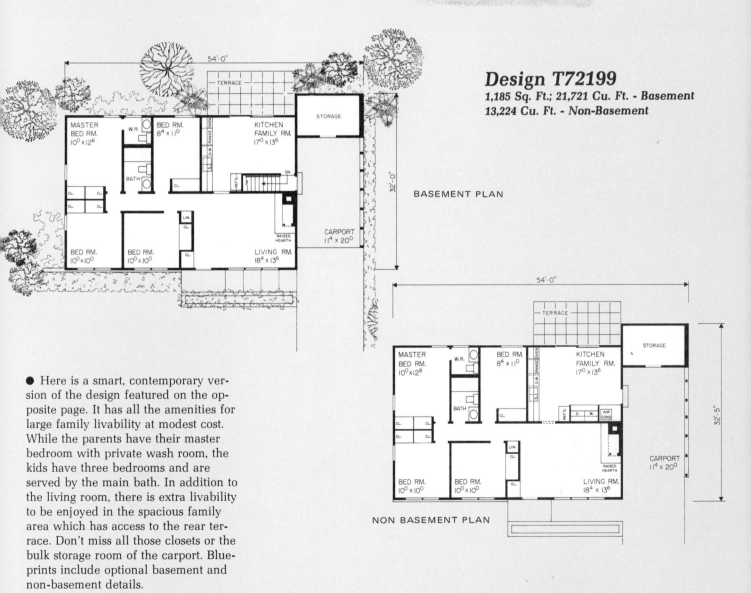

Design T72199
1,185 Sq. Ft.; 21,721 Cu. Ft. - Basement
13,224 Cu. Ft. - Non-Basement

BASEMENT PLAN

54'-0"

TERRACE

MASTER BED RM.
$10^0 \times 12^6$

W.R.

BED RM.
$8^4 \times 11^0$

BATH

KITCHEN FAMILY RM.
$17^0 \times 13^6$

STORAGE

32'-0"

DN.

REFG.

BED RM.
$10^0 \times 10^0$

BED RM.
$10^0 \times 10^0$

LIN.
CL.

LIVING RM.
$18^4 \times 13^6$

RAISED HEARTH

CARPORT
$11^4 \times 20^0$

NON BASEMENT PLAN

54'-0"

TERRACE

MASTER BED RM.
$10^0 \times 12^8$

W.R.

BATH

BED RM.
$8^4 \times 11^0$

KITCHEN FAMILY RM.
$17^0 \times 13^6$

STORAGE

32'-5"

REF'G.

D.

W.

AIR COND.

BED RM.
$10^0 \times 10^0$

BED RM.
$10^0 \times 10^0$

LIN.
CL.

LIVING RM.
$18^4 \times 13^6$

RAISED HEARTH

CARPORT
$11^4 \times 20^0$

● Here is a smart, contemporary version of the design featured on the opposite page. It has all the amenities for large family livability at modest cost. While the parents have their master bedroom with private wash room, the kids have three bedrooms and are served by the main bath. In addition to the living room, there is extra livability to be enjoyed in the spacious family area which has access to the rear terrace. Don't miss all those closets or the bulk storage room of the carport. Blueprints include optional basement and non-basement details.

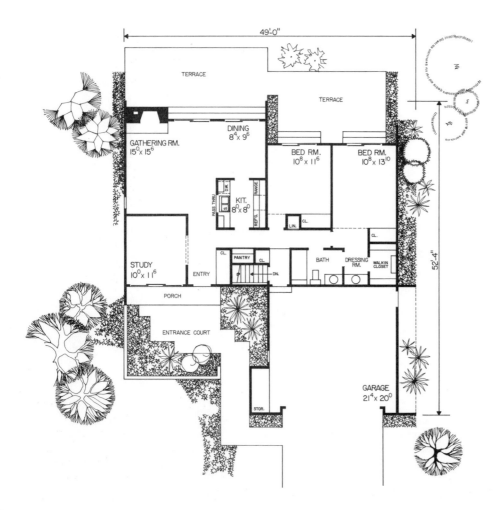

Design T72755
1,200 Sq. Ft.; 23,925 Cu. Ft.

● Here is truly an outstanding, low-cost design created to return all the pride of ownership and livability a small family or retired couple would ask of a new home. The living/dining area measures a spacious 23 feet. It has a fireplace and two sets of sliding glass doors leading to the large rear terrace. The two bedrooms also have access to this terrace. The kitchen is a real step-saver and has a pantry nearby. The study, which has sliding glass doors to the front porch, will function as that extra all-purpose room. Use it for sewing, guests, writing or reading or just plain napping. The basement offers the possibility for the development of additional recreation space. Note the storage area at the side of the garage. Many years of enjoyable living will surely be obtained in this home designed in the contemporary fashion.

MORE ONE-STORY HOMES
...Over 2,000 Sq. Ft.

This group of exciting one-story homes caters to the needs of large, active families with expanded building budgets. These spacious homes can be cost-effective and incorporate added features that contribute to more enjoyable living patterns.

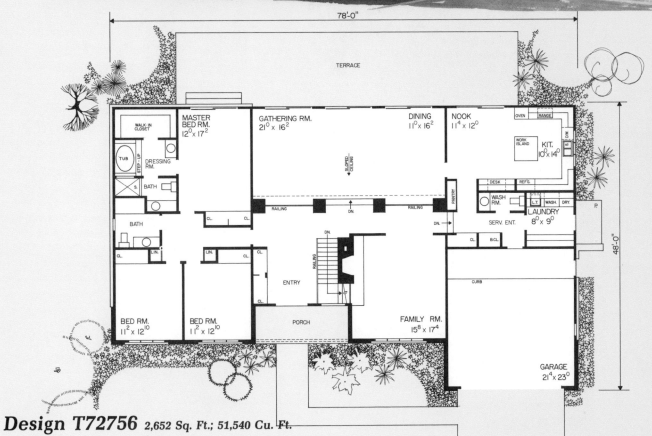

Design T72756 2,652 Sq. Ft.; 51,540 Cu. Ft.

● This one-story, contemporary design is bound to serve your family well. It will assure the best in contemporary living with its many fine features. Notice the bath with tub and stall shower, dressing room and walk-in closet featured with the master bedroom. Two more family bedrooms are adjacent. The sunken gathering room/dining room is highlighted by the sloped ceiling and sliding glass doors to the large, rear terrace. This formal area is a full 32' x 16'. Imagine the great furniture placement that can be done in this area. In addition to the gathering room, there is an informal family room with a fireplace. You will enjoy the efficient kitchen and get much use out of the work island, pantry and built-in desk. Note the service entrance with washroom and laundry.

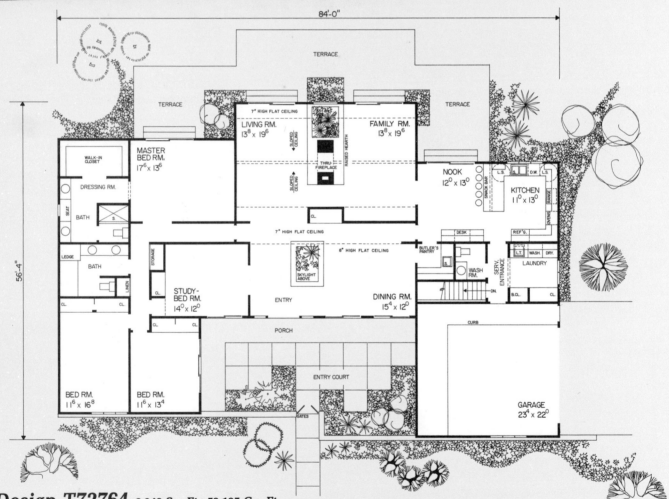

Design T72764 2,946 Sq. Ft.; 59,185 Cu. Ft.

● If uniqueness is what you're looking for in your new home then this three (optional four) bedroom design will be ideal. Notice the large gated-in entry court, vertical paned windows and contrasting exterior materials. All of these features compose an attractive design suitable for any location. Within but a second after entering this home one will be confronted with features galore. The entry/dining area has a focal point of a built-in planter with skylight above. The living room and family room both have an attractive sloped ceiling. They share a raised hearth thru-fireplace and both have access to the large wrap-around terrace. The kitchen-nook area also has access to the terrace and has the features of a snack bar, built-in desk and large butler's pantry.

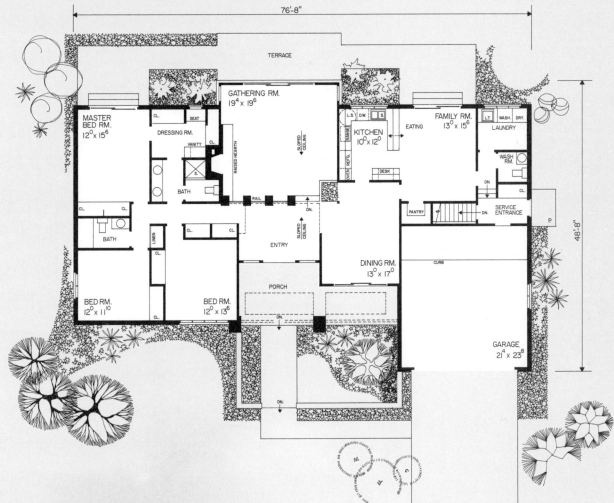

Design T72717 *2,310 Sq. Ft.; 51,680 Cu. Ft.*

● Great for family life! There's a spacious family room for casual activities. And a "work efficient" kitchen that features a built-in desk and appliances, a large pantry plus a pass-through to the family room for added conven-ience. A first floor laundry, too, with adjacent washroom and stairs to the basement. Want glamour? There's a sloped ceiling in the entry hall plus a delightful "over the railing" view of the sunken gathering room. And the gathering room itself! More than 19' by 19' . . . with a sloped ceiling, raised hearth fireplace and sliding glass doors to the rear terrace. A 13' by 17' formal dining room, too. The curb area in garage is convenient.

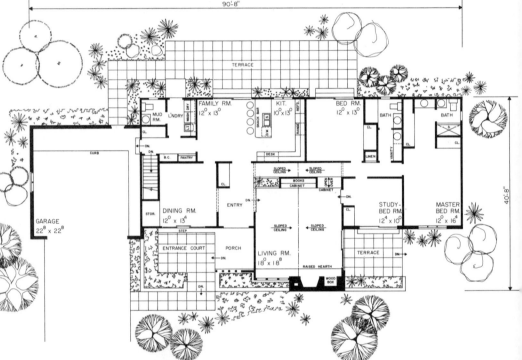

Design T72523
2,055 Sq. Ft.; 43,702 Cu. Ft.

● You'll want the investment in your new home to be one of the soundest you'll ever make. And certainly the best way to do this is to make sure your new home has unexcelled exterior appeal and outstanding interior livability. For those who like refreshing contemporary lines, this design will rate at the top. The wide overhanging roof, the brick masses, the glass areas, the raised planters, and the covered front entrance highlight the facade. As for the interior, all the elements are present to assure fine living patterns. Consider the room relationships and how they function with one another. Note how they relate to the outdoors.

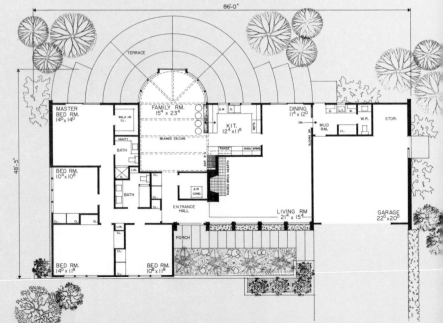

Design T71111
2,248 Sq. Ft.; 18,678 Cu. Ft.

● "Great", will be just the word to characterize the ownership of this home. The trim hip-roof with its wide overhang, the massiveness of the vertical brick piers, and the extension of the brick wall to form a front court are but a few of the features. Among the other features include the four bedrooms, two full baths and extra wash room, a spacious L-shaped living and dining area, a dramatic family room and a mud room.

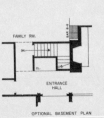

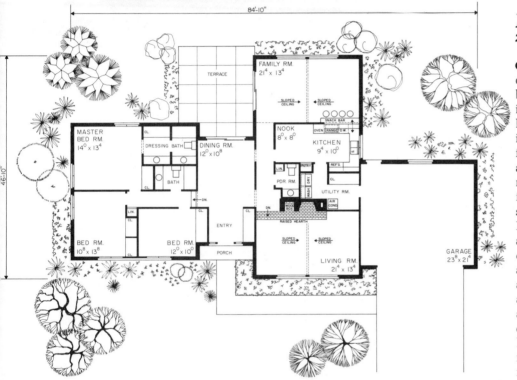

Design T72359
2,078 Sq. Ft.; 22,400 Cu. Ft.

● The low-pitched, wide-overhanging roof with its exposed beams, acts as a visor for the dramatic glass gable end of the projecting living room. This will be an exceedingly pleasant room with its sunken floor, sloped ceiling, large glass area, and raised hearth fireplace. At the rear of this living rectangle is the family room. This room also has a sloped ceiling and a glass gable end. In addition, there is the snack bar and sliding glass doors to the protected terrace. Between these two living areas is the efficient kitchen with its adjacent eating area. The utility room and its laundry equipment is nearby, as is the powder room. A separate dining room acts as the connecting link to the bedroom zone. Note the master bedroom with its dressing room, twin lavatories and two closets.

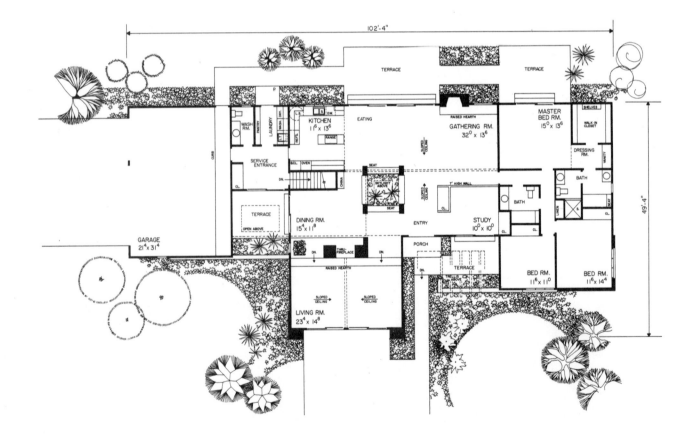

Design T72745 2,890 Sq. Ft.; 44,650 Cu. Ft.

● Just imagine the fun everyone will have living in this contemporary home with its frame exterior and accents of stone veneer (make it brick, if you prefer). The living areas revolve around the dramatic atrium-type planting area flooded with natural light from the skylight above. The formal living room is sunken and has a thru-fireplace to the dining room. Also a large gathering room with a second raised hearth fireplace, sloped ceiling, sliding glass doors to a rear terrace and informal eating area. Observe the sloping ceilings, the laundry with pantry, the washroom and the study. Master bedroom has a stall shower, a tub with seat, a vanity and two lavatories.

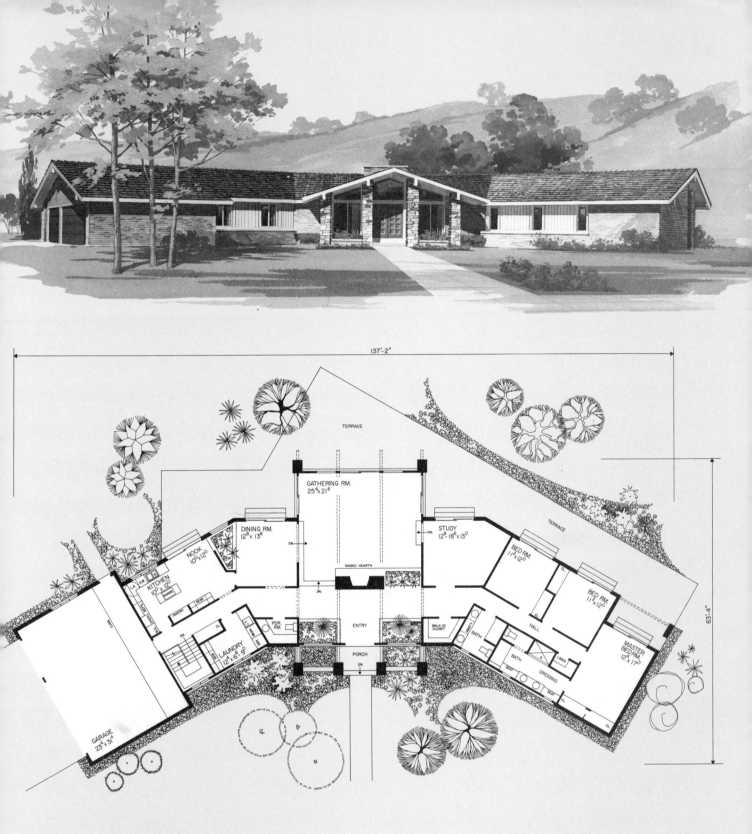

Design T72720 *3,130 Sq. Ft.; 45,700 Cu. Ft.*

● A raised hearth fireplace lights up the sunken gathering room which is exceptionally large and located at the very center of this home! For more living space, a well-located study and formal dining room each having a direct entrance to the gathering room. Plus a kitchen with all the right features . . . an island range, pantry, built-in desk and separate breakfast nook. There's an extended terrace, too . . . accessible from every room! And a master suite with double closets, dressing room and private bath. Plus two family bedrooms, a first-floor laundry and lots of storage space. A basement too, for additional space. This is a liveable home! You can entertain easily or you can hide-out with a good book. Study this plan with your family and pick out your favorite features. Don't miss the dramatic front entry planting areas, or the extra curb area in the garage.

Design T72594
2,294 Sq. Ft.; 42,120 Cu. Ft.

● A spectacular foyer! It is fully 21' long and offers double entry to the heart of this home. Other highlights include a 21' by 21' gathering room complete with sloped ceiling, raised hearth fireplace and sliding glass doors. There's a formal dining room, too. Plus a well-located study which insures space for solitude or undisturbed work. The kitchen features a snack bar and a breakfast nook with another set of sliding doors. For more convenience, a pantry and first-floor laundry. In the master suite, a dressing room with entry to the bath, four closets and sliding doors onto the terrace! Two more bedrooms if you wish to convert the study or one easily large enough for two children with a dressing area and private entry to the second bath.

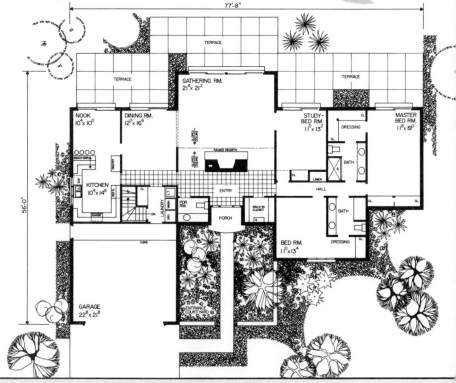

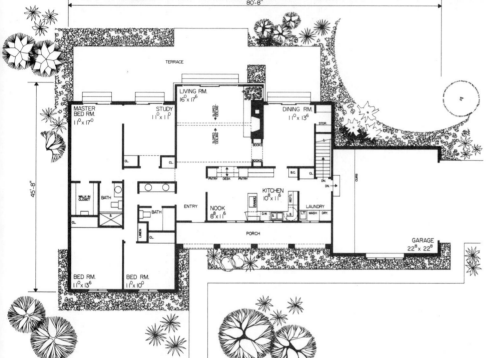

Design T72557
1,955 Sq. Ft.; 43,509 Cu. Ft.

● This eye-catching design with a flavor of the Spanish Southwest will be as interesting to live in as it will be to view from the street. The character of the exterior is set by the wide overhanging roof with its exposed beams; the massive arched pillars; the arching of the brick over the windows; the panelled door and the vertical siding that contrasts with the brick. The elegantly large master bedroom/study suite is a focal point of the interior. However, if necessary, the study could become the fourth bedroom. The living and dining rooms are separated by a massive raised hearth fireplace. All of the work center is in the front of the plan. It also has easy access to the garage and the basement.

Design T72287
2,394 Sq. Ft.; 26,933 Cu. Ft.

● Here is a flat roof contemporary designed to be in harmony with the surroundings of the Far West. Yet, its fine proportions and sleek appearance would be a credit wherever built. Here, again, the covered court fosters a peaceful, welcoming atmosphere on the way to the front door. The center entrance hall routes traffic efficiently to the main areas. The kitchen is strategically located — handy to the front door, only a step from the two eating areas and just around the corner from the laundry and entrance from the garage. The formal, living room functions well with the dining room. The family room is ideally located, too. It is close to the kitchen and directly accessible to the outdoors. Study the sleeping area.

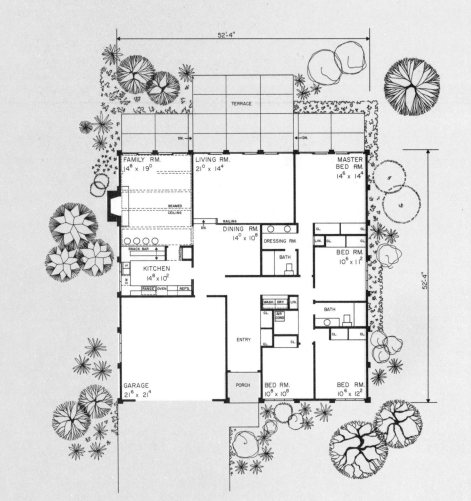

Design T72357
2,135 Sq. Ft.; 24,970 Cu. Ft.

● Palm trees on your site are not a prerequisite for the building of this distinctive home. If you and your family have a flair for things unique, the exterior, as well as the interior, of this attractive design will excite you. The low-pitched, wide overhanging hip roof has a slag surface. The equally spaced pillars and the spaces between the vertical boards are finished in stucco. This house is a perfect square measuring 52'-4". The resulting plan is one that is practical and efficient. The kitchen will be a joy in which to work. A pass-thru provides the access to the snack bar of the beamed ceilinged family room. The formal dining area is but a couple steps away and overlooks the sunken living room. Four bedrooms and two baths make up the delightful sleeping zone.

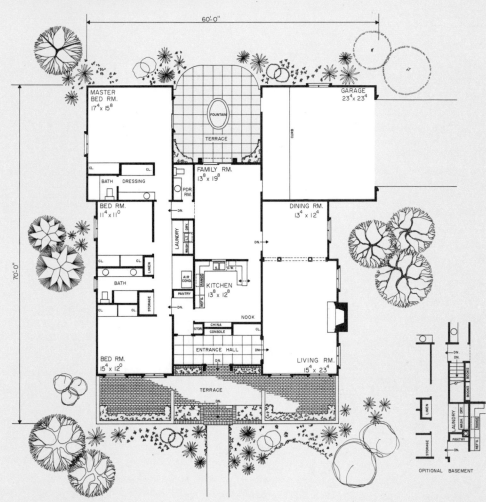

OPTIONAL BASEMENT

Design T72347 2,322 Sq. Ft.; 26,572 Cu. Ft.

● The regal character of this distinctive home is most inviting. The symmetry of the front exterior is enhanced by the raised terrace. The recessed front entrance shelters panelled double doors which open to the formal hall. Traffic may pass to the right directly into the sunken living room. To the left is the sunken three bedroom, two-bath sleeping area. The center of the plan features the efficient kitchen with nook space and the family room. The rear terrace, enclosed on three sides to assure privacy, is accessible from master bedroom, as well as family room, through sliding glass doors. Separating the formal living and dining rooms are finely proportioned, round wood columns. Don't overlook the first floor laundry. Blueprints include details for optional partial basement.

Design T72882

2,832 Sq. Ft.; 59,635 Cu. Ft.

● This contemporary, one-story design should be oriented on a west-facing site if it is built in the northern regions of the country. The result will be minimal exposure to the cold northern winds during the winter. Study the north side of this plan. There is only one small window and it will be protected by the privacy wall. This means that the rooms on the opposite side of the house will have the desirable southern exposure. A westerly exposure for the living room will be most beneficial in many areas of the country. This plan reflects interesting living patterns and excellent indoor/outdoor relationships. Wide overhanging roofs, skylights, glass gables, vented walkways, wind-buffering privacy fences and 2x6 construction are among this design's energy oriented features.

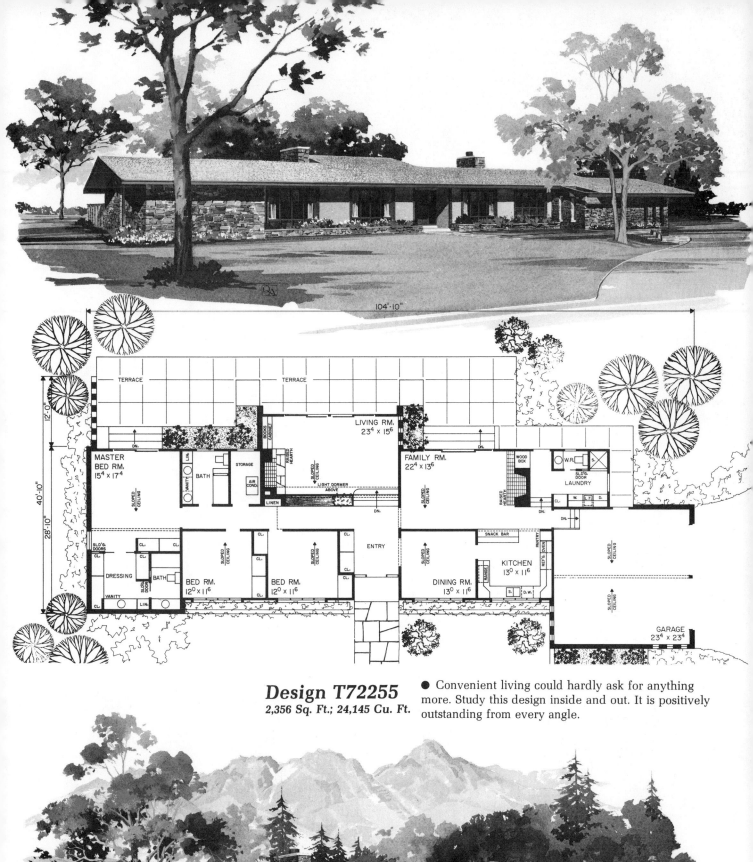

TERRACE

TERRACE

LIVING RM.
23⁴ x 15⁶

MASTER
BED RM.
15⁴ x 17⁴

BATH

STORAGE

BOOKS
CABINET

RAISED HEARTH

SLOPED CEILING

AIR COND.

FAMILY RM.
22⁴ x 13⁶

WOOD BOX

W.R.

SLD'G. DOOR

LAUNDRY

SLOPED CEILING

LIGHT DORMER ABOVE

LINEN

DN.

CL.

W.   L.T.   D.

DN.

SLD'G & DOORS

CL.   CL.

DRESSING

BATH

SLOPED CEILING

BED RM.
12⁰ x 11⁶

CL.

CL.

SLOPED CEILING

BED RM.
12⁰ x 11⁶

CL.

CL.

CL.

ENTRY

SNACK BAR

PANTRY

REF'G. OVEN

KITCHEN
13⁰ x 11⁶

SLOPED CEILING

SLOPED CEILING

VANITY

LIN.

DINING RM.
13⁰ x 11⁶

RANGE

S.   D.W.

SLOPED CEILING

GARAGE
23⁴ x 23⁴

104'-10"

12'-0"

40'-10"

28'-10"

Design T72255
2,356 Sq. Ft.; 24,145 Cu. Ft.

● Convenient living could hardly ask for anything more. Study this design inside and out. It is positively outstanding from every angle.

Design T71897
2,628 Sq. Ft.; 38,859 Cu. Ft.

● A home can have many faces. This refreshingly simple, yet delightfully impressive design has a contemporary flavor. The low-pitched roof has a wide overhang. Its exposed rafter tails protrude at each gable end for a distinctive look. Appealing architectural detailing highlights the projecting bedroom wing. Four bedrooms and two baths are in this wing. Note that the master bedroom has access to a private terrace. The living areas are separated in this plan. The formal areas, living and dining rooms, are in the front; while the informal areas overlook the backyard.

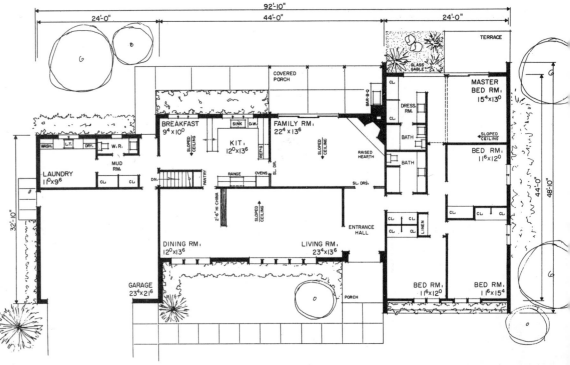

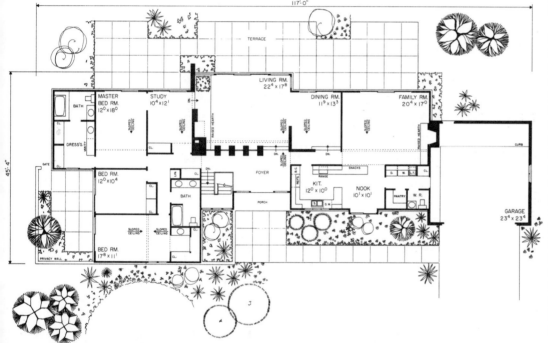

Design T72506
2,851 Sq. Ft.; 47,525 Cu. Ft.

● Here is a home that is sure to add an extra measure of fun to your family's living patterns. The exterior is extremely pleasing with the use of paned glass windows, the hipped roof and the double front doors. The initial impact of the interior begins dramatically in the large foyer. The ceiling is sloped, while straight ahead one views the sunken living room. Impressive are the masonry columns with a railing between each. The stairwell to the partial basement is open and has a view of the outdoor planter. The sleeping area consists of three bedrooms, baths and a study (or fourth bedroom if you prefer). Two raised hearth fireplaces, pantry, washroom and more. List your favorite features.

Design T71820
2,730 Sq. Ft.; 36,335 Cu. Ft.

● Whatever the location, snugly tucked in among the hills or impressively oriented on the flatlands - this trim hip-roof ranch home will be fun to own. Here is a gracious exterior whose floor plan has "everything". Traffic patterns are excellent. The zoning of the sleeping wing, as well as the formal and informal living areas, is outstanding. Indoor-outdoor living relationships are most practical and convenient.

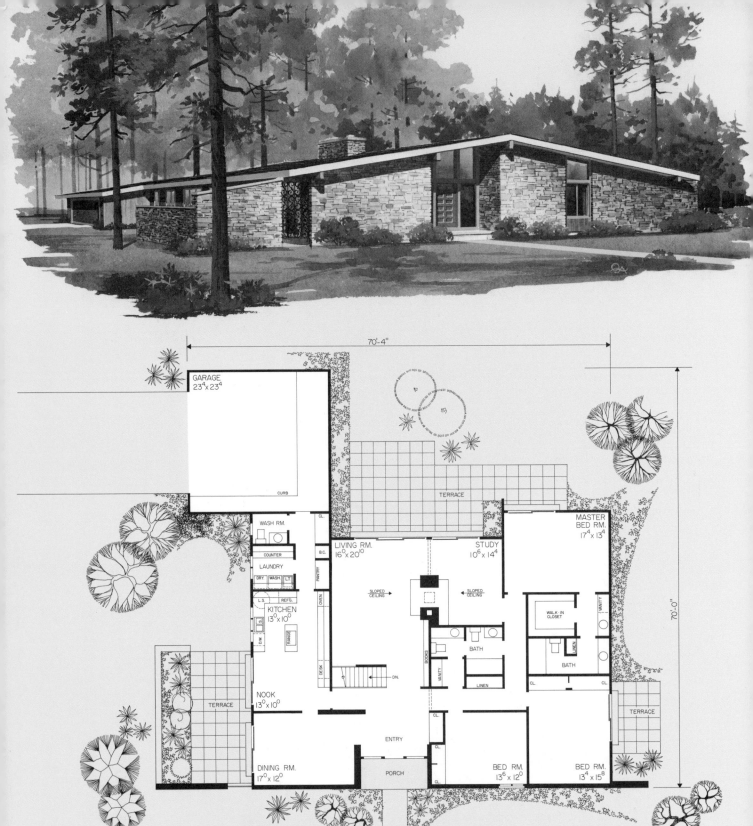

GARAGE
23⁴ x 23⁴

CURB

70'-4"

70'-0"

TERRACE

WASH RM.

COUNTER

LAUNDRY

DRY. WASH L.T.

L.S. REFG.

KITCHEN
13⁰ x 10⁰

D.W. RANGE

B.C.

CL.

PANTRY

OVEN

DESK

LIVING RM.
16⁶ x 20¹⁰

SLOPED CEILING

DN.

NOOK
13⁰ x 10⁰

TERRACE

DINING RM.
17⁰ x 12⁰

PORCH

ENTRY

CL.

CL.

CL.

STUDY
10⁶ x 14⁴

SLOPED CEILING

BOOKS

VANITY

BATH

LINEN

CL.

MASTER BED RM.
17⁴ x 13⁴

WALK-IN CLOSET

LINEN

BATH

VANITY

CL.

CL.

TERRACE

BED RM.
13⁶ x 12⁰

BED RM.
13⁴ x 15⁸

Design T72537 2,602 Sq. Ft.; 41,731 Cu. Ft.

● A low-pitched, wide overhanging roof and masses of quarried stone (make it some other material of your choice if you wish) set the character of this contemporary design. The recessed front entrance with its patterned door and glass panels is, indeed, dramatic.

An attractive wrought iron gate opens to the private, side eating terrace. Sloping ceilings and raised hearth through-fireplace highlight the living room/study area. Spaciousness is further enhanced by the open stairwell to the recreation area which may be devel-

oped below. The kitchen, with its island cooking range and plenty of counter and cupboard space will be a joy in which to function. The area between kitchen and garage is well-planned. The separate laundry has extra counter space.

Design T72303 2,330 Sq. Ft.; 26,982 Cu. Ft.

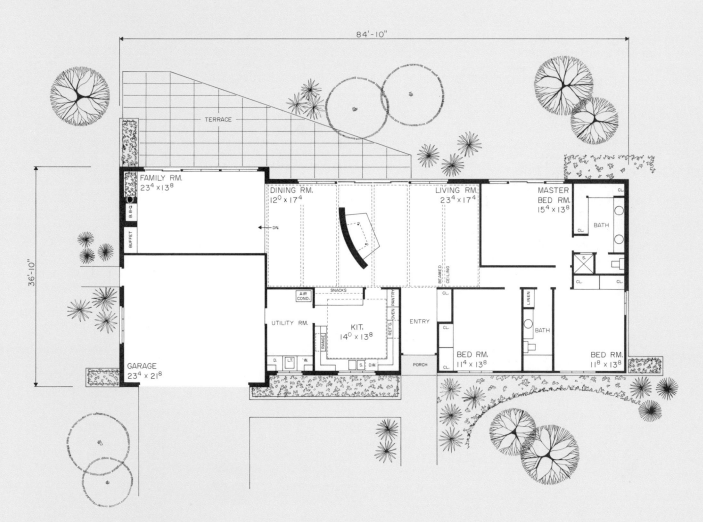

● This hip-roof ranch home has a basic floor plan that is the favorite of many. The reasons for its popularity are, of course, easy to detect. The simple rectangular shape means relatively economical construction. The living areas are large and are located to the rear to function through sliding glass doors with the terrace. The front kitchen is popular because of its view of approaching callers and its proximity to the front entry. The big utility room serves as a practical buffer between the garage and the kitchen.

Worthy of particular note is the efficiency of the kitchen, the stylish living room fireplace, the beamed ceiling, the sunken family room with its wall of built-ins (make that a music wall if you wish). Observe the snack bar and the fine master bath.

Design T71026
2,506 Sq. Ft.; 26,313 Cu. Ft.

● When you move into this attractive home you'll find you and your family will begin to experience new dimensions in living. All areas will be forever conscious of the beauty of the out-of-doors. The front entry court provides both the quiet living room and the formal dining room with a delightful view. The functional terraces will expand the horizons of each of the other rooms. While the raised hearth fireplaces of the two living areas are major focal points, there are numerous convenient living features which will make everyday living a joy. Some of these features are the mud room, the pantry, the planning desk with china storage above, the snack bar and pass-thru. As noted in the illustration, an optional basement plan is included.

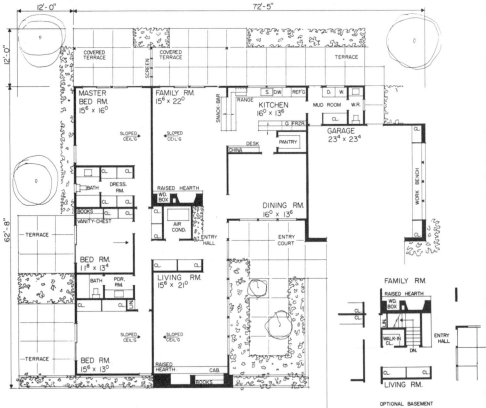

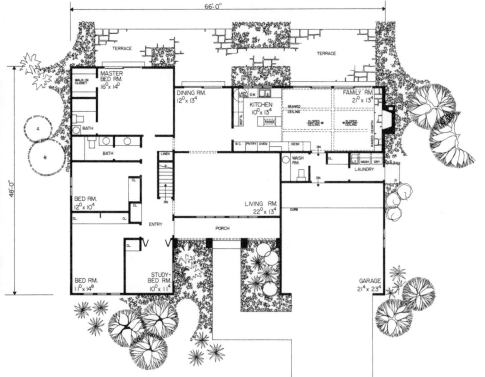

Design T72532
2,112 Sq. Ft.; 42,300 Cu. Ft.

● Here is a refreshing, modified U-shaped contemporary that is long on both looks and livability. The board and batten exterior creates simple lines which are complimented by the low-pitched roof with its wide overhang and exposed rafters. The appeal of the front court is enhanced by the massive stone columns at the edge of the covered porch. A study of the floor plan reveals interestingly different and practical living patterns. The location of the entry hall represents a fine conservation of space for the living areas. The L-shaped formal living-dining zone has access to both front and rear yards. The informal living area is a true family kitchen. Its open planning produces a spacious and cheerful area. Note sloping, beamed ceiling, raised hearth fireplace and sliding glass doors.

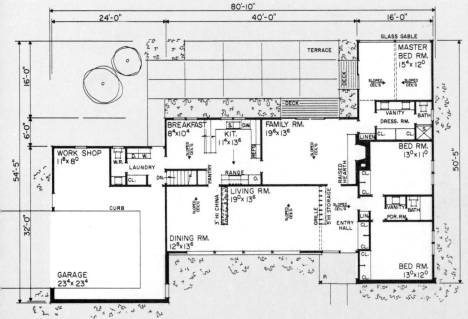

Design T71844
2,047 Sq. Ft.; 32,375 Cu. Ft.

● A sparkling contemporary with all the elements to help assure a lifetime of complete livability. This one-story home is essentially a frame dwelling with two dramatic areas of durable and colorful quarried stone. The low-pitched, wide-overhanging roof provides shelter for the front porch. In addition, it acts as a visor for the large glass areas. The plan is positively outstanding. The informal areas are to the rear of the plan and overlook the rear terrace. The formal, separate dining room and living room are strategically located to the front. The sleeping zone comprises a wing of its own with the master bedroom suite apart from the children's room. Don't miss the extra wash room, laundry and shop. Basement stairs are near this work area.

Design T72114
2,665 Sq. Ft.; 29,819 Cu. Ft.

● When you study this plan you will find that it offers a lot of livability. Note the good-sized living room and equally sized family room. These spacious rooms are perfect for entertaining. The kitchen is conveniently located to provide easy access to the dining room and eating area. Two bedrooms a full bath and a master bedroom are in the sleeping area.

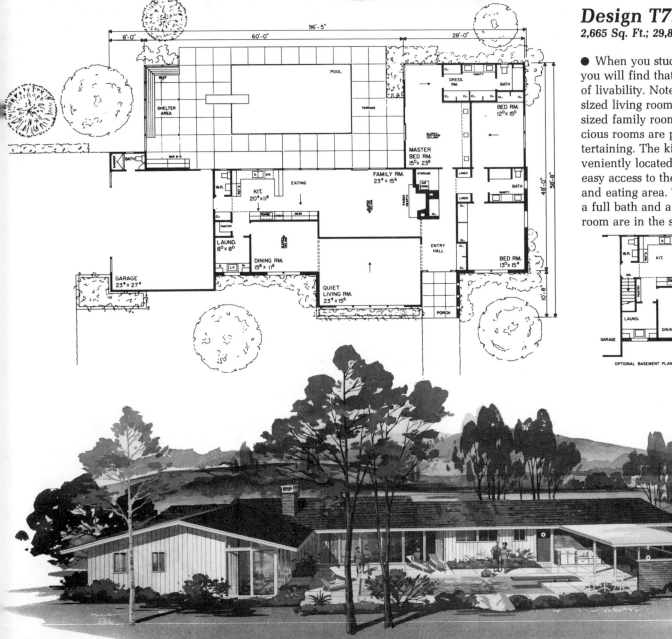

OPTIONAL BASEMENT PLAN

LEISURE LIVING HOUSES
...for Recreation, Vacation or Year-Round Fun!

Enjoy the informality of leisure living with the designs on the following pages. An investment in leisure-time living adds up to quality vacation time and possibly more. Many vacation homes can make excellent year-round residences for seniors who want a fun retirement nest among others.

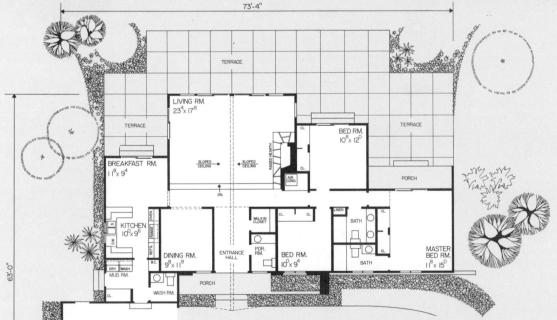

Design T72483 1,775 Sq. Ft.; 21,394 Cu. Ft.

● Floor-to-ceiling windows are a delightful attraction in the living room. They are good looking and a way to take advantage of the beautiful outdoor scenery. For more good looks, sloped ceilings, a raised hearth fireplace plus a terrace that runs the length of the house. A formal dining room is convenient to the efficient, U-shaped kitchen with a separate breakfast room. The laundry/mud room will allow immediate cleanup after a day spent fishing or on the beach. Three bedrooms! Including one with a private bath.

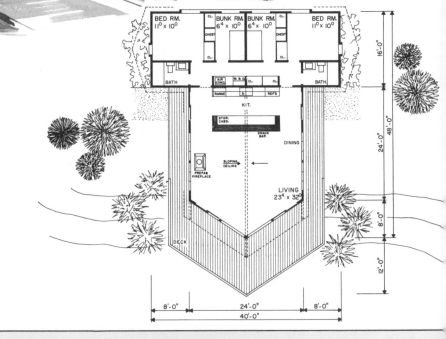

Design T72439
1,312 Sq. Ft.; 17,674 Cu. Ft.

❧ A wonderfully organized plan with an exterior that will command the attention of each and every passerby. And what will catch the eye? Certainly the roof lines and the pointed glass gable end wall will be noticed immediately. The delightful deck will be quickly noticed, too. Inside a visitor will be thrilled by the spaciousness of the huge living room. The ceilings slope upward to the exposed ridge beam. A free-standing fireplace will make its contribution to a cheerful atmosphere. What could improve upon the sleeping zone when it has two bedrooms, two bunk rooms, two full baths, two built-in chests and fine closet space?

Design T72417
1,520 Sq. Ft.; 19,952 Cu. Ft.

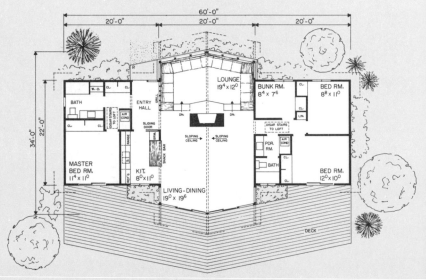

● Have you ever seen a vacation home design that is anything quite like this one? Probably not! The picturesque exterior is dominated by a projecting gable with its wide, overhanging roof acting as a dramatic sun visor for the large glass area below. Effectively balancing this 20 foot center section are two 20 foot wings. Inside, and below the high, sloping, beamed ceiling is the huge living area. In addition to the living-dining area, there is the spacious sunken lounge. This pleasant area has a built-in seating arrangement and a cozy fireplace. The parents' and children's sleeping areas are separated and a full bath.

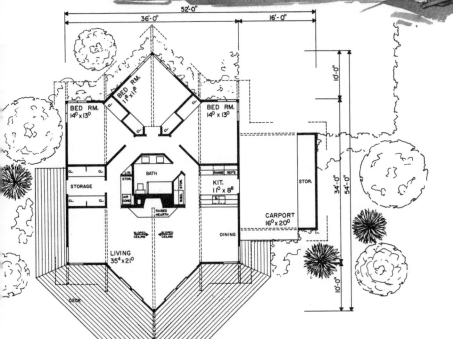

Design T72418
1,424 Sq. Ft.; 17,891 Cu. Ft.

● You'll search a long time before locating a vacation home that is any more exciting than this fascinating angular retreat. Whatever its setting, it will command attention and also provide its happy owners with a lifetime of carefree living. The soaring roof lines, the cedar shakes, the appealing glass areas and the sloping, beamed ceilings are features. Three bedrooms and a centered bath are clustered together. Family activities will take place in the spacious living room.

Design T71458 576 Sq. Ft.; 5,904 Cu. Ft.

Design T71495 800 Sq. Ft.; 9,108 Cu. Ft.

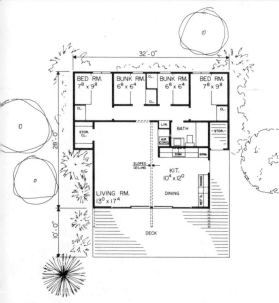

Design T71403 698 Sq. Ft.; 7,441 Cu. Ft.

Design T72424 1,456 Sq. Ft.; 16,760 Cu. Ft.

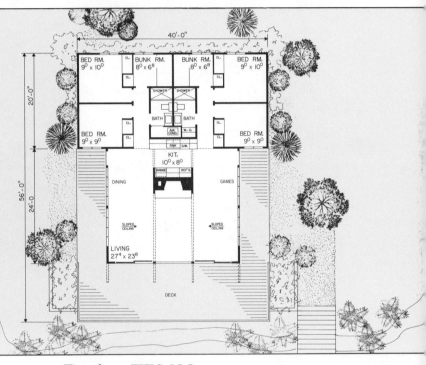

● Here are five outstanding second homes which, in spite of their variation in size, have many things in common. Perhaps the most significant common denominator is the location of the living area and its unrestricted view of the outdoors. Each of the designs feature a glass gable end and sloping ceiling which assures the living zone of a bright and cheerful atmosphere. A study of the sizes and the livability of these designs is interesting. They range in size from a 576 square foot, one bedroom cottage, to a 1,456 square foot lodge with four bedrooms plus two bunk rooms. Regardless of the overall size of the interior, the open planning of the living areas results in plenty of space for your family and visitors to just sit around and talk.

Design T72423 864 Sq. Ft.; 9,504 Cu. Ft.

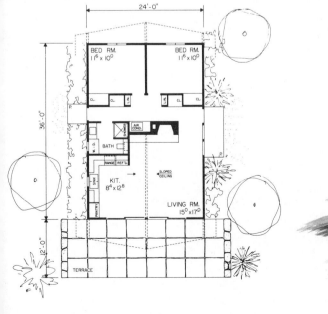

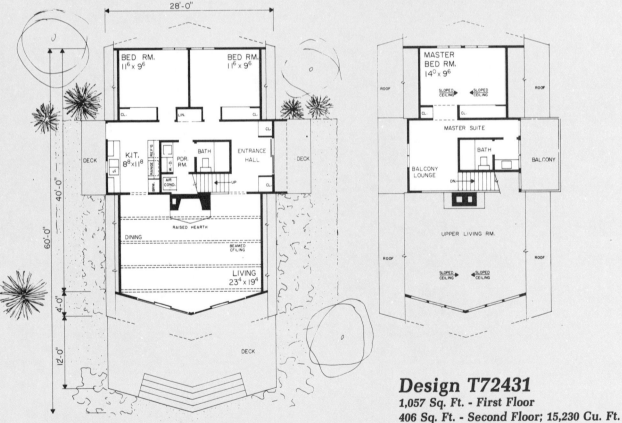

BED RM. 11⁶ x 9⁶

BED RM. 11⁶ x 9⁶

28'-0"

40'-0"

60'-0"

4'-0"

12'-0"

DECK

DECK

DECK

CL.

LIN.

CL.

CL.

CL.

K.I.T. 8⁸ x 11⁸

RANGE

REF'G

BRM.

W.C.

PDR. RM.

BATH

ENTRANCE HALL

AIR COND.

UP

RAISED HEARTH

DINING

BEAMED CEILING

LIVING 23⁴ x 19⁴

MASTER BED RM. 14⁰ x 9⁶

ROOF

ROOF

SLOPED CEILING

SLOPED CEILING

CL.

CL.

MASTER SUITE

BATH

BALCONY LOUNGE

BALCONY

DN.

UPPER LIVING RM.

ROOF

ROOF

SLOPED CEILING

SLOPED CEILING

Design T72431
1,057 Sq. Ft. - First Floor
406 Sq. Ft. - Second Floor; 15,230 Cu. Ft.

● A favorite everywhere – the A-frame vacation home. Its popularity is easily discernible at first glance. The stately appearance is enhanced by the soaring roof lines and the dramatic glass areas. Inside, the breathtaking beauty of outstanding architectural detailing also is apparent. The high ceiling of the living room slopes and has exposed beams. The second floor master suite is a great feature. Observe the raised hearth fireplace and the outdoor balcony. This outdoor spot certainly will be a quiet perch for sunbathing on a warm afternoon.

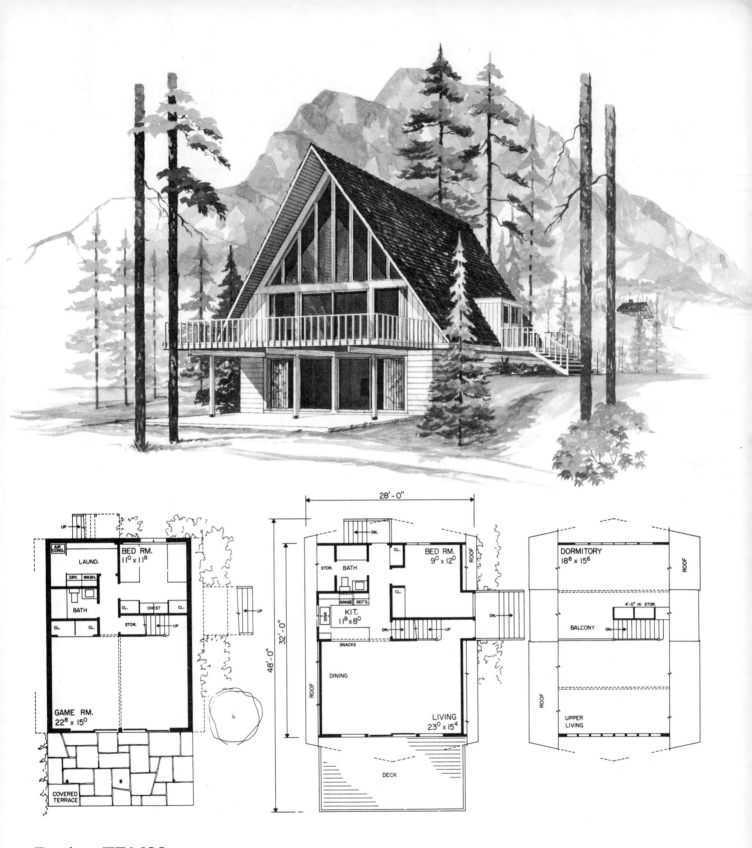

Design T71499 *896 Sq. Ft. - Main Level; 298 Sq. Ft. - Upper Level; 896 Sq. Ft. - Lower Level; 18,784 Cu. Ft.*

● Three level living results in family living patterns which will foster a delightful feeling of informality. Upon arrival at this charming second home, each family member will enthusiastically welcome the change in environment – both indoors and out. Whether looking down into the living room from the dormitory balcony, or walking through the sliding doors onto the huge deck, or participating in some family activity in the game room, everyone will count the hours spent here as relaxing ones. Study the plan carefully. Note the sleeping facilities on each of the three levels. Two bedrooms and a dormitory in all to sleep the family and friends comfortably. There are two full baths, a separate laundry room and plenty of storage. Don't miss the efficient U-shaped kitchen.

Design T72488 1,113 Sq. Ft. - First Floor
543 Sq. Ft. - Second Floor; 36,055 Cu. Ft.

● A cozy cottage for the young at heart! Whether called upon to serve the young, active family as a leisure-time retreat at the lake, or the retired couple as a quiet haven in later years, this charming design will perform well. As a year round second home, the upstairs with its two sizable bedrooms, full bath and lounge area, looking down into the gathering room below, will ideally accommodate the younger generation.

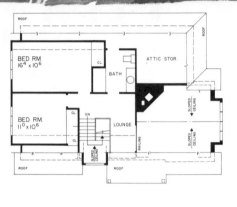

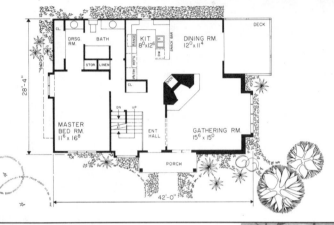

● Here's a chalet right from the pages of the travel folders. Whether the setting reflects the majestic beauty of a winter scene or the tranquil splendor of a summer landscape, this design will serve its occupants well. In addition to the big bedrooms on the first floor, there are three more upstairs. The large master bedroom has a balcony which looks down into the lower wood deck. There are two full baths. The first floor bath is directly accessible from the outdoors. Note snack bar and pantry of the kitchen. Laundry area is adjacent to side door.

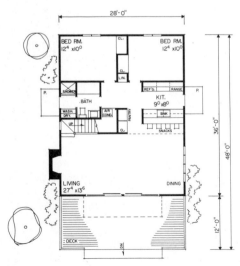

Design T71482
1,008 Sq. Ft. - First Floor
637 Sq. Ft. - Second Floor
16,657 Cu. Ft.

Design T72479
1,547 Sq. Ft.; 14,878 Cu. Ft.

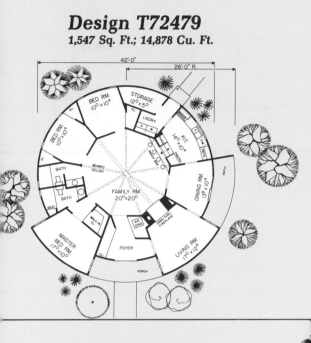

● Here is a unique round house with an equally unique floor plan. The centrally located family room is the focal point. There is much to study and admire in this plan. For instance, the use of space is most efficient. Notice the strategic location of the kitchen. Don't miss the storage room and laundry. Observe the snack bar, the two-way fireplace, the separate dining room and the two full baths. Fixed glass windows at the beamed ceiling provide natural light from above for the family room.

Design T72457
1,288 Sq. Ft.; 13,730 Cu. Ft.

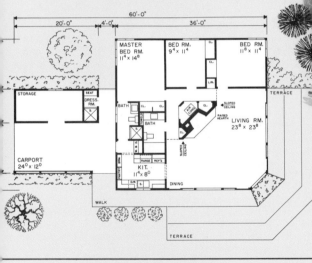

● Leisure living will be graciously experienced in this second home. The wide overhanging roof affords protection from the sun. This home is a perfect square measuring 36 x 36 feet, not counting the clipped corner. The 23 foot square living room enjoys a great view of the surrounding environment by virtue of the expanses of glass. "Open planning" adds to the spaciousness of the interior. Three bedrooms are served by two full baths which are accessible to other areas. The kitchen, looking out upon the water, will be a delight. What great planning for a leisure-time second home.

Design T72461
1,400 Sq. Ft.; 13,742 Cu. Ft.

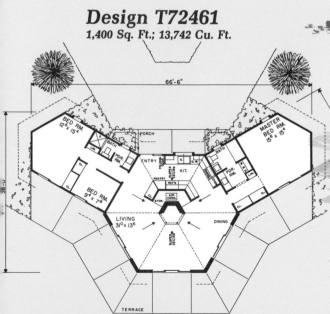

● If you have the urge to make your vacation home one that has a distinctive flair of individuality, you should give consideration to this design. Not only will you love the unique exterior appeal of your new home but, also, the exceptional living patterns offered by the interior. Here, the basic living area is a hexagon. The sleeping wings with bath are added to this space conscious geometric shape.

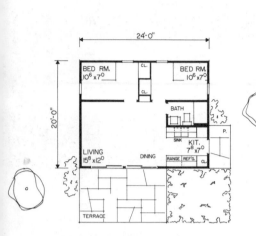

Design T71486
480 Sq. Ft.; 4,118 Cu. Ft.

● You'll be anxious to start building this delightful little vacation home. Whether you do-it-yourself, or engage professional help, you will not have to wait long for its completion.

Design T72425
1,106 Sq. Ft.; 14,599 Cu. Ft.

● You'll adjust to living in this vacation cottage with the greatest of ease. And forevermore the by-word will be, "fun". Imagine, a thirty-one foot living room with access to a large deck!

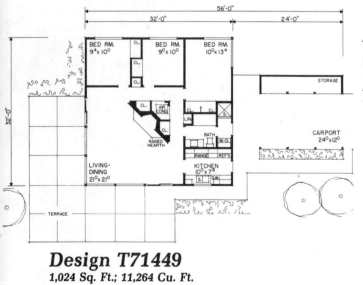

Design T71449
1,024 Sq. Ft.; 11,264 Cu. Ft.

● If yours is a preference for a vacation home with a distinctive flair, then you need not look any further. Here is a simple and economically built 32 foot rectangle to meet your needs.

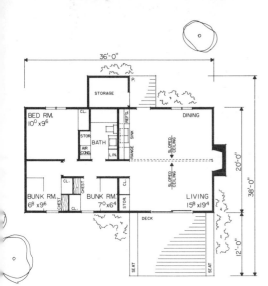

Design T71488
720 Sq. Ft.; 8,518 Cu. Ft.

● The kids won't be able to move into this vacation retreat soon enough. Two bunk rooms plus another bedroom for Mom and Dad. Open-planned living area. A real leisure-time home.

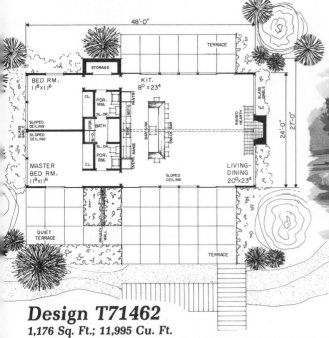

Design T71462
1,176 Sq. Ft.; 11,995 Cu. Ft.

● A second home with the informal living message readily apparent both inside and out. The zoning of this home is indeed most interesting – and practical, too. Study the plan carefully.

Design T71485
784 Sq. Ft.; 10,192 Cu. Ft.

● Here's a perfect 28 foot square that will surely open up new dimensions in living for its occupants. A fine, lower budget version of 51449 on the opposing page yet retaining many of the fine qualities.

How To Read Floor Plans and Blueprints

Selecting the most suitable house plan for your family is a matter of matching your needs, tastes, and life-style against the many designs we offer. When you study the floor plans in this issue, and the blueprints that you may subsequently order, remember that they are simply a two-dimensional representation of what will eventually be a three-dimensional reality.

Floor plans are easy to read. Rooms are clearly labeled, with dimensions given in feet and inches. Most symbols are logical and self-explanatory: The location of bathroom fixtures, planters, fireplaces, tile floors, cabinets and counters, sinks, appliances, closets, sloped or beamed ceilings will be obvious.

A blueprint, although much more detailed, is also easy to read; all it demands is concentration. The blueprints that we offer come in many large sheets, each one of which contains a different kind of information. One sheet contains foundation and excavation drawings, another has a precise plot plan. An elevations sheet deals with the exterior walls of the house; section drawings show precise dimensions, fittings, doors, windows, and roof structures. Our detailed floor plans give the construction information needed by your contractor. And each set of blueprints contains a lengthy materials list with size and quantities of all necessary components. Using this list, a contractor and suppliers can make a start at calculating costs for you.

When you first study a floor plan or blueprint, imagine that you are walking through the house. By mentally visualizing each room in three dimensions, you can transform the technical data and symbols into something more real.

Start at the front door. It's preferable to have a foyer or entrance hall in which to receive guests. A closet here is desirable; a powder room is a plus.

Look for good traffic circulation as you study the floor plan. You should not have to pass all the way through one main room to reach another. From the entrance area you should have direct access to the three principal areas of a house—the living, work, and sleeping zones. For example, a foyer might provide separate entrances to the living room, kitchen, patio, and a hallway or staircase leading to the bedrooms.

Study the layout of each zone. Most people expect the living room to be protected from cross traffic. The kitchen, on the other hand, should connect with the dining room—and perhaps also the utility room, basement, garage, patio or deck, or a secondary entrance. A homemaker whose workday centers in the kitchen may have special requirements: a window that faces the backyard; a clear view of the family room where children play; a garage or driveway entrance that allows for a short trip with groceries; laundry facilities close at hand. Check for efficient placement of kitchen cabinets, counters, and appliances. Is there enough room in the kitchen for additional appliances, for eating in? Is there a dining nook?

Perhaps this part of the house contains a family room or a den/bedroom/office. It's advantageous to have a bathroom or powder room in this section.

As you study the plan, you may encounter a staircase, indicated by a group of parallel lines, the number of lines equaling the number of steps. Arrows labeled "up" mean that the staircase leads to a higher level, and those pointing down mean it leads to a lower one. Staircases in a split-level will have both up and down arrows on one staircase because two levels are depicted in one drawing and an extra level in another.

Notice the location of the stairways. Is too much floor space lost to them? Will you find yourself making too many trips?

Study the sleeping quarters. Are the bedrooms situated as you like? You may want the master bedroom near the kids, or you may want it as far away as possible. Is there at least one closet per person in each bedroom or a double one for a couple? Bathrooms should be convenient to each bedroom—if not adjoining, then with hallway access and on the same floor.

Once you are familiar with the relative positions of the rooms, look for such structural details as:

• Sufficient uninterrupted wall space for furniture arrangement.

• Adequate room dimensions.

• Potential heating or cooling problems—i.e., a room over a garage or next to the laundry.

• Window and door placement for good ventilation and natural light.

• Location of doorways—avoid having a basement staircase or a bathroom in view of the dining room.

• Adequate auxiliary space—closets, storage, bathrooms, countertops.

• Separation of activity areas. (Will noise from the recreation room disturb sleeping children or a parent at work?)

As you complete your mental walk through the house, bear in mind your family's long-range needs. A good house plan will allow for some adjustments now and additions in the future.

Each member of your family may find the listing of his, or her, favorite features a most helpful exercise. Why not try it?

How To Choose a Contractor

A contractor is part craftsman, part businessman, and part magician. As the person who will transform your dreams and drawings into a finished house, he will be responsible for the final cost of the structure, for the quality of the workmanship, and for the solving of all problems that occur quite naturally in the course of construction. Choose him as carefully as you would a business partner, because for the next several months that will be his role in your life.

As soon as you have a building site and house plans, start looking for a contractor, even if you do not plan to break ground for several months. Finding one suitable to build your house can take time, and once you have found him, you will have to be worked into his schedule. Those who are good are in demand and, where the season is short, they are often scheduling work up to a year in advance.

There are two types of residential contractors: the construction company and the carpenter-builder, often called a general contractor. Each of these has its advantages and disadvantages.

The carpenter-builder works directly on the job as the field foreman. Because his background is that of a craftsman, his workmanship is probably good—but his paperwork may be slow or sloppy. His overhead—which you pay for—is less than that of a large construction company. However, if the job drags on for any reason, his interest may flag because your project is overlapping his next job and eroding his profits.

Construction companies handle several projects concurrently. They have an office staff to keep the paperwork moving and an army of subcontractors they know they can count on. Though you can be confident that they will meet deadlines, they may sacrifice workmanship in order to do so. Because they emphasize efficiency, they are less personal to work with than a general contractor. Many will not work with an individual unless he is represented by an architect. The company and the architect speak the same language; it requires far more time to deal directly with a homeowner.

To find a reliable contractor, start by asking friends who have built homes for recommendations. Check with local lumber yards and building supply outlets for names of possible candidates.

Once you have several names in hand, ask the Chamber of Commerce, Better Business Bureau, or local department of consumer affairs for any information they might have on each of them. Keep in mind that these watchdog organizations can give only the number of complaints filed; they cannot tell you what percent of those claims were valid. Remember, too, that a large-volume operation is logically going to have more complaints against it than will an independent contractor.

Set up an interview with each of the potential candidates. Find out what his specialty is—custom houses, development houses, remodeling, or office buildings. Ask each to take you into—not just to the site of—houses he has built. Ask to see projects that are complete as well as work in progress, emphasizing that you are interested in projects comparable to yours. A $300,000 dentist's office will give you little insight into a contractor's craftsmanship.

Ask each contractor for bank references from both his commercial bank and any other lender he has worked with. If he is in good financial standing, he should have no qualms about giving you this information. Also ask if he offers a warranty on his work. Most will give you a one-year warranty on the structure; some offer as much as a ten-year warranty.

Ask for references, even though no contractor will give you the name of a dissatisfied customer. While previous clients may be pleased with a contractor's work overall, they may, for example, have had to wait three months after they moved in before they had any closet doors. Ask about his follow-through. Did he clean up the building site, or did the owner have to dispose of the refuse? Ask about his business organization. Did the paperwork go smoothly, or was there a delay in hooking up the sewer because he forgot to apply for a permit?

Talk to each of the candidates about fees. Most work on a "cost plus" basis; that is, the basic cost of the project—materials, subcontractors' services, wages of those working directly on the project, but not office help—plus his fee. Some have a fixed fee; others work on a percentage of the basic cost. A fixed fee is usually better for you if you can get one. If a contractor works on a percentage, ask for a cost breakdown of his best estimate and keep very careful track as the work progresses. A crafty contractor can always use a cost overrun to his advantage when working on a percentage.

Do not be overly suspicious of a contractor who won't work on a fixed fee. One who is very good and in great demand may not be willing to do so. He may also refuse to submit a competitive bid.

If the top two or three candidates are willing to submit competitive bids, give each a copy of the plans and your specifications for materials. If they are not each working from the same guidelines, the competitive bids will be of little value. Give each the same deadline for turning in a bid; two or three weeks is a reasonable period of time. If you are willing to go with the lowest bid, make an appointment with all of them and open the envelopes in front of them.

If one bid is remarkably low, the contractor may have made an honest error in his estimate. Do not try to hold him to it if he wants to withdraw his bid. Forcing him to build at too low a price could be disastrous for both you and him.

Though the above method sounds very fair and orderly, it is not always the best approach, especially if you are inexperienced. You may want to review the bids with your architect, if you have one, or with your lender to discuss which to accept. They may not recommend the lowest. A low bid does not necessarily mean that you will get quality with economy.

If the bids are relatively close, the most important consideration may not be money at all. How easily you can talk with a contractor and whether or not he inspires confidence are very important considerations. Any sign of a personality conflict between you and a contractor should be weighed when making a decision.

Once you have financing, you can sign a contract with the builder. Most have their own contract forms, but it is advisable to have a lawyer draw one up or, at the very least, review the standard contract. This usually costs a small flat fee.

A good contract should include the following:

• Plans and sketches of the work to be done, subject to your approval.

• A list of materials, including quantity, brand names, style or serial numbers. (Do not permit any "or equal" clause that will allow the contractor to make substitutions.)

• The terms—who (you or the lender) pays whom and when.

• A production schedule.

• The contractor's certification of insurance for workmen's compensation, damage, and liability.

• A rider stating that all changes, whether or not they increase the cost, must be submitted and approved in writing.

Of course, this list represents the least a contract should include. Once you have signed it, your plans are on the way to becoming a home.

A frequently asked question is: "Should I become my own general contractor?" Unless you have knowledge of construction, material purchasing, and experience supervising subcontractors, we do not recommend this route.

How To Shop For Mortgage Money

Most people who are in the market for a new home spend months searching for the right house plan and building site. Ironically, these same people often invest very little time shopping for the money to finance their new home, though the majority will have to live with the terms of their mortgage for as long as they live in the house.

The fact is that all banks are not alike, nor are the loans that they offer—and banks are not the only financial institutions that lend money for housing. The amount of down payment, interest rate, and period of the mortgage are all, to some extent, negotiable.

• Lending practices vary from one city and state to another. If you are a first-time builder or are new to an area, it is wise to hire a real estate (not divorce or general practice) attorney to help you unravel the maze of your specific area's laws, ordinances, and customs.

• Before talking with lenders, write down all your questions. Take notes during the conversation so you can make accurate comparisons.

• Do not be intimidated by financial officers. Keep in mind that you are not begging for money, you are buying it. Do not hesitate to reveal what other institutions are offering; they may be challenged to meet or better the terms.

• Use whatever clout you have. If you or your family have been banking with the same firm for years, let them know that they could lose your business if you can get a better deal elsewhere.

• Know your credit rights. The law prohibits lenders from considering only the husband's income when determining eligibility, a practice that previously kept many people out of the housing market. If you are turned down for a loan, you have a right to see a summary of the credit report and change any errors in it.

A GUIDE TO LENDERS

Where can you turn for home financing? Here is a list of sources for you to approach:

Savings and loan associations are the best place to start because they write well over half the mortgages in the United States on dwellings that house from one to four families. They generally offer favorable interest rates, require lower down payments, and allow more time to pay off loans than do other banks.

Savings banks, sometimes called mutual savings banks, are your next best bet. Like savings and loan associations, much of their business is concentrated in home mortgages.

Commercial banks write mortgages as a sideline, and when money is tight many will not write mortgages at all. They do hold about 15 percent of the mortgages in the country, however, and when the market is right, they can be very competitive.

Mortgage banking companies use the money of private investors to write home loans. They do a brisk business in government-backed loans, which other banks are reluctant to handle because of the time and paperwork required.

Some credit unions are now allowed to grant mortgages. A few insurance companies, pension funds, unions, and fraternal organizations also offer mortgage money to their membership, often at terms more favorable than those available in the commercial marketplace.

A GUIDE TO MORTGAGES

The types of mortgages available are far more various than most potential home buyers realize.

Traditional Loans

Conventional home loans have a fixed interest rate and fixed monthly payments. About 80 percent of the mortgage money in the United States is lent in this manner. Made by private lending institutions, these fixed rate loans are available to anyone whom the bank officials consider a good credit risk. The interest rate depends on the prevailing market for money and is slightly negotiable if you are willing to put down a large down payment. Most down payments range from 15 to 33 percent.

You can borrow as much money as the lender believes you can afford to pay off over the negotiated period of time—usually 20 to 30 years. However, a 15 year mortgage can save you considerably and enable you to own your home in half the time. For example, a 30 year, $60,800 mortgage at 12% interest will have a monthly payment of $625.40 per month vs $729.72 per month for a 15 year loan at the same interest rate. At the end of 30 years you have paid $164,344 in interest vs $70,550 for the 15 year. Remember - this is only $104.32 more per month. Along with saving with a 15 year mortgage, additional savings

can be realized with a biweekly payment plan. So be sure to consult your borrowing institution for all of your options.

The FHA does not write loans; it insures them against default in order to encourage lenders to write loans for first-time buyers and people with limited incomes. The terms of these loans make them very attractive, and you may be allowed to take as long as 25 to 30 years to pay it off.

The down payment also is substantially lower with an FHA-backed loan. At present it is set at 3 percent of the first $25,000 and 5 percent of the remainder, up to the $75,300 limit. This means that a loan on a $75,300 house would require a $750 down payment on the first $25,000 plus $2,515 on the remainder, for a total down payment of $3,265. In contrast, the down payment for the same house financed with a conventional loan could run as high as $20,000.

Anyone may apply for an FHA-insured loan, but both the borrower and the house must qualify.

The VA guarantees loans for eligible veterans, and the husbands and wives of those who died while in the service or from a service-related disability. The VA guarantees up to 60 percent of the loan or $27,500, whichever is less. Like the FHA, the VA determines the appraised value of the house, though with a VA loan, you can borrow any amount up to the appraised value.

The Farmers Home Administration offers the only loans made directly by the government. Families with limited incomes in rural areas can qualify if the house is in a community of less than 10,000 people and is outside of a large metropolitan area; if their income is less than $18,000; and if they can prove that they do not qualify for a conventional loan.

For more information, write Farmers Home Administration, Department of Agriculture, Washington, D.C. 20250, or your local office.

New loan instruments

If you think that the escalating cost of housing has squeezed you out of the market, take a look at the following new types of mortgages.

The graduated payment mortgage features a monthly obligation that gradually increases over a negotiated period of time—usually five to ten years. Though the payments begin lower, they stabilize at a higher monthly rate than a standard fixed rate mortgage. Little or no equity is built in the first years, a disadvantage if you decide to sell early in the mortgage period.

These loans are aimed at young people who can anticipate income increases that will enable them to meet the escalating payments. The size of the down payment is about the same or slightly higher than for a conventional loan, but you can qualify with a lower income. As of last year, savings and loan associations can write these loans, and the FHA now insures five different types.

The flexible loan insurance program (FLIP) requires that part of the down payment, which is about the same as a conventional loan, be placed in a pledged savings account. During the first five years of the mortgage, funds are drawn from this account to supplement the lower monthly payments.

The deferred interest mortgage, another graduated program, allows you to pay a lower rate of interest during the first few years and a higher rate in the later years of the mortgage. If the house is sold, the borrower must pay back all the interest, often with a prepayment penalty. Both the FLIP and deferred interest loans are very new and not yet widely available.

The variable rate mortgage is most widely available in California, but its popularity is growing. This instrument features a fluctuating interest rate that is linked to an economic indicator—usually the lender's cost of obtaining funds for lending. To protect the consumer against a sudden and disastrous increase, regulations limit the amount that the interest rate can increase over a given period of time.

To make these loans attractive, lenders offer them without prepayment penalties and with "assumption" clauses that allow another buyer to assume your mortgage should you sell.

Flexible payment mortgages allow young people who can anticipate rising incomes to enter the housing market sooner. They pay only the interest during the first few years; then the mortgage is amortized and the payments go up. This is a valuable option only for those people who intend to keep their home for several years because no equity is built in the lower payment period.

The reverse annuity mortgage is targeted for older people who have fixed incomes. This new loan allows those who qualify to tap into the equity on their houses. The lender pays them each month and collects the loan when the house is sold or the owner dies.

All The "TOOLS" You And Your Builder Need

. . . to, first select an exterior and a floor plan for your new house that satisfy your tastes and your family's living patterns . . .

. . . then, to review the blueprints in great detail and obtain a construction cost figure . . . also, to price out the structural materials required to build . . . and, finally, to review and decide upon the specifications to which your home is to be built. Truly, an invaluable set of "tools" to launch your home planning and building programs.

1. THE PLAN BOOKS

Home Planners' unique Design Category Series makes it easy to look at and study only the types of designs for which you and your family have an interest. Each of six plan books features a specific type of home, namely: Two-Story, 1½ Story, One-Story Over 2000 Sq. Ft., One-Story Under 2000 Sq. Ft., Multi-Levels and Vacation Homes. In addition to the convenient Design Category Series, there is an impressive selection of other current titles. While the home plans featured in these books are also to be found in the Design Category Series, they, too, are edited for those with special tastes and requirements. Your family will spend many enjoyable hours reviewing the delightfully designed exteriors and the practical floor plans. Surely your home or office library should include a selection of these popular plan books. Your complete satisfaction is guaranteed.

2. THE CONSTRUCTION BLUEPRINTS

There are blueprints available for each of the designs published in Home Planners' current plan books. Depending upon the size, the style and the type of home, each set of blueprints consists of from five to ten large sheets. Only by studying the blueprints is it possible to give complete and final consideration to the proper selection of a design for your next home. The blueprints provide the opportunity for all family members to familiarize themselves with the features of all exterior elevations, interior elevations and details, all dimensions, special built-in features and effects. They also provide a full understanding of the materials to be used and/or selected. The low-cost of our blueprints makes it possible and indeed, practical, to study in detail a number of different sets of blueprints before deciding upon which design to build.

3. THE MATERIALS LIST

A list of materials is an integral part of the plan package. It comprises the last sheet of each set of blueprints and serves as a handy reference during the period of construction. Of course, at the pricing and the material ordering stages, it is indispensable.

4. THE SPECIFICATION OUTLINE

Each order for blueprints is accompanied by one Specification Outline. You and your builder will find this a time-saving tool when deciding upon your own individual specifications. An important reference document should you wish to write your own specifications.

The Design Category Series

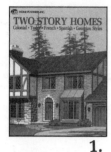

360 TWO STORY HOMES

English Tudors, Early American Salt ·Boxes, Gambrels, Farmhouses, Southern Colonials, Georgians, French Mansards, Contemporaries. Interesting floor plans for both small and large families. Efficient kitchens, 2 to 6 bedrooms, family rooms, libraries, extra baths, mud rooms. Homes for all budgets.

1. 288 Pages, $6.95

150 1½ STORY HOMES

Cape Cod, Williamsburg, Georgian, Tudor and Contemporary versions. Low budget and country-estate feature sections. Expandable family plans. Formal and informal living and dining areas along with gathering rooms. Spacious, country kitchens. Indoor-outdoor livability with covered porches and functional terraces.

2. 128 Pages, $3.95

210 ONE STORY HOM OVER 2,000 Sq. Ft.

All popular styles. Includ Spanish, Western, Tud French, and other traditio versions. Contemporari Gracious, family living p terns. Sunken living roo master bedroom suites, a ums, courtyards, pools. F indoor-outdoor living re tionships. For modest country-estate budgets.

3. 192 Pages, $4.95

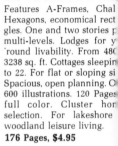

315 ONE STORY HOMES UNDER 2,000 Sq. Ft.

A great selection of traditional and contemporary exteriors for medium and restricted budgets. Efficient, practical floor plans. Gathering rooms, formal and informal living and dining rooms, mud rooms, indoor-outdoor livability. Economically built homes. Designs with bonus space livability for growing families.

4. 192 Pages, $4.95

215 MULTI-LEVEL HOMES

For new dimensions in family living. A captivating variety of exterior styles, exciting floor plans for flat and sloping sites. Exposed lower levels. Balconies, decks. Plans for the active family. Upper level lounges, excellent bath facilities. Sloping ceilings. Functional outdoor terraces. For all building budgets.

5. 192 Pages, $4.95

223 VACATION HOM

Features A-Frames, Chal Hexagons, economical re gles. One and two stories p multi-levels. Lodges for y 'round livability. From 480 3238 sq. ft. Cottages sleepin to 22. For flat or sloping si Spacious, open planning. O 600 illustrations. 120 Page full color. Cluster hor selection. For lakeshore woodland leisure living.

6. 176 Pages, $4.95

The Exterior Style Series

330 EARLY AMERICAN PLANS

Our new *Essential Guide to Early American Home Plans* traces Early American architecture from our Colonial Past to Traditional styles popular today with a written history of designs and colorful sections devoted to styles. Many of our designs are patterned after historic homes.

7. 304 Pages, $9.95

335 CONTEMPORARY HOME PLANS

Our new *Essential Guide to Contemporary Home Plans* offers a colorful directory to modern architecture, including a history of American Contemporary styling and more than 335 home plans of all sizes and popular designs. 304 colorful pages!

8. 304 Pages, $9.95

135 ENGLISH TUDOR HOMES

and other Popular Fam Plans is a favorite of ma The current popularity of English Tudor home desig phenomenal. Here is a b which is loaded with Tud for all budgets. There one-story, 1½ and two-st designs, plus multi-levels hillsides from 1,176 to 3,849 ft. There is a special 20 p section of Early Ameri Adaptations.

9. 104 Pages, $3.95

The Budget Series

175 LOW BUDGET HOMES

A special selection of home designs for the modest or restricted building budget. An excellent variety of Traditional and Contemporary designs. One-story, 1½ and two-story and split-level homes. Three, four and five bedrooms. Family rooms, extra baths, formal and informal dining rooms. Basement and non-basement designs. Attached garages an covered porches.

13. 96 Pages, $2.95

165 AFFORDABLE HOME PLANS

This outstanding book was specially edited with a wide selection of houses and plans for those with a medium building budget. While none of these designs are considered low-cost; neither do they require an unlimited budget to build. Square footages range from 1,428. Exteriors of Tudor, French, Early American, Spanish and Contemporary are included.

14. 112 Pages, $2.95

142 HOME DESIGNS FOR EXPANDED BUILDING BUDGETS

A family's ability to fina and need for a larger ho grows as its size and inco increases. This selection h lights designs which house average square footage 2,551. One-story plans ave 2,069; two-stories, 2,7 multi-levels, 2,825. Spac homes featuring raised he fireplaces, open planning efficient kitchens.

15. 112 Pages, $2.95

The Full Color Series

116 TRADITIONAL and CONTEMPORARY PLANS

A beautifully illustrated home plan book in complete, full color. One, 1½, two-story and split-level designs featured in all of the most popular exterior styles. Varied building budgets will be satisfied by the numerous plans for all budget sizes. Designs for flat and hillside sites, including exposed lower levels. It will make an ideal gift item.

17.

96 Pages in Full Color, $5.95

122 HOME DESIGNS

This book has full color throughout. More than 120 eye-pleasing, colored illustrations. Tudor, French, Spanish, Early American and Contemporary exteriors featuring all design types. The interiors house efficient, step-saving floor plans. Formal and informal living areas along with convenient work centers. Two to six bedroom sleeping areas. A delightful book for one's permanent library.

18.

96 Pages in Full Color, $5.95

114 TREND HOMES

Heritage Houses, Energy Designs, Family Plans - these, along with Vacation Homes, are in this new plan book in full color. The Trend Homes feature unique living patterns. The revered Heritage Houses highlight the charm and nostalgia of Early America. Solariums, greenhouses, earth-sheltered and super-insulated houses are the Energy Designs. Vacation homes feature A-frames and chalets.

19.

104 Pages in Full Color, $5.95

450 HOUSE PLANS

For those who wish to review and study perhaps the largest selection of designs available in a single volume. This edition will provide countless hours of enjoyable family home planning. Varying exterior styles, plus interesting and practical floor plans for all building budgets. Formal, informal living patterns; indoor-outdoor livability; small, growing and large family facilities.

23.

320 Pages, $9.95

136 SPANISH & WESTERN HOME DESIGNS

Stucco exteriors, arches, tile roofs, wide-overhangs, courtyards and rambling ranches are characteristics which make this design selection distinctive. These sun-country designs highlight indoor-outdoor relationships. Solar oriented livability is featured. Their appeal is not limited to the Southwest region of our country.

10.

120 Pages, $2.95

The Plan Books

. . . are a most valuable tool for anyone planning to build a new home. A study of the hundreds of delightfully designed exteriors and the practical, efficient floor plans will be a great learning and fun-oriented family experience. You will be able to select your preferred styling from among Early American, Tudor, French, Spanish and Contemporary adaptations. Your ideas about floor planning and interior livability will expand. And, of course, after you have selected an appealing home design that satisfies your long list of living requirements, you can order the blueprints for further study of your favorite design in greater detail. Surely the hours spent studying the portfolio of Home Planners' designs will be both enjoyable and rewarding ones.

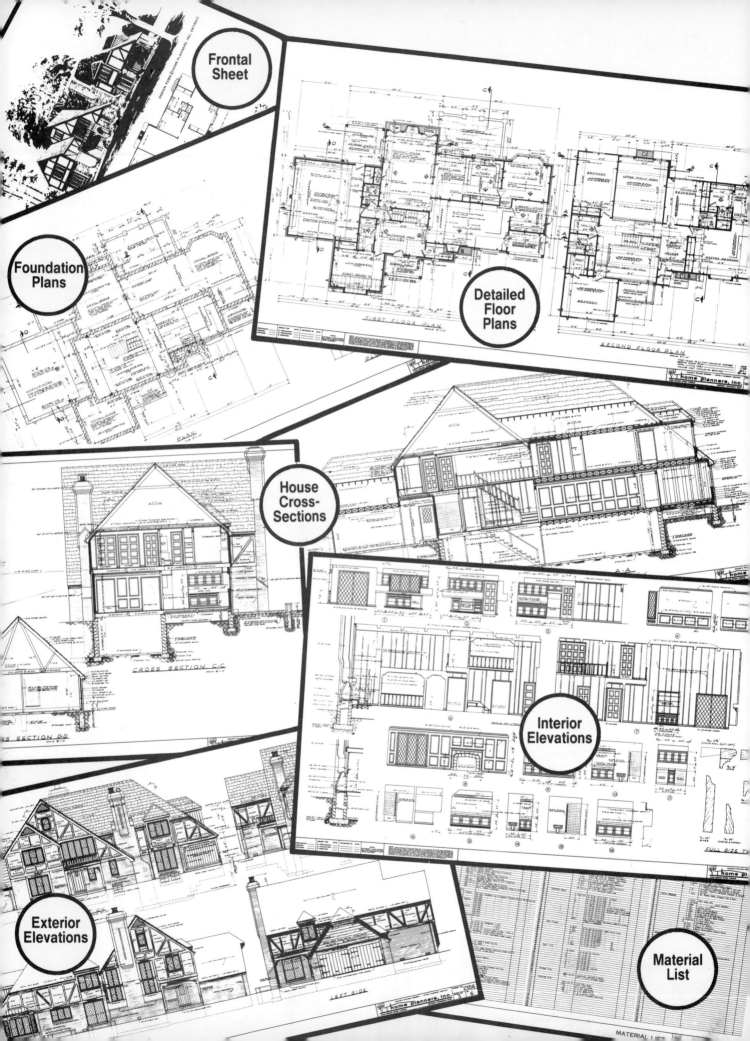

Frontal Sheet

Detailed Floor Plans

Foundation Plans

House Cross-Sections

Interior Elevations

Exterior Elevations

Material List

The Blueprints

1. FRONTAL SHEET.
Artist's landscaped sketch of the exterior and ink-line floor plans are on the frontal sheet of each set of blueprints.

2. FOUNDATION PLAN.
¼" Scale basement and foundation plan. All necessary notations and dimensions. Plot plan diagram for locating house on building site.

3. DETAILED FLOOR PLAN.
¼" Scale first and second floor plans with complete dimensions. Cross-section detail keys. Diagrammatic layout of electrical outlets and switches.

4. HOUSE CROSS-SECTIONS.
Large scale sections of foundation, interior and exterior walls, floors and roof details for design and construction control.

5. INTERIOR ELEVATIONS.
Large scale interior details of the complete kitchen cabinet design, bathrooms, powder room, laundry, fireplaces, paneling, beam ceilings, built-in cabinets, etc.

6. EXTERIOR ELEVATIONS.
¼" Scale exterior elevation drawings of front, rear, and both sides of the house. All exterior materials and details are shown to indicate the complete design and proportions of the house.

7. MATERIAL LIST.
Complete lists of all materials required for the construction of the house as designed are included in each set of blueprints.

THIS BLUEPRINT PACKAGE will help you and your family take a major step forward in the final appraisal and planning of your new home. Only by spending many enjoyable and informative hours studying the numerous details included in the complete package, will you feel sure of, and comfortable with, your commitment to build your new home. To assure successful and productive consultation with your builder and/or architect, reference to the various elements of the blueprint package is a must. The blueprints, material list and specification outline will save much consultation time and expense. Don't be without them.

The Material List

With each set of blueprints you order you will receive a material list. Each list shows you the quantity, type and size of the non-mechanical materials required to build your home. It also tells you where these materials are used. This makes the blueprints easy to understand.

Influencing the mechanical requirements are geographical differences in availability of materials, local codes, methods of installation and individual preferences. Because of these factors, your local heating, plumbing and electrical contractors can supply you with necessary material take-offs for their particular trades.

Material lists simplify your material ordering and enable you to get quicker price quotations from your builder and material dealer. Because the material list is an integral part of each set of blueprints, it is not available separately.

Among the materials listed:

• Masonry, Veneer & Fireplace • Framing Lumber • Roofing & Sheet Metal • Windows & Door Frames • Exterior Trim & Insulation • Tile Work, Finish Floors • Interior Trim, Kitchen Cabinets • Rough & Finish Hardware

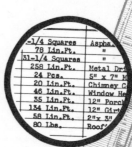

The Specification Outline

This fill-in type specification lists over 150 phases of home construction from excavating to painting and includes wiring, plumbing, heating and air-conditioning. It consists of 16 pages and will prove invaluable for specifying to your builder the exact materials, equipment and methods of construction you want in your new home. One Specification Outline is included free with each order for blueprints. Additional Specification Outlines are available at $3.00 each.

CONTENTS

• General Instructions, Suggestions and Information • Excavating and Grading • Masonry and Concrete Work • Sheet Metal Work • Carpentry, Millwork, Roofing, and Miscellaneous Items • Lath and Plaster or Drywall Wallboard • Schedule for Room Finishes • Painting and Finishing • Tile Work • Electrical Work • Plumbing • Heating and Air-Conditioning

Before You Order

1. STUDY THE DESIGNS . . . found in Home Planners current publications. As you review these delightful custom homes, you should keep in mind the total living requirements of your family — both indoors and outdoors. Although we do not make changes in plans, many minor changes can be made prior to the period of construction. If major changes are involved to satisfy your personal requirements, you should consider ordering one set of blueprints and having them redrawn locally. Consultation with your architect is strongly advised when contemplating major changes.

2. HOW TO ORDER BLUEPRINTS . . . After you have chosen the design that satisfies your requirements, or if you have selected one that you wish to study in more detail, simply clip the accompanying order blank and mail with your remittance. However, if it is not convenient for you to send a check or money order, you can use your credit card, or merely indicate C.O.D. shipment. Postman will collect all charges, including postage and C.O.D. fee. C.O.D. shipments are not permitted to Canada or foreign countries. Should time be of essence, as it sometimes is with many of our customers, your telephone order usually can be processed and shipped in the next day's mail. Simply call toll free 1-800-521-6797, (Michigan residents call collect 0-313-477-1854).

3. OUR SERVICE . . . Home Planners makes every effort to process and ship each order for blueprints and books within 48 hours. Because of this, we have deemed it unnecessary to acknowledge receipt of our customers orders. See order coupon for the postage and handling charges for surface mail, air mail or foreign mail.

4. A NOTE REGARDING REVERSE BLUEPRINTS . . . As a special service to those wishing to build in reverse of the plan as shown, we do include an extra set of reversed blueprints for only $25.00 additional with each order. Even though the lettering and dimensions appear backward on reversed blueprints, they make a handy reference because they show the house just as it's being built in reverse from the standard blueprints — thereby helping you visualize the home better.

5. OUR EXCHANGE POLICY . . . Since blueprints are printed up in specific response to your individual order, we cannot honor requests for refunds. However, the first set of blueprints in any order (or the one set in a single set order) for a given design may be exchanged for a set of another design at a fee of $20.00 plus $3.00 for postage and handling via surface mail; $4.00 via air mail.

TO: HOME PLANNERS, INC., 23761 RESEARCH DRIVE FARMINGTON HILLS, MICHIGAN 48024

Please rush me the following:

_____ SET(S) BLUEPRINTS FOR DESIGN NO(S). _____ $_____
Single Set, $110.00; Additional Identical Sets in Same Order $25.00 ea.
4 Set Package of Same Design, $165.00 (Save $20.00)
7 Set Package of Same Design, $195.00 (Save $65.00)
(Material Lists and 1 Specification Outline included)

_____ SPECIFICATION OUTLINES @ $3.00 EACH . . . . $_____

Michigan Residents add 4% sales tax $_____

FOR POSTAGE ☐ $3.00 Added to Order for Surface Mail (UPS) - Any Mdse.
AND HANDLING ☐ $4.00 Added for Priority Mail of One-Three Sets of Blueprints.
PLEASE CHECK ☐ $6.00 Added for Priority Mail of Four or more Sets of Blueprints. } $_____
✔ & REMIT ☐ For Canadian orders add $2.00 to above applicable rates

☐ C.O.D. PAY POSTMAN
(C.O.D. Within U.S.A. Only)   TOTAL in U.S.A. funds $_____

PLEASE PRINT
Name _____
Street _____
City _____ State _____ Zip _____

CREDIT CARD ORDERS ONLY: Fill in the boxes below   **Prices subject to change without notice**

Credit Card No. ☐☐☐☐☐☐☐☐☐☐☐☐☐☐   Expiration Date Month/Year ☐☐☐☐

CHECK ONE: ☐ **VISA** ☐ **MasterCard**

Order Form Key TB7BP   Your Signature _____

BLUEPRINT ORDERS SHIPPED WITHIN 48 HOURS OF RECEIPT!

TO: HOME PLANNERS, INC., 23761 RESEARCH DRIVE FARMINGTON HILLS, MICHIGAN 48024

Please rush me the following:

_____ SET(S) BLUEPRINTS FOR DESIGN NO(S). _____ $_____
Single Set, $110.00; Additional Identical Sets in Same Order $25.00 ea.
4 Set Package of Same Design, $165.00 (Save $20.00)
7 Set Package of Same Design, $195.00 (Save $65.00)
(Material Lists and 1 Specification Outline included)

_____ SPECIFICATION OUTLINES @ $3.00 EACH . . . . $_____

Michigan Residents add 4% sales tax $_____

FOR POSTAGE ☐ $3.00 Added to Order for Surface Mail (UPS) - Any Mdse.
AND HANDLING ☐ $4.00 Added for Priority Mail of One-Three Sets of Blueprints.
PLEASE CHECK ☐ $6.00 Added for Priority Mail of Four or more Sets of Blueprints. } $_____
✔ & REMIT ☐ For Canadian orders add $2.00 to above applicable rates

☐ C.O.D. PAY POSTMAN
(C.O.D. Within U.S.A. Only)   TOTAL in U.S.A. funds $_____

PLEASE PRINT
Name _____
Street _____
City _____ State _____ Zip _____

CREDIT CARD ORDERS ONLY: Fill in the boxes below   **Prices subject to change without notice**

Credit Card No. ☐☐☐☐☐☐☐☐☐☐☐☐☐☐   Expiration Date Month/Year ☐☐☐☐

CHECK ONE: ☐ **VISA** ☐ **MasterCard**

Order Form Key TB7BP   Your Signature _____

How many sets of blueprints should be ordered?

This question is often asked. The answer can range anywhere from 1 to 7 sets, depending upon circumstances. For instance, a single set of blueprints of your favorite design is sufficient to study the house in greater detail. On the other hand, if you are planning to get cost estimates, or if you are planning to build, you may need as many as seven sets of blueprints. Because the first set of blueprints in each order is $110.00, and because additional sets of the same design in each order are only $25.00 each (and with package sets even more economical), you save considerably by ordering your total requirements now. To help you determine the exact number of sets, please refer to the handy check list.

How Many Blueprints Do You Need?

__OWNER'S SET

__BUILDER (Usually requires at least 3 sets: 1 as legal document; 1 for inspection; and at least 1 for tradesmen — usually more.)

__BUILDING PERMIT (Sometimes 2 sets are required.)

__MORTGAGE SOURCE (Usually 1 set for a conventional mortgage; 3 sets for F.H.A. or V.A. type mortgages.)

__SUBDIVISION COMMITTEE (If any.)

__TOTAL NO. SETS REQUIRED

Blueprint Ordering Hotline –

Phone toll free: 1-800-521-6797.
Orders received by 11 a.m. (Detroit time) will be processed the same day and shipped to you the following day. Use of this line restricted to blueprint ordering only. Michigan residents simply call collect 0-313-477-1854.

Kindly Note: When ordering by phone, please state Order Form Key No. located in box at lower left corner of blueprint order form.

In Canada Mail To:
Home Planners, Inc., 20 Cedar St. North Kitchener, Ontario N2H 2W8
Phone: (519) 743-4169

TRADITIONAL FACADE DESIGNS

. . . with Contemporary Living Patterns Many homes with Traditional exteriors sport modern floor plans with Contemporary lifestyle features on the inside. For many, this may present an excellent way to have the best of both worlds – plus all the personality of Modern lifestyle patterns.

Design T72909 1,221 Sq. Ft. - First Floor
767 Sq. Ft. - Second Floor; 38,954 Cu. Ft.

● This charming traditional home with striking good looks offers the modern family plenty of contemporary amenities. The first floor features a large gathering room with fireplace, media room for stereos and VCRs, a convenient kitchen with breakfast room, plus a dining room.

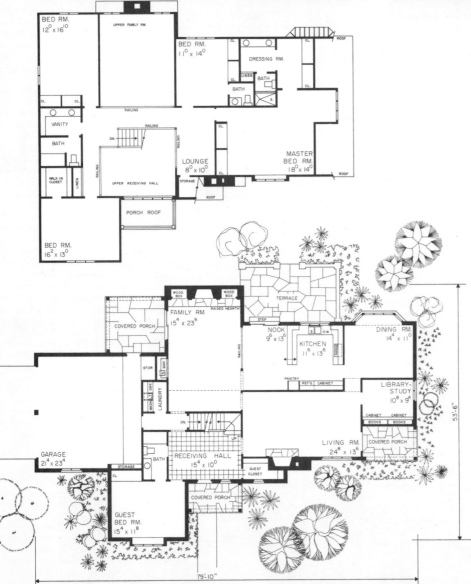

Floor plan labels:

BED RM. 12⁰ x 16¹⁰
UPPER FAMILY RM.
BED RM. 11⁰ x 14⁰
DRESSING RM.
CL
LINEN
BATH
BATH
S.
ROOF
CL
CL
RAILING
VANITY
BATH
WALK IN CLOSET
LINEN
DN
RAILING
RAILING
LOUNGE 8⁰ x 10⁰
CL
STORAGE
CL
MASTER BED RM. 18⁰ x 14⁰
ROOF
UPPER RECEIVING HALL
ROOF
PORCH ROOF
BED RM. 16² x 13⁰

WOOD BOX
WOOD BOX
FAMILY RM. 15⁴ x 23⁶
RAISED HEARTH
TERRACE
COVERED PORCH
STEP
NOOK 9⁶ x 13⁵
S DW
DINING RM. 14⁴ x 11⁰
KITCHEN 11⁵ x 13⁶
STOR
BAR
PANTRY
REF'S. CABINET
LIBRARY-STUDY 10⁸ x 9⁴
LAUNDRY
WASHER DRYER
CABINET CABINET
BOOKS BOOKS
DN
UP
LIVING RM. 24⁸ x 13⁶
COVERED PORCH
BATH
RECEIVING HALL 15⁴ x 10⁰
GUEST CLOSET
GARAGE 21⁰ x 23⁴
STORAGE
CL
COVERED PORCH
GUEST BED RM. 15⁴ x 11⁸
53'-6"
79'-10"

Design T72356

1,969 Sq. Ft. - First Floor
1,702 Sq. Ft. - Second Floor
55,105 Cu. Ft.

● Here is truly an exquisite Tudor adaptation. The exterior, with its interesting roof lines, window treatment, stately chimney and its appealing use of brick and stucco, could hardly be more dramatic. Inside, the drama really begins to unfold as one envisions his family's living patterns. The delightfully large receiving hall has a two story ceiling and controls the flexible traffic patterns. The living and dining rooms, with the library nearby, will cater to the formal living pursuits. The guest room offers another haven for the enjoyment of peace and quiet. Observe the adjacent full bath. Just inside the entrance from the garage is the laundry room. For the family's informal activities there are the interactions of the family room - covered porch - nook - kitchen zone. Notice the raised hearth fireplace, the wood boxes, the sliding glass doors, built-in bar and the kitchen pass-thru. Adding to the charm of the family room is its high ceiling. From the second floor hall one can look down and observe the activities below.

Design T72543

2,345 Sq. Ft. - First Floor
1,687 Sq. Ft. - Second Floor; 76,000 Cu. Ft.

● Certainly a dramatic French adaptation highlighted by effective window treatment, delicate cornice detailing, appealing brick quoins and excellent proportion. Stepping through the double front doors the drama is heightened by the spacious entry hall with its two curving staircases to the second floor. The upper hall is open and looks down to the hall below. There is a study and a big gathering room which look out on the raised terrace. The work center is outstanding. The garage will accommodate three cars.

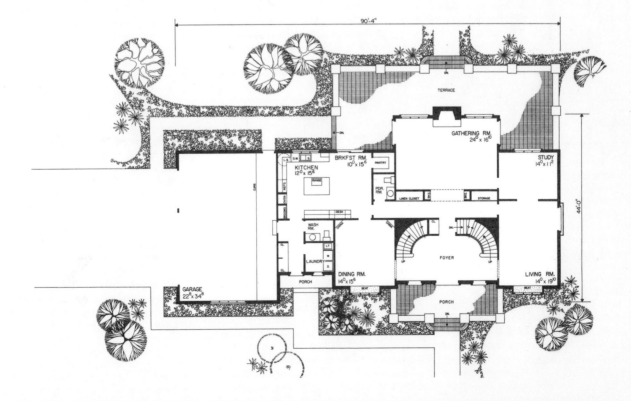

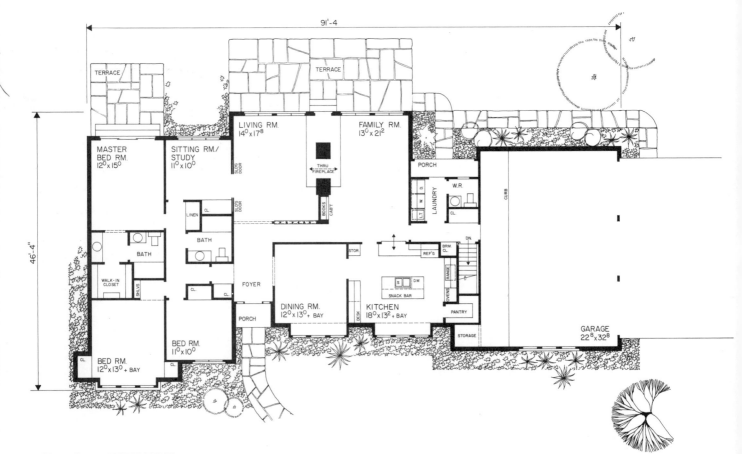

Design T72785 *2,375 Sq. Ft.; 47,805 Cu. Ft.*

● Exceptional Tudor design! Passersby will take a second glance at this fine home wherever it may be located. And the interior is just as pleasing. As one enters the foyer and looks around, the plan will speak for itself in the areas of convenience and efficiency.

Cross room traffic will be avoided. There is a hall leading to each of the three bedrooms and study of the sleeping wing and another leading to the living room, family room, kitchen and laundry with washroom. The formal dining room can be entered from both

the foyer and the kitchen. Efficiency will be the by-word when describing the kitchen. Note the fine features: a built-in desk, pantry, island snack bar with sink and pass-thru to the family room. The fireplace will be enjoyed in the living and family rooms.

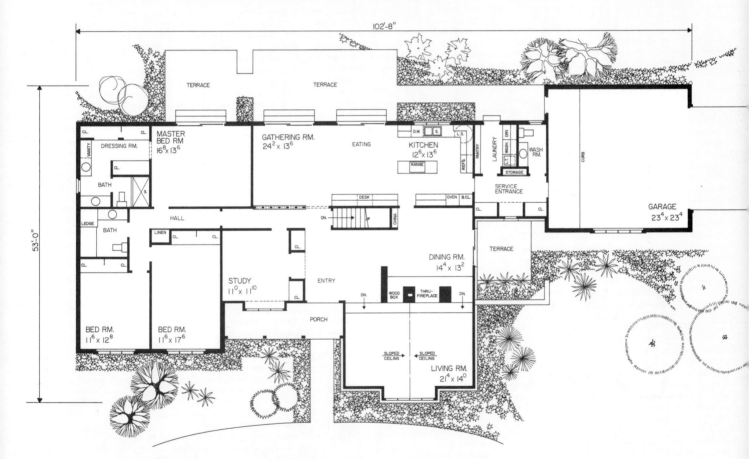

Design T72746 *2,790 Sq. Ft.; 57,590 Cu. Ft.*

● This impressive one-story will be the talk-of-the-town. And not surprisingly, either. It embodies all of the elements to assure a sound investment and years of happy family livability. The projecting living room with its stucco, simulated wood beams and effective window treatment adds a dramatic note. Sunken by two steps, this room will enjoy privacy. The massive double front doors are sheltered by the covered porch and lead to the spacious entry hall. The interior is particularly well-zoned. The large, rear gathering room will cater to the family's gregarious instincts. Outdoor enjoyment can be obtained on the three terraces. Also, a study is available for those extra quiet moments. Be sure to observe the plan closely for all of the other fine features.

Design T71974 1,680 Sq. Ft. - Main Level; 1,344 Sq. Ft. - Lower Level; 34,186 Cu. Ft.

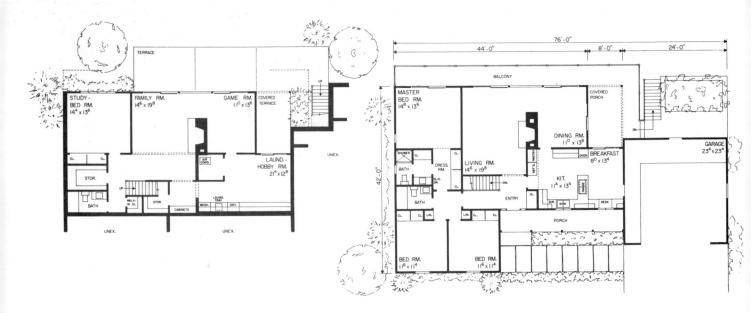

● You would never guess from looking at the front of this traditional design that it possessed such a strikingly different rear. From the front, you would guess that all of its livability is on one floor. Yet, just imagine the tremendous amount of livability that is added to the plan as a result of exposing the lower level - 1,344 square feet of it. Living in this hillside house will mean fun. Obviously, the most popular spot will be the balcony. Then again, maybe it could be the terrace adjacent to the family room. Both the terrace and the balcony have a covered area to provide protection against unfavorable weather. The interior of the plan also will serve the family with ease.

● Organized zoning by room functions makes this Traditional design a comfortable home for living, as well as classic in its styling. A central foyer facilitates flexible traffic patterns. Quiet areas of the house include a media room and luxurious master bedroom suite with fitness area, spacious closet space and bath, as well as a lounge or writing area. Informal living areas of the house include a sun room, large country kitchen, and efficient kitchen with an island. Service areas include a room just off the garage for laundry, sewing, or hobbies. The second floor garage can double as a practical shop. Formal living areas include a living area and formal dining room. The second floor holds two bedrooms that would make a wonderful children's suite, with a study or TV area also upstairs.

Design T72921

3,215 Sq. Ft. - First Floor
296 Sq. Ft. - Sun Room
711 Sq. Ft. - Second Floor
69,991 Cu. Ft.

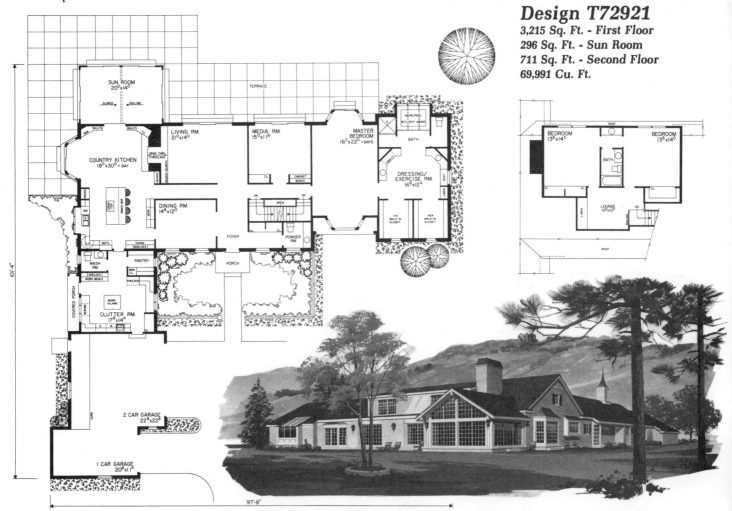

Design T72888
3,018 Sq. Ft.; 59,769 Cu. Ft.

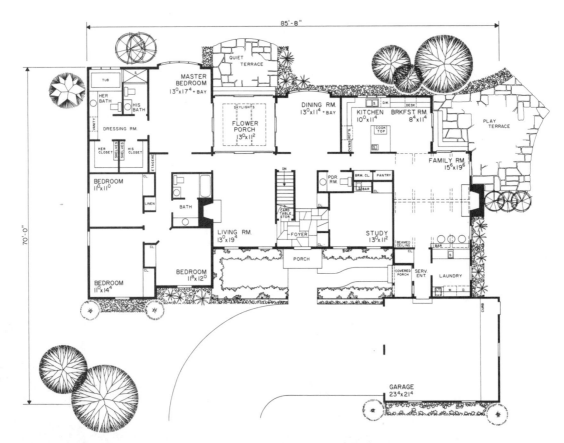

● This is an outstanding Early American design for the 20th-Century. The exterior detailing with narrow clapboards, multi-paned windows and cupola are the features of yesteryear. Interior planning, though, is for today's active family. Formal living room, informal family room plus a study are present. Every activity will have its place in this home. Picture yourself working in the kitchen. There's enough counter space for two or three helpers. Four bedrooms are in the private area. Stop and imagine your daily routine if you occupied the master bedroom. Both you and your spouse would have plenty of space and privacy. The flower porch, accessible from the master bedroom, living and dining rooms, is a very delightful "plus" feature. Study this design's every detail.

Design T72615 2,563 Sq. Ft. - First Floor
552 Sq. Ft. - Second Floor; 59,513 Cu. Ft.

● The exterior detailing of this design recalls 18th-Century New England architecture. Enter by way of the centered front door and you are greeted into the foyer. Directly to the right is the study or optional bedroom or to the left is the living room. This large formal room features sliding glass doors to the sun-drenched solarium. The beauty of the solarium will be appreciated from the master bedroom and the dining room along with the living room.

Design T72779
3,225 Sq. Ft.; 70,715 Cu. Ft.

● This design is impressive, indeed, with French roof, paned-glass windows, masonry, brick privacy wall, and double front doors. A large entry hall leads to each of the areas in this large home. While serving in the formal dining room, one can enter by a butler's pantry with sink. There's also a sizable parlor just off the entry. Other features include a gathering room with fireplace, an adjacent study, a work center, U-shaped modern kitchen with snack bar and nook, pantry with washroom, large laundry room, and basement.

Design T72778
2,761 Sq. Ft.; 4,145 Cu. Ft.

● No matter what the occasion, family and friends alike should enjoy the spacious gathering room of this large one-story brick Traditional home. This 20' x 23' gathering room features a thru fireplace to the study and two sets of sliding glass doors that lead to a large rear terrace. Indoor-outdoor living also can be enjoyed from a formal dining room, study, and master bedroom. The master suite includes its own exercise room and large storage. All three bedrooms are isolated at one end of the house for privacy. There is also a covered porch accessible through sliding glass doors in the dining room and breakfast nook.

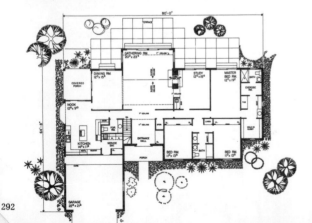

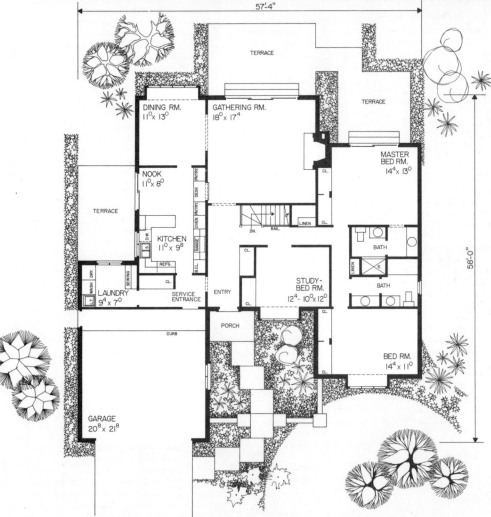

TERRACE

DINING RM.
11⁰ x 13⁰

GATHERING RM.
18⁰ x 17⁴

TERRACE

NOOK
11⁰ x 8⁰

TERRACE

MASTER BED RM.
14⁴ x 13⁰

CL.

PANTRY

OVEN PANTRY DESK

RANGE

D.W.

S.

KITCHEN
11⁰ x 9⁸

REFG.

DN. RAIL

LINEN

CL.

LINEN

BATH

SEWING

WASH DRY

L.T.

CL.

B.CL.

CL.

LAUNDRY
9⁴ x 7⁰

SERVICE ENTRANCE

ENTRY

CL.

STUDY-BED RM.
12⁴ 10⁰ 12⁰

CL.

S.

BATH

CURB

PORCH

CL.

BED RM.
14⁴ x 11⁰

GARAGE
20⁸ x 21⁸

57'-4"

58'-0"

Design T72738
1,898 Sq. Ft.; 36,140 Cu. Ft.

● Impressive architectural work is indeed apparent in this three bedroom home. The three foot high entrance court wall, the high pitched roof and the paned glass windows all add to this home's exterior appeal. It is also apparent that the floor plan is very efficient with the side, U-shaped kitchen and nook with two pantry closets. Overlooking the backyard, the dining and gathering rooms will serve your every family occasion. Three (or make it two with a study) bedrooms and two baths are in the sleeping wing. Indoor-outdoor living also will be enjoyed in this home with a dining terrace off the nook and a living terrace off the gathering room and master bedroom. Note the fireplace in the gathering room and bay window in dining room. This design will be very livable.

Design T72883 1,919 Sq. Ft. - First Floor
895 Sq. Ft. - Second Floor; 46,489 Cu. Ft.

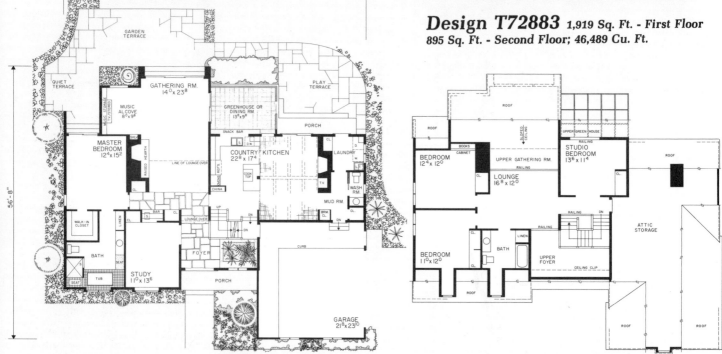

● A country-style home is part of America's fascination with the rural past. This home's emphasis of the traditional home is in its gambrel roof, dormers and fanlight windows. Having a traditional exterior from the street view, this home has window walls and a greenhouse, which opens the house to the outdoors in a thoroughly contemporary manner. The interior meets the requirements of today's active family. Like the country houses of the past, it has a gathering room for family get-togethers or entertaining. The adjacent two-story greenhouse doubles as the dining room. There is a pass-thru snack bar to the country kitchen here. This country kitchen just might be the heart of the house with its two areas - work zone and sitting room. There are four bedrooms on the two floors - the master bedroom suite on the first floor; three more on the second floor. A lounge, overlooking the gathering room and front foyer, is also on the second floor.

Design T72826
1,112 Sq. Ft. - First Floor
881 Sq. Ft. - Second Floor; 32,770 Cu. Ft.

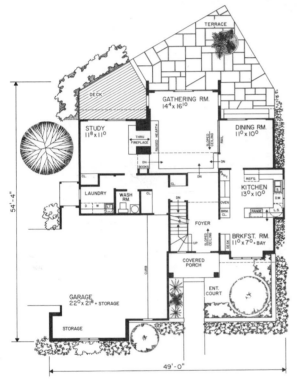

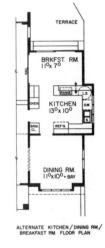

ALTERNATE KITCHEN / DINING RM. / BREAKFAST RM. FLOOR PLAN

● This is an outstanding example of the type of informal, traditional-style architecture that has captured the modern imagination. The interior plan houses all of the features that people want most - a spacious gathering room, formal and informal dining areas, efficient, U-shaped kitchen, master bedroom, two children's bedrooms, second floor lounge, entrance court and rear terrace and deck. Study all areas of this plan carefully.

POST-MODERN VARIATIONS
. . . Modern Facelifts for Classic Period Architecture

Designs on the following pages represent a Contemporary architectural trend of modernizing traditional architectural styles of different periods. Contemporary features such as lines and angles mark many of these new designs, while the flavor of the original architectural style is maintained.

Design T72876 1,462 Sq. Ft. - First Floor; 1,132 Sq. Ft. - Second Floor; 41,140 Cu. Ft.

● This Early American design has received a modern facelift that includes large view windows and a floor plan for Contemporary living patterns. The charm of traditional covered porch and vertical lines have been maintained, along with practical dormer windows that pierce the gable roof line. A front dining room and a living room on either side of the central foyer both enjoy bay windows. There's also a rear family room downstairs, as well as a modern kitchen that incorporates a breakfast room and island cook top in its open planning expanse. Upstairs are three large bedrooms including a master bedroom suite and five cozy dormers with window-ledge seats. Also note the covered side porch that allows handy entry to the laundry, kitchen, or garage.

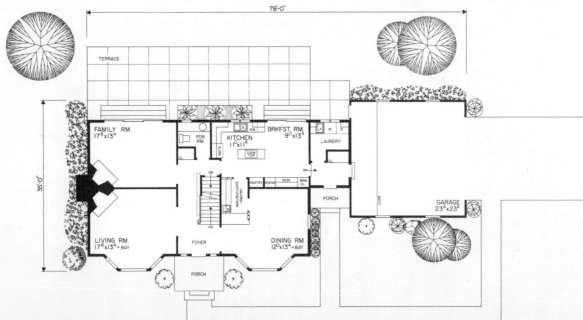

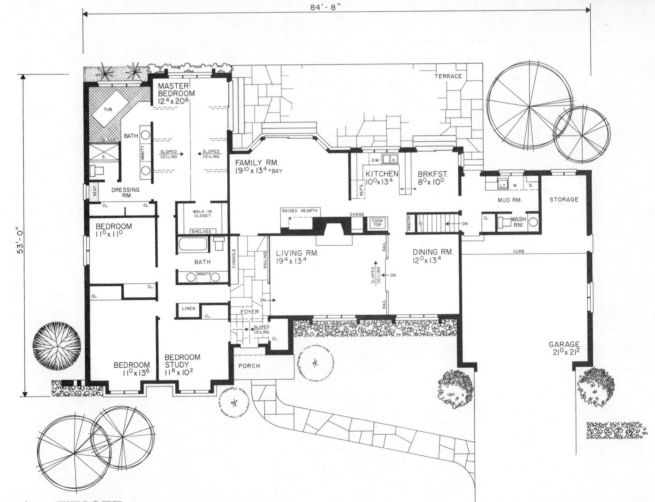

Design T72877 2,612 Sq. Ft.; 67,175 Cu. Ft.

● Here's a dramatic, Post-Modern exterior with a popular plan featuring an outstanding master bedroom suite. The bedroom itself is spacious, has a sloped ceiling, a large walk-in closet and sliding glass doors to the terrace. Now examine the bath and dressing area. Two large closets, twin vanities, built-in seat and a dramatically presented corner tub are present. The tub will be a great place to spend the evening hours after a long, hard day. Along with this bedroom, there are three more served by a full bath. The living area of this plan has the formal areas in the front and the informal areas in the rear. Both have a fireplace. The spacious work center is efficiently planned.

Design T72874

1,661 Sq. Ft. - First Floor
1,808 Sq. Ft. - Second Floor
436 Sq. Ft. - Third Floor
64,260 Cu. Ft.

● This Post-Modern design with its many gables offers plenty of roomy comfort in a stylish home sure to draw heads. The first floor includes a living room with fireplace and bay window, study with its own bay window, family room with fireplace, formal dining room, modern kitchen with snack bar and breakfast room, and large foyer. The second floor includes a master bedroom suite, three other large bedrooms, and a large studio that could also double as room for hobbies or storage. The third floor includes a guest bedroom with bath and an upper lounge. Note the covered porch, window treatments and overhangs in this lovely design. This is a modernization of classic period architecture, with a modern floor plan and Contemporary view windows.

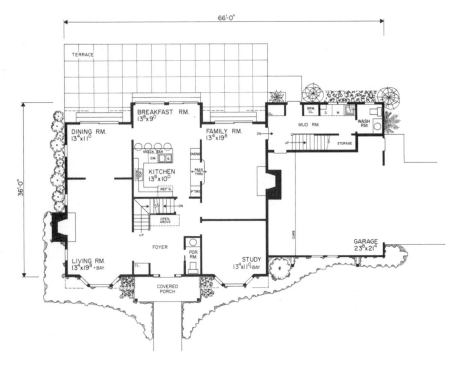

BEDROOM
12⁰x13⁴

UPPER FAMILY RM.

BALCONY

BEDROOM
11⁰x14⁴

ROOF

SLOPED CEILING

SLOPED CEILING

HIS BATH

TUB

HER BATH

LOUNGE
15⁸x9⁴

BALCONY RAIL

DRESSING RM.

VANITY

WALK-IN CLOSET

SHELVES

RAILING

DN

SHOES

CL.

DRESSING RM.

BATH

UPPER RECEIVING HALL

LINEN

CL.

MASTER BEDROOM
25⁸x13⁴

BATH

RAILING

CL.

WALK-IN CLOSET

LINEN

ROOF

ROOF

SLOPED CEILING

SLOPED CEILING

BALCONY

BEDROOM
15⁸x13⁰

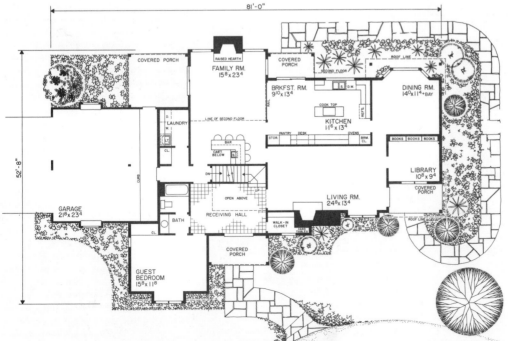

81'-0"

52'-8"

COVERED PORCH

RAISED HEARTH

FAMILY RM.
15⁸x23⁴

COVERED PORCH

ROOF LINE

SECOND FLOOR

BRKFST. RM.
9¹⁰x13⁴

DINING RM.
14⁰x11⁴+BAY

LINE OF SECOND FLOOR

COOK TOP

LAUNDRY

KITCHEN
11⁶x13⁴

REFG.

BAR
CAB'T BELOW

STOR.

PANTRY

DESK

OVENS

BRM. CL.

BOOKS

BOOKS

BOOKS

DN

UP

LIBRARY
10⁸x9⁴

OPEN ABOVE

GARAGE
21⁸x23⁴

BATH

RECEIVING HALL

LIVING RM.
24⁸x13⁴

COVERED PORCH

WALK-IN CLOSET

ROOF LINE

GUEST BEDROOM
15⁸x11⁸

COVERED PORCH

Design T72829

2,044 Sq. Ft. - First Floor
1,962 Sq. Ft. - Second Floor; 74,360 Cu. Ft.

● The architecture of this design is Post-Modern with a taste of Victorian styling. Detailed with gingerbread woodwork and a handsome double-width chimney, this two-story design is breathtaking. Enter this home to the large, tiled receiving hall and begin to explore this very livable floor plan. Formal areas consist of the front living room and the dining room. Each has features to make it memorable. The living room is spacious, has a fireplace and access to the covered porch; the dining room has a delightful bay window and is convenient to the kitchen for ease in meal serving. The library is tucked between these two formal areas. Now let's go to the informal area. The family room will welcome many an explorer. It will be a great place for many family activities. Note the L-shaped snack bar with cabinets below. Onward to the second floor, where the private area will be found. Start with the two bedrooms that have two full bathrooms joining them together. The older children will marvel at this area's efficiency and privacy. A third family bedroom is nearby. Then, there is the master bedroom suite. Its list of features is long, indeed. Begin with the "his" and "her" baths and see how many features you can list. A guest bedroom and bath are on the first floor.

Design T72646 1,274 Sq. Ft. - First Floor
1,322 Sq. Ft. - Second Floor; 42,425 Cu. Ft.

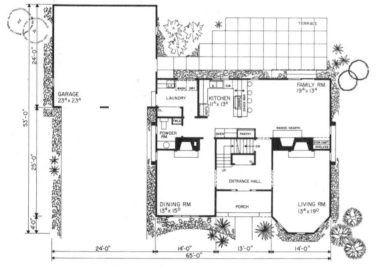

● What a stylish departure from today's usual architecture. This refreshing exterior may be referred to as Neo-Victorian. Its vertical lines, steep roofs and variety of gables remind one of the old Victorian houses of yesteryear. Inside, there is an efficiently working floor plan that is delightfully spacious.

Design T72647 2,104 Sq. Ft. - First Floor; 1,230 Sq. Ft. - Second Floor; 56,395 Cu. Ft.

● Another Neo-Victorian, and what an impressive and unique design it is. Observe the roof lines, the window treatment, the use of contrasting exterior materials and the arched, covered front entrance.

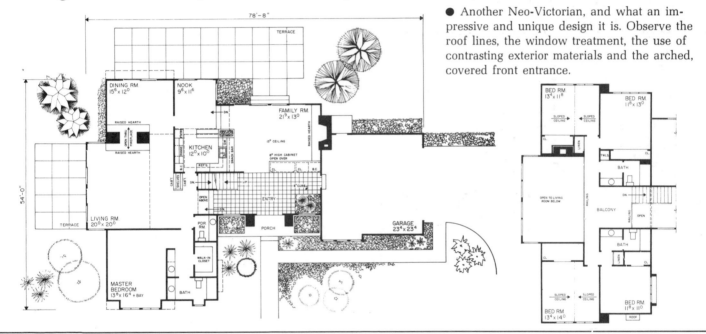

Design T72645 1,600 Sq. Ft. - First Floor; 1,305 Sq. Ft. - Second Floor
925 Sq. Ft. - Third Floor; 58,355 Cu. Ft.

● Reminiscent of the Gothic Victorian style of the mid-19th Century, this delightfully detailed, three-story house has a wrap-around veranda for summertime relaxing. The parlor and family room, each with fireplaces, provide excellent formal and informal living facilities. The third floor houses two more great areas plus bath.

Design T72892
1,623 Sq. Ft.; 38,670 Cu. Ft.

● What a striking contemporary! It houses an efficient floor plan with many outstanding features. The foyer has a sloped ceiling and an open stair-case to the basement. To the right of the foyer is the work center. Note the snack bar, laundry and covered dining porch, along with the step-saving kitch-en. Both the gathering and dining rooms overlook the backyard. Each of the three bedrooms has access to an outdoor area. Now, just think of the potential use of the second floor loft. Its 160 square feet of livability could be used as a den, sewing room, lounge or any of many other activities. It over-looks the gathering room and front foyer and has two large skylights.

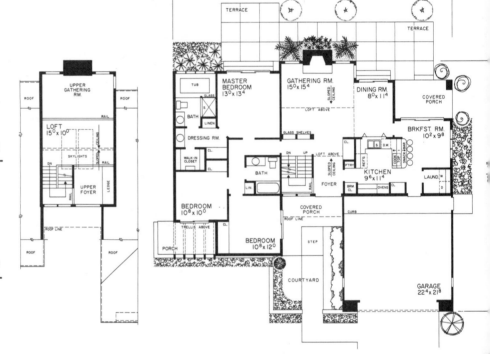

Design T72809
1,551 Sq. Ft.; 42,615 Cu. Ft.

● One-story living can be very rewarding and this contemporary home will be just that. Study the indoor-outdoor living relationships which are offered in the back of the plan. Sliding glass doors are in each of the rear rooms leading to the terrace. The formal dining room has a second set of doors to the porch. Many enjoyable hours will be spent here in the hot tub. A sloped ceiling with skylights is above the hot tub area. Back to the interior, there is a large gathering room. It, too, has a sloped ceiling which will add to its spacious appearance. The interior kitchen is con-veniently located between the formal and infor-mal dining areas. Two, or optional three, bed-rooms are ready to serve the small family.

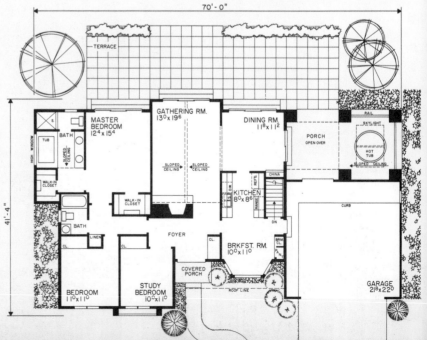

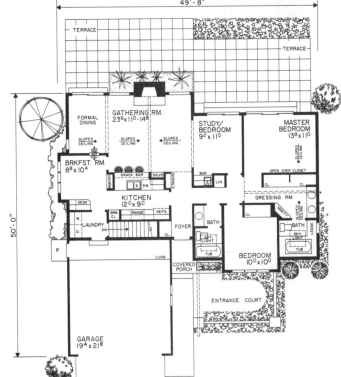

TERRACE

TERRACE

FORMAL DINING

GATHERING RM.
23⁶ x 11⁰-14⁸

STUDY/
BEDROOM
9² x 11⁰

MASTER
BEDROOM
13⁸ x 11⁰

SLOPED CEILING

SLOPED CEILING

SLOPED CEILING

BRKFST. RM.
8⁸ x 10⁴

SNACK BAR

BAR

PANTRY

SHLVS

OPEN OVER CLOSET

DESK

KITCHEN
12 x 9⁰

LIN.

CL.

CL.

DRESSING RM.

RANGE

REF'G.

VANITY

SLOPED CEILING

LAUNDRY

FOYER

BATH

CL.

BATH

LEDGE

LIGHT

TUB

BEDROOM
10⁰ x 10⁰

TUB

CURB

COVERED PORCH

ENTRANCE COURT

GARAGE
19⁴ x 21⁸

49'-8"

50'-0"

Design T72864
1,387 Sq. Ft.; 29,160 Cu. Ft.

● Projecting the garage to the front of a house is very economical in two ways. One, it reduces the required lot size for building (in this case the overall width is under 50 feet). And, two, it will protect the interior from street noise and unfavorable winds. Many other characteristics about this design deserve mention, too. The entrance court and covered porch are a delightful way to enter this home. Upon entering, the foyer will take you to the various areas. The interior kitchen has an adjacent breakfast room and a snack bar on the gathering room side. Here, one will enjoy a sloped ceiling and a fireplace. A study with a wet bar is adjacent. If need be, adjust the plan and make the study the third bedroom. Sliding glass doors in the study and master bedroom open to the terrace.

Design T72872

2,148 Sq. Ft. - First Floor
1,126 Sq. Ft. - Second Floor; 51,370 Cu. Ft.

● This Post-Modern design is stylistic, indeed, with angles and broken lines that reach for the sky. The downstairs provides excellent terrace views for a master bedroom suite, study, and a large living room with fireplace. A formal dining room and family room near the three-car garage also enjoy terrace views. A modern kitchen area with island cook top includes a breakfast room. Two other bedrooms with bath are located upstairs, along with an upper foyer, balcony lounge, storage areas, and outer balconies.